Junior Dictionary

First edition for the United States, its territories and possessions,
Canada, and the Philippine Republic published by
Barron's Educational Series, Inc., 2001

First published in 2000 by HarperCollins*Publishers* Ltd

Copyright © 2000 by HarperCollins*Publishers* Ltd

All rights reserved.
No part of this book may be reproduced in any form, by photostat,
microfilm, xerography, or any other means, or incorporated into
any information retrieval system, electronic or mechanical,
without the written permission of the copyright owner.

All inquiries should be addressed to:
Barron's Educational Series, Inc.
250 Wireless Boulevard
Hauppauge, New York 11788
http://www.barronseduc.com

International Standard Book No. 0-7641-5435-4
Library of Congress Catalog Card No. 2001087621

Printed in Scotland

9 8 7 6 5 4 3 2 1

Compiler   Evelyn Goldsmith

Literacy consultants   Kay Hiatt, Rosemary Boys
Numeracy consultant   Jan Henley
Science consultant   Rona Wyn Davies

Cover designer   Susi Martin
Design   Neil Adams, Grasshopper Design Co.
Illustrators   Tim Archbold, Tamsin Cook,
             Felicity House, Pat Murray,
             Sarah Wimperis, Sue Woollatt
             (all of Graham-Cameron Illustration)

Photos
All commissioned photos by Steve Lumb.

The publishers wish to thank the following for permission to use
photographs:
Cover photos by NASA (planet) and Bruce Coleman (moth).
Andes Press: p. 61 Diwali; **Art Directors & Trip**: p. 7 acorn,
p. 9 airplane, p. 12 antelope, p. 29 bridge, p. 31 butterfly,
p. 32 cactus, p. 34 carnival, p. 48 coral, p. 62 dragonfly,
p. 64 duck, p. 65 Earth, p. 65 eclipse, p. 68 erupt, p. 69 evergreen,
p. 86 giraffe, p. 95 harvest, p. 101 horse, p. 102 hurricane,
p. 103 illuminations, p. 107 ivy, p. 113 ladybug, p. 115 leaves,
p. 128 mill, p. 147 pagoda, p. 172 ray, p. 174 reflection,
p. 178 rhinoceros, p. 180 rose, p. 209 statue, p. 223 thatched,
p. 230 tractor; **BBC**: p. 213 studio; **Biofotos/Heather Angel**:
p. 18 badger, p. 57 desert, p. 81 fox, p. 158 polar bear; **Oxford
Scientific Films**: p. 13 ape, p. 14 aquarium, p. 32 camel, p. 38
cheetah, p. 52 crystal, p. 85 gerbil, p. 88 gorilla, p. 103 iceberg,
p. 108 jellyfish, p. 148 panda, p. 157 plow, p. 171 rainbow, p. 191
shark, p. 206 springbok, p. 218 swan, p. 226 tiger, p. 253 x-ray;
Papilio: p. 25 bluebells, p. 56 deer, p. 117 lighthouse.

All other photos and illustrations © HarperCollins*Publishers* Ltd
2000.

Acknowledgments
The publishers would like to thank all the teachers, staff, and
pupils who contributed to this book:

Models
Lauren Carroll   Elizabeth Fison   Petra Pavlovic
Stacey Cleary   Jesse Johnson   Milo Petrie-Foxell
Tom Crane   Ismael Khan   Dexter Sampson
Katherine Davis   Margaret Omoboade   Mauri-Joy Smith
William Davis   Zina Patel   Tom Symonds
Ruby Feroze   Dunia Pavlovic   Rosie Ward

Schools
Aberhill Primary, Fife; ASDAC, Fife; Canning St Primary,
Newcastle upon Tyne; Cowgate Primary, Newcastle upon Tyne;
Crombie Primary, Fife; the Literacy Team at Dryden Professional
Development Centre, Gateshead; Dunshalt Primary, Fife; Ecton
Brook Lower, Northampton; English Martyrs RC Primary,
Newcastle upon Tyne; Hotspur Primary, Newcastle upon Tyne;
John Betts Primary, London; Lemington First, Newcastle upon
Tyne; LMTC Education Development Centre, Northumberland;
Melcombe Primary, London; Methilhill Primary, Fife; Newcastle
Literacy Centre, Newcastle upon Tyne; Northampton High,
Northampton; Pitcoudie Primary, Fife; Pitreavie Primary, Fife;
Ravenswood Primary, Newcastle upon Tyne; St Andrew's
CE Primary, London; Simon de Senlis Lower, Northampton;
Sinclairtown Primary, Fife; Standens Barn Lower, Northampton;
Touch Primary, Fife; Towcester Infants, Northampton; Wooton
Primary, Northampton.

Contents

Using this dictionary

A dictionary tells you what a word means and how to spell it. The words in a dictionary are listed in alphabetical order.

How to find a word

Look up the word **fossil**. What letter does it begin with? Use the alphabet line at the side of the page. The green box tells you that the words on this page start with **f**.

Think about the second letter of the word. You are looking for a word beginning with **fo**. Use the guide word at the top of the page. A guide word at the top left tells you the *first word* on that page. A guide word at the top right tells you the *last word* on that page. The guide word for this page is **frequent** – it starts with **fr**. Does **fo** come before **fr**?

When you think you have the right page, look at the blue words. These are called headwords. The headwords are in alphabetical order. If you run your finger down the headwords on this page, you will see more than one that begins with **fo**. Think about the next letter or letters in your word and look for a headword that begins with **fos**.

Keep looking until you find the word **fossil**.

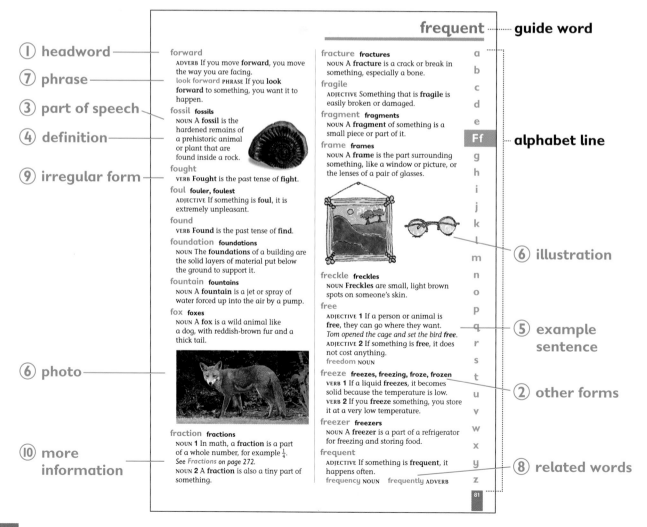

- ① headword
- ⑦ phrase
- ③ part of speech
- ④ definition
- ⑨ irregular form
- ⑥ photo
- ⑩ more information

frequent guide word

forward
ADVERB If you move **forward**, you move the way you are facing.
look forward PHRASE If you **look forward** to something, you want it to happen.

fossil fossils
NOUN A **fossil** is the hardened remains of a prehistoric animal or plant that are found inside a rock.

fought
VERB **Fought** is the past tense of **fight**.

foul fouler, foulest
ADJECTIVE If something is **foul**, it is extremely unpleasant.

found
VERB **Found** is the past tense of **find**.

foundation foundations
NOUN The **foundations** of a building are the solid layers of material put below the ground to support it.

fountain fountains
NOUN A **fountain** is a jet or spray of water forced up into the air by a pump.

fox foxes
NOUN A **fox** is a wild animal like a dog, with reddish-brown fur and a thick tail.

fraction fractions
NOUN **1** In math, a **fraction** is a part of a whole number, for example $\frac{1}{4}$.
See *Fractions on page 272.*
NOUN **2** A **fraction** is also a tiny part of something.

fracture fractures
NOUN A **fracture** is a crack or break in something, especially a bone.

fragile
ADJECTIVE Something that is **fragile** is easily broken or damaged.

fragment fragments
NOUN A **fragment** of something is a small piece or part of it.

frame frames
NOUN A **frame** is the part surrounding something, like a window or picture, or the lenses of a pair of glasses.

freckle freckles
NOUN **Freckles** are small, light brown spots on someone's skin.

free
ADJECTIVE **1** If a person or animal is **free**, they can go where they want. *Tom opened the cage and set the bird free.*
ADJECTIVE **2** If something is **free**, it does not cost anything.
freedom NOUN

freeze freezes, freezing, froze, frozen
VERB **1** If a liquid **freezes**, it becomes solid because the temperature is low.
VERB **2** If you **freeze** something, you store it at a very low temperature.

freezer freezers
NOUN A **freezer** is a part of a refrigerator for freezing and storing food.

frequent
ADJECTIVE If something is **frequent**, it happens often.
frequency NOUN **frequently** ADVERB

a
b
c
d
e
Ff
g
h
i
j
k
l
m
n
o
p
q
r
s
t
u
v
w
x
y
z

- alphabet line
- ⑥ illustration
- ⑤ example sentence
- ② other forms
- ⑧ related words

Using this dictionary

Finding out about a word

① The headword is the word you are looking up.

② On the same line as the headword, you will see how to spell other forms of the word, such as plural nouns, verb tenses or other adjective forms, called comparatives and superlatives.

③ Next you will see the part of speech. This tells you what type of word the headword is, such as a noun, verb, adjective, adverb, or pronoun.

④ After the part of speech, you will find the definition. The definition tells you what the word means. The definitions are numbered if there is more than one. Each definition has its own part of speech.

⑤ Some words have an example sentence in *italics*. This shows you how the word might be used in speech or writing.

⑥ Some words have a photo or other illustration to help you read the word and understand its meaning.

⑦ A phrase may also be included. For example, under the word **forward**, you will also find the definition of the phrase **look forward**.

⑧ Sometimes, other related words are given at the end, with their parts of speech. These tell you, for example, the noun or adverb form of the word.

⑨ An irregular form of a word is a plural noun or verb tense which does not follow the usual spelling rules. You can find many irregular forms in this dictionary.

⑩ Some definitions tell you where to look for more information, such as another headword, or the pages at the back of the dictionary.

Other features of this dictionary

● Pronunciation is how you say a word. Some words can be spelled the same, but sound different and mean different things – these words are called homographs. This dictionary gives you pronunciation help for some words, including homographs. For example:

tear **tears, tearing, tore, torn**
(*rhymes with* **fear**) NOUN **1** Tears are the drops of liquid that come out of your eyes when you cry.
(*rhymes with* **fair**) VERB **2** If you **tear** something, such as paper or fabric, you pull it apart.

● Some definitions include a label, such as FORMAL, INFORMAL, or TRADEMARK. This tells you a little more about the word or how it is used. For example:

Rollerblade **Rollerblades**
NOUN; TRADEMARK **Rollerblades** are roller skates which have the wheels set in one straight line on the bottom of the boot.

Picture pages, word banks, and number banks

There are special topic pages at the back of this dictionary to support your writing.

Picture pages have labeled illustrations of things such as fruit and vegetables, parts of the body, different types of animals, and shapes and colors.

Other pages help you understand parts of speech, punctuation, and prefixes and suffixes.

Word banks and **number banks** help you learn and spell time words, weather words, synonyms and antonyms, confusing words, abbreviations, measures, numbers, and fractions.

Aa

abacus **abacuses**

NOUN An **abacus** is a frame with beads that slide along rods. It is used for counting.

abandon **abandons, abandoning, abandoned**

VERB **1** If you **abandon** something, you leave it and do not return. *The cub had been **abandoned** by its mother.*

VERB **2** If you **abandon** a piece of work, you stop doing it before it is finished.

abbreviation **abbreviations**

NOUN An **abbreviation** is a short form of a word or phrase. *The **abbreviation** for compact disc is CD.*

See *Abbreviations* on page 270.

ability **abilities**

NOUN If you have the **ability** to do something, you are able to do it.

able **abler, ablest**

ADJECTIVE If you are **able** to do something, you can do it.

aboard

PREPOSITION If you are **aboard** a ship or plane, you are on or in it.

about

ADVERB **1** You say **about** in front of a number to show it is not exact. *I'll be home at **about** five o'clock.*

PREPOSITION **2** If you talk or write **about** something, you say things to do with that subject. *He is talking **about** boats.*

above

PREPOSITION If something is **above** something else, it is over it, or higher up.

abroad

ADVERB When you go **abroad**, you go to a different country.

absent

ADJECTIVE If someone is **absent**, they are not here.

absolutely

ADVERB You can use **absolutely** to make what you are saying sound stronger. *You must stay **absolutely** still.*

absorb **absorbs, absorbing, absorbed**

VERB If something **absorbs** a liquid, it soaks it up or takes it in.

absurd

ADJECTIVE Something that is **absurd** seems silly, because it is quite different from what you would expect. *It's **absurd** to wear your sweatshirt in this heat.*

abuse

NOUN **Abuse** is cruel treatment of someone.

accelerate **accelerates, accelerating, accelerated**

VERB When a car **accelerates**, it speeds up.

accept **accepts, accepting, accepted**

VERB If you **accept** something you have been offered, you say yes to it.

accident **accidents**

NOUN An **accident** is something nasty that happens by chance. *He broke his leg in a climbing **accident**.*

accidentally ADVERB

Aa
b
c
d
e
f
g
h
i
j
k
l
m
n
o
p
q
r
s
t
u
v
w
x
y
z

account accounts

NOUN **1** An **account** is something written or spoken that tells you what has happened.

NOUN **2** An **account** is also money that you keep at a bank.

accurate

ADJECTIVE An **accurate** measurement or description is exactly right.

ache aches

NOUN An **ache** is a dull, lasting pain.

achieve achieves, achieving, achieved

VERB If you **achieve** something, you usually get it by hard work.

achievement NOUN

acid acids

NOUN Some **acids** give food a sharp, sour taste. Lemons and vinegar contain acid. Strong acid can burn your skin.

acid rain

NOUN **Acid rain** is rain that is mixed with dirty gases in the air. It can damage buildings, trees, and fish.

acorn acorns

NOUN An **acorn** is a nut. Acorns grow on oak trees.

acrobat acrobats

NOUN An **acrobat** is someone who does difficult and exciting tricks, like balancing on a high wire.

across

PREPOSITION If you go **across** something, you go from one side to the other.

act acts, acting, acted

VERB **1** When you **act**, you do something. *He had to **act** quickly to put out the fire.*

VERB **2** If you **act** in a play or film, you have a part in it.

NOUN **3** An **act** is something that you do.

action actions

NOUN An **action** is a movement of part of your body.

active

ADJECTIVE **1** Someone who is **active** moves about a lot, or is very busy.

ADJECTIVE **2** In grammar, a verb in the **active** voice is one where the subject does the action, rather than having it done to them. See **voice**.

activity activities

NOUN **Activity** is when there are a lot of things happening.

actor actors

NOUN An **actor** is a man or woman whose job is to act in plays or movies.

actress actresses

NOUN A female actor is sometimes called an **actress**. See **actor**.

actual

ADJECTIVE You describe something as **actual** when you mean it is real. *The shop said the paint was red, but the **actual** color was pink.*

actually ADVERB

adapt adapts, adapting, adapted

VERB **1** If you **adapt** to something new, you change in some way that helps you.

VERB **2** If you **adapt** something, you change it to suit your needs. *The book was **adapted** to make a movie.*

adaptable

ADJECTIVE Someone who is **adaptable** can change to deal with new situations.

add adds, adding, added

VERB **1** If you **add** something, you put it with whatever you have already. *Put flour in the bowl and **add** an egg.*

VERB **2** If you **add** numbers of things together, you find out how many you have. The sign + means add. *I have two marbles in the bag. If I **add** these three, it makes five altogether.* 2 + 3 = 5

addition

NOUN **Addition** is adding numbers or things together.

address

b
c
d
e
f
g
h
i
j
k
l
m
n
o
p
q
r
s
t
u
v
w
x
y
z

address **addresses**

NOUN Your **address** is the name or number of your house, and the street and town where you live.

adjective **adjectives**

NOUN An **adjective** is a word that describes someone or something. "Beautiful" and "green" are adjectives. See *Adjective* on page 263.

admire **admires, admiring, admired**

VERB **1** When you **admire** someone, you think very highly of them.

VERB **2** When you **admire** something, you enjoy looking at it. *They stopped the car to **admire** the view.*

admit **admits, admitting, admitted**

VERB **1** If you **admit** something, you agree that it is true.

VERB **2** If people are **admitted** to a place, they are allowed to go in.

adopt **adopts, adopting, adopted**

VERB If a person **adopts** a child, they make the child their own by law.

adore **adores, adoring, adored**

VERB If you **adore** someone, you love them very much.

adult **adults**

NOUN An **adult** is a grown-up person or animal.

advance **advances, advancing, advanced**

VERB If someone **advances**, they move forward. *The army **advanced** nine miles in one day.*

advantage **advantages**

NOUN An **advantage** is something that helps you do better than other people. *His long legs gave him an **advantage** in the race.*

adventure **adventures**

NOUN If you are having an **adventure**, you are doing something exciting.

adverb **adverbs**

NOUN An **adverb** is a word that answers questions like how, when, where, and why. In the sentence "The girl came quietly into the room," the word "quietly" is an adverb telling you how the girl came in.

See *Adverb* on page 263.

advertise **advertises, advertising, advertised**

VERB If you **advertise** something, you tell people about it through newspapers, posters, or TV.

advertisement **advertisements**

NOUN An **advertisement** is a notice in the paper, or on a poster or TV, about a job or things for sale.

advice

NOUN If you give someone **advice**, you say what you think they should do.

advise **advises, advising, advised**

VERB When you **advise** someone, you tell them what you think they should do.

aerial **aerials**

NOUN An **aerial** is a wire that sends or receives radio or television signals.

affect **affects, affecting, affected**

VERB When something **affects** someone or something else, it changes them in some way.

affection

NOUN **Affection** is a feeling of caring for someone.

afford **affords, affording, afforded**
VERB If you can **afford** something, you have enough money to buy it or do it.

afraid
ADJECTIVE Someone who is **afraid** thinks that something scary might happen.

after
PREPOSITION If something happens **after** something else, it happens at a later time. *We'll watch television **after** supper.*

afternoon **afternoons**
NOUN The **afternoon** is the time of day between 12 o'clock (noon) and about six o'clock in the evening.

again
ADVERB If you do something **again**, you do it once more.

against
PREPOSITION **1** If you play **against** someone, you are not on their side.
PREPOSITION **2** If you are **against** something, you are touching it and leaning on it. *She felt tired and leaned **against** the tree.*

age **ages**
NOUN **1** Your **age** is how old you are.
NOUN **2** An **age** is a special period in history, like the Stone Age.

ago
ADVERB If something happened four days **ago**, it is four days since it happened.

agree **agrees, agreeing, agreed**
VERB **1** If you **agree** with someone, you think the same about something.
VERB **2** If you **agree** to do something, you say you will do it.
agreement NOUN

ahead
ADVERB Something or someone who is **ahead** of you is in front of you. *She walked fast and went on **ahead** of me.*

aim **aims, aiming, aimed**
VERB **1** If you **aim** at something, you point at it.
VERB **2** If you **aim** to do something, you plan to do it.

air
NOUN **Air** is the mixture of gases that we breathe.

aircraft
NOUN An **aircraft** is a vehicle that flies. Helicopters and airplanes are aircraft.

air force **air forces**
NOUN An **air force** is a force that a country uses for fighting in the air.

airplane **airplanes**
NOUN An **airplane** is a flying vehicle with wings and one or more engines.

airport **airports**
NOUN An **airport** is a place where aircraft land and take off.

alarm **alarms**
NOUN **1** An **alarm** is something like a bell or flashing light that warns you of something.
NOUN **2** **Alarm** is a feeling of fear. *He looked at the hungry bear in **alarm**.*

album **albums**
NOUN An **album** is a book that you put things like stamps or photographs in.

alien **aliens**
NOUN In science fiction, an **alien** is a creature from outer space.

alight
ADJECTIVE If something is **alight**, it is lighted up.

alike
ADJECTIVE If two or more things are **alike**, they are the same in some way.

alive
ADJECTIVE If a person, animal, or plant is **alive**, they are living now.

all
ADJECTIVE You say **all** when you mean the whole of a particular group or thing. *Put **all** your toys away.*

allergy allergies
NOUN If you have an **allergy** to something, it makes you ill. *Tom has an **allergy** to nuts, so he must not eat them.*

alley alleys
NOUN An **alley** is a narrow path with buildings or walls on both sides.

alligator alligators
NOUN An **alligator** is a reptile. It is of the same family as a crocodile, but smaller. See *Reptiles* on page 259.

alliteration
NOUN **Alliteration** is the use of words close together which begin with the same sound, for example "hundreds of huge hairy horses."

allow allows, allowing, allowed
VERB If someone **allows** you to do something, they let you do it.

all right
ADJECTIVE **1** If someone is **all right**, they are well or safe. *See if the baby's **all right**.*
INTERJECTION **2** You say **all right** if you agree to something.

almost
ADVERB **Almost** means very nearly, but not quite. *He tripped and **almost** fell.*

alone
ADJECTIVE If you are **alone**, there is nobody with you.

along
PREPOSITION If you go **along** something, you move toward the end of it.

aloud
ADVERB If you read something **aloud**, you read it so that people can hear you.

alphabet alphabets
NOUN An **alphabet** is all the letters used to write words, written in a special order.

alphabetical
ADJECTIVE **Alphabetical** means arranged in the order of the letters of the alphabet. *She read out the names on the register in **alphabetical** order.*

already
ADVERB If you have done something **already**, you did it earlier.

also
ADVERB You say **also** when you want to add to something you have just said.

alter alters, altering, altered
VERB When you **alter** something, you change it in some way.

alternate alternates, alternating, alternated
VERB When two things **alternate**, they regularly happen one after the other. *He **alternates** between being friendly and completely ignoring me.*

although
CONJUNCTION You say **although** when you expected something different. ***Although** my dad was cross, he still gave me pocket money.*

altogether

ADVERB If you say there are a number of things **altogether**, you are counting all of them. *I've picked four apples and you've picked two, so that's six **altogether**.*

aluminum

NOUN **Aluminum** is a light, silver-colored metal. It is used for making rolls of foil and containers like cans and pie dishes.

always

ADVERB **1** If you **always** do something, you do it every time. *He **always** puts his things away when he has used them.*
ADVERB **2** If something has **always** been so, it has been that way at all times. *They have **always** been good friends.*

a.m.

ADVERB **a.m.** is the time between midnight and noon. *I get up at 7 **a.m.*** See **p.m.**

amaze   amazes, amazing, amazed

VERB If something **amazes** you, it surprises you very much.
amazement NOUN

amazing

ADJECTIVE Something that is **amazing** is very surprising or wonderful.

ambition   ambitions

NOUN If you have an **ambition** to do something, you want to do it very much.

ambulance   ambulances

NOUN An **ambulance** is a vehicle that is used to take people to a hospital.

among

PREPOSITION **1** If something is **among** a number of things, it is surrounded by them. *He sat **among** piles of books.*
PREPOSITION **2** If something is divided **among** several people, they all have a share.

amount   amounts

NOUN An **amount** of something is how much there is of it.

amphibian   amphibians

NOUN An **amphibian** is an animal that is able to live on land and in water.
amphibious ADJECTIVE

See *Amphibians* on page 259.

amuse   amuses, amusing, amused

VERB If you **amuse** somebody, you make them smile or stop them feeling bored.

analog

ADJECTIVE An **analog** watch or clock shows the time with hands that move around a dial. See **digital**.

anchor   anchors

NOUN An **anchor** is a heavy metal hook on a long chain. It is dropped over the side of a boat to stop it from moving.

ancient

ADJECTIVE If something is **ancient**, it is very old.

and

CONJUNCTION You use **and** to join two or more words or phrases together. *I like chocolate, **and** my brother does too.*

angel   angels

NOUN **Angels** are beings some people believe act as messengers for God.

anger

NOUN **Anger** is the strong feeling you have about something that is unfair.

angle   angles

NOUN An **angle** is the shape that is made when two lines or surfaces join. The size of an angle is measured in degrees.

angry

Aa
b
c
d
e
f
g
h
i
j
k
l
m
n
o
p
q
r
s
t
u
v
w
x
y
z

angry **angrier, angriest**
ADJECTIVE If you feel **angry**, you are very cross.
angrily ADVERB

animal **animals**
NOUN **Animals** are living things which are not plants. Humans, dogs, birds, fish, reptiles, and insects are all animals.

ankle **ankles**
NOUN Your **ankle** is the joint between your foot and your leg.

anniversary **anniversaries**
NOUN An **anniversary** is the yearly recurrence of a day marking a special event, like a wedding.

announce **announces, announcing, announced**
VERB If you **announce** something important, you tell people about it publicly. *My sister's engagement was **announced** last week.*

annoy **annoys, annoying, annoyed**
VERB If you do something which **annoys** someone, you make them cross.

annual **annuals**
ADJECTIVE **1** Something that is **annual** happens once a year, like a birthday.
NOUN **2** An **annual** is a book that comes out once a year.

another
ADJECTIVE **Another** means one more. *Amy finished her chocolate and took **another** one immediately.*

answer **answers, answering, answered**
VERB **1** When you **answer**, you say or write something to someone who has asked you a question.
NOUN **2** Your **answer** is what you say or write to a question.

ant **ants**
NOUN **Ants** are small insects which live in large groups called colonies.
See *Insects* on page 259.

antelope **antelopes**
NOUN **Antelopes** are animals that look like deer, but their horns are not branch-shaped. They live in Africa and Asia.

antenna **antennae** or **antennas**
NOUN The **antennae** of an insect are the two long, thin parts on its head that it uses to feel with.

anthology **anthologies**
NOUN An **anthology** is a book of writings by different authors.

anti-
PREFIX **Anti-** is put in front of a word to mean against or opposite to that word. See *Prefixes* on page 264.

antibiotic
NOUN An **antibiotic** is a type of drug given by a doctor to treat various types of bacterial infections. *I'm taking an **antibiotic** for my strep throat.*

antique **antiques**
NOUN An **antique** is an old object which is valuable because it is beautiful or rare.

antiseptic **antiseptics**
NOUN An **antiseptic** is a substance that prevents infection by killing germs.

antonym **antonyms**
NOUN An **antonym** is a word that means the opposite of another word. See *Antonyms* on page 267.

anxious
ADJECTIVE Someone who is **anxious** is nervous or worried about something.

any
ADJECTIVE **1** **Any** means one, some, or several. *Do you have **any** milk?*
ADJECTIVE **2** **Any** can also mean even the smallest amount. *I mustn't eat **any** nuts.*

anybody
PRONOUN **Anybody** is any person.

anyone
PRONOUN **Anyone** is any person.

anything
PRONOUN **Anything** means any object, event, situation, or action.

anywhere
ADVERB **Anywhere** means in, at, or to any place. *Just put it down* ***anywhere***.

apart
ADJECTIVE If something is **apart** from something else, there is a space between them. *He stood with his feet* ***apart***.

ape **apes**
NOUN **Apes** are like monkeys but are larger and have no tails. Chimpanzees and gorillas are apes. The ape in the photo is an orangutan.

apex **apexes**
NOUN The **apex** is the highest point of something.

apologize **apologizes, apologizing, apologized**
VERB When you **apologize**, you say you are sorry for something you have done.

apology **apologies**
NOUN An **apology** is something you say or write to tell someone you are sorry.

apostrophe **apostrophes**
NOUN An **apostrophe** is a punctuation mark (') used in contractions and to show belonging.
See *Punctuation* on page 264.

apparatus
NOUN The **apparatus** for a particular task is the equipment you use for it.

appear **appears, appearing, appeared**
VERB **1** When something **appears**, it moves into a place where you can see it.
VERB **2** If something **appears** to be a certain way, that is how it seems.

appearance **appearances**
NOUN **1** Someone's **appearance** in a place is their sudden arrival there.
NOUN **2** Your **appearance** is the way you look to other people.

appetite **appetites**
NOUN If you have an **appetite**, you are looking forward to eating something.

applause
NOUN **Applause** is clapping your hands to show that you liked something.

apple **apples**
NOUN An **apple** is a round crisp fruit which grows on a tree.
See *Fruit* on page 257.

apply **applies, applying, applied**
VERB If you **apply** for something, like a job, you usually ask for it in writing.

appreciate **appreciates, appreciating, appreciated**
VERB If you **appreciate** something, you feel grateful for it.

approach **approaches, approaching, approached**
VERB When someone **approaches** you, they get nearer to you.

approve **approves, approving, approved**
VERB If you **approve** of something, you think it is good.
approval NOUN

approximate
ADJECTIVE An **approximate** answer may not be exactly right. *What is the* ***approximate*** *distance between those trees?*

approximately

ADVERB If you say **approximately**, you mean about. *It is **approximately** 5 miles away.*

apricot **apricots**

NOUN An **apricot** is a small, round yellow-orange fruit with a large pit in the center.

April

NOUN **April** is the fourth month of the year. It has 30 days.

apron **aprons**

NOUN An **apron** is a piece of material that you wear to keep your clothes clean when you are cooking.

aquarium **aquariums** or **aquaria**

NOUN An **aquarium** is a glass tank for fish and other underwater animals.

arch **arches**

NOUN An **arch** is a curved part of a bridge, wall, or building.

archery

NOUN **Archery** is a sport in which people shoot at a target with a bow and arrow.

architect **architects**

NOUN An **architect** is a person who designs buildings.

area **areas**

NOUN **1** The **area** of something is the size of its surface. To find the area of a rectangle, you multiply the length by the width. The area of this rectangle is 12 square inches.

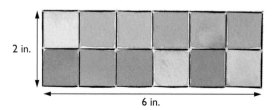

2 in.

6 in.

NOUN **2** You use the word **area** to mean in or around a place. *There are lots of shops in this **area**.*

argue **argues, arguing, argued**

VERB If you **argue** with someone, you say that you do not agree with them, and give your reasons.

argument **arguments**

NOUN An **argument** is a talk between people who do not agree. In some arguments, people shout angrily.

arithmetic

NOUN **Arithmetic** is about adding, subtracting, multiplying, and dividing numbers.

arm **arms**

NOUN Your **arm** is the part of your body between the shoulder and the hand.

armchair **armchairs**

NOUN An **armchair** is a chair with a support on each side for your arms.

armor

NOUN **Armor** is metal clothing that soldiers used to wear in battle.

army **armies**

NOUN An **army** is a large organized group of people who are trained to fight in case of war.

around

PREPOSITION **1** You say **around** when things are in various places. *There are lots of lamps **around** the house.*

PREPOSITION **2** You can use **around** when something is on all sides of something else. *The Earth's atmosphere is the air **around** it.*

arrange **arranges, arranging, arranged**
VERB **1** If you **arrange** something like a party, you make plans and organize it.
VERB **2** If you **arrange** things like flowers, you group them in a special way.

array **arrays**
NOUN **1** An **array** is a group of things set out neatly in columns and rows.
NOUN **2** An **array** is also a large number of things displayed together. *Ben's mouth watered at the **array** of cakes.*

arrest **arrests, arresting, arrested**
VERB If the police **arrest** someone, they take them to the police station.

arrive **arrives, arriving, arrived**
VERB When you **arrive** at a place, you reach it at the end of your journey.
arrival NOUN

arrow **arrows**
NOUN **1** An **arrow** is a thin stick with a pointed end, which is shot from a bow.
NOUN **2** An **arrow** can also be a sign that shows people which way to go.

art
NOUN **Art** is something like a painting or sculpture, which is beautiful or has a special meaning.

artery **arteries**
NOUN An **artery** is a tube which carries blood from your heart to the rest of your body.

article **articles**
NOUN **1** An **article** is a piece of writing in a magazine or newspaper.
NOUN **2** An **article** can also be an object. *What is this strange **article**?*

artificial
ADJECTIVE **Artificial** things are made by people. They do not occur naturally.

artist **artists**
NOUN An **artist** is a person who creates things like a painting or sculpture.

ascend **ascends, ascending, ascended**
VERB When you **ascend**, you move upward. *He **ascended** the stairs to his room.*

ascending
ADJECTIVE When things are arranged in **ascending** order, each thing is higher than the one before it. *The numbers 21, 37, and 49 are in **ascending** order.*

ash **ashes**
NOUN **1** **Ash** is the dust left after a fire.
NOUN **2** An **ash** is a large tree.

ashamed
ADJECTIVE If you are **ashamed**, you feel sorry about something you have done. *She was **ashamed** after calling her friend a liar.*

ask **asks, asking, asked**
VERB **1** If you **ask** someone a question, you are trying to find something out.
VERB **2** If you **ask** someone for something, you want them to give it to you.

asleep
ADJECTIVE If you are **asleep**, your eyes are closed and your body is resting.

aspirin **aspirins**
NOUN **Aspirin** is a drug that is used to treat pain or a fever. An **aspirin** is a tablet of this drug.

assassin **assassins**
NOUN An **assassin** is someone who commits murder.
assassinate VERB

assemble **assembles, assembling, assembled**
VERB **1** If you **assemble** something, you fit the parts of it together.
VERB **2** When people **assemble**, they come together in a group.

Aa
b
c
d
e
f
g
h
i
j
k
l
m
n
o
p
q
r
s
t
u
v
w
x
y
z

assembly assemblies
NOUN **Assembly** is a gathering of all the teachers and pupils in a school.

assistant assistants
NOUN **1** A person's **assistant** is someone whose job is to help them.
NOUN **2** A shop **assistant** is a person who works in a shop selling things.

asthma
NOUN **Asthma** is a disease that causes wheezing and makes it difficult for you to breathe properly.

astonish astonishes, astonishing, astonished
VERB If you are **astonished** by something or someone, you are very surprised.

astronaut astronauts
NOUN An **astronaut** is a person who travels in space.

astronomer astronomers
NOUN An **astronomer** is a scientist who studies the stars and planets.

ate
VERB **Ate** is the past tense of **eat**.

atlas atlases
NOUN An **atlas** is a book of maps.

atmosphere atmospheres
NOUN **1** A planet's **atmosphere** is the layer of air or other gas around it.
NOUN **2** You can use **atmosphere** to talk about the general mood of a place. *In the classroom the **atmosphere** was relaxed.*

atom atoms
NOUN An **atom** is the smallest part of any substance.

attach attaches, attaching, attached
VERB When you **attach** something to an object, you join the two things together.

attack attacks, attacking, attacked
VERB If a person **attacks** somebody, they try to hurt them.

attempt attempts, attempting, attempted
VERB If you **attempt** something difficult, you try to do it.

attend attends, attending, attended
VERB If someone **attends** something like a meeting, they are present at it.

attention
NOUN **1** If something attracts your **attention**, you notice it suddenly.
NOUN **2** If you pay **attention** to someone, you listen carefully to them.

attic attics
NOUN An **attic** is a room at the top of a house, just under the roof.

attract attracts, attracting, attracted
VERB **1** If something or somebody **attracts** you, you find them interesting. *Joe was **attracted** to the fair by the lights.*
VERB **2** If something like a magnet **attracts** an object, it makes it move toward it.

attractive
ADJECTIVE If something is **attractive**, it is nice to look at.

audience audiences
NOUN An **audience** is a group of people watching or listening to something like a play, film, speech, or piece of music.

August
NOUN **August** is the eighth month of the year. It has 31 days.

aunt aunts
NOUN Your **aunt** is the sister of one of your parents, or the wife of your uncle.

author **authors**

NOUN The **author** of a book is the person who wrote it.

authority **authorities**

NOUN **1** **Authority** is a quality that someone has that makes people take notice of what they say.

NOUN **2** The **authorities** are people like the police who have a lot of power.

autograph **autographs**

NOUN An **autograph** is the signature of a famous person.

automatic

ADJECTIVE An **automatic** machine is one that can do things on its own.

automatically ADVERB

autumn **autumns**

NOUN **Autumn** is the season between summer and winter. The weather cools and many trees lose their leaves.

available

ADJECTIVE If something is **available**, you can get it. *Tickets are **available** now.*

avalanche **avalanches**

NOUN An **avalanche** is a huge mass of snow and ice that falls down a mountain.

avenue **avenues**

NOUN An **avenue** is a wide road with trees on either side.

avocado **avocados**

NOUN An **avocado** is a fruit with dark green skin and a large pit.
See Fruit on page 257.

avoid **avoids, avoiding, avoided**

VERB If you **avoid** someone or something, you keep away from them.

awake

ADJECTIVE If you are **awake**, you are not sleeping.

award **awards**

NOUN An **award** is a prize that you are given for doing something well.

aware

ADJECTIVE If you are **aware** of something, you know about it.

away

ADVERB **1** If you move **away** from somewhere, you move so that you are farther from that place.

ADVERB **2** If you are **away** from somewhere, you are not in that place. *Katherine is **away** from school today.*

awful

ADJECTIVE Something **awful** is very unpleasant or bad.

awkward

ADJECTIVE **1** If something is **awkward**, it is difficult to do or use.

ADJECTIVE **2** If people are **awkward**, they move in a clumsy way.

ax **axes**

NOUN An **ax** is a tool with a long handle and a heavy sharp blade at one end. It is used for chopping wood.

axis **axes**

NOUN **1** An **axis** is an imaginary line through the center of something, around which it moves.

NOUN **2** An **axis** is also one of the two sides of a graph. A graph has a horizontal axis and a vertical axis.

Bb

baby **babies**
NOUN A **baby** is a very young child.

back **backs**
NOUN **1** The **back** of something is the part opposite the front.
ADVERB **2** If you go **back** to a place, you go somewhere you have been before.
NOUN **3** Your **back** is the part of your body which is behind you, from your neck to the top of your legs.
NOUN **4** The **back** of an animal is the part on top, between its neck and the beginning of its tail.

background **backgrounds**
NOUN The **background** of a picture is everything behind the main part.

backlog **backlogs**
NOUN A **backlog** is a buildup of tasks that have yet to be done.

backward
ADVERB **1** If you move **backward**, you move with your back facing in the direction you are going.
ADVERB **2** If you do something **backward**, you do it in the opposite of the usual way. *Counting **backward** from one hundred.*

bacon
NOUN **Bacon** is salted meat from a pig.

bacteria
PLURAL NOUN **Bacteria** are very tiny living things which break down waste. They can cause diseases.

bad **worse, worst**
ADJECTIVE **1** You say somebody is **bad** if they are naughty or wicked.
ADJECTIVE **2** If something is **bad**, it can hurt or upset you in some way.

badge **badges**
NOUN A **badge** is a sign people wear to show they belong to a school or club.

badger **badgers**
NOUN A **badger** is a strongly built animal with short legs and neck. It has long gray fur and a striped head.

badminton
NOUN **Badminton** is a game in which players use rackets to hit a small feathered object called a shuttlecock across a net.

bag **bags**
NOUN A **bag** is a soft container for carrying or holding things.

bait
NOUN **Bait** is food used to trap animals.

bake **bakes, baking, baked**
VERB When you **bake** food, you cook it in an oven.

baker **bakers**
NOUN A **baker** makes and sells bread, cakes, and pies.

balance **balances, balancing, balanced**
VERB When you **balance**, you keep steady. *She tried to **balance** on one leg.*

balcony **balconies**
NOUN A **balcony** is a platform on the outside of a building. Balconies have a railing or wall around them.

bald **balder, baldest**
ADJECTIVE People who are **bald** have no hair on the top of their head.

ball **balls**
NOUN Anything round can be called a **ball**. You need a ball for lots of games, like tennis and soccer.

ballet ballets

NOUN A **ballet** is a sort of play where the story is told with dancing and music.

balloon balloons

NOUN A **balloon** is a small rubber bag. If you blow hard into it, it gets bigger and makes a very light toy or decoration.

bamboo

NOUN **Bamboo** is a kind of grass with strong hollow stems which are useful as garden canes or for making furniture.

ban bans, banning, banned

VERB If someone is **banned** from doing something, they are told by people in charge that they must not do it.

banana bananas

NOUN A **banana** is a long yellow fruit which grows on trees in hot countries. See *Fruit* on page 257.

band bands

NOUN **1** A **band** is a small number of people, like a gang of robbers or a group of musicians.

NOUN **2** A **band** can also be a strip of material such as cloth or rubber.

bandage bandages

NOUN A **bandage** is a strip of cloth used to cover a wound.

bang bangs, banging, banged

NOUN **1** A **bang** is a sudden loud noise.

VERB **2** If you **bang** something like your knee, you hit it sharply.

bank banks

NOUN **1** A **bank** is a business that looks after people's money.

NOUN **2** The **bank** of a river is the ground on either side of the water.

banner banners

NOUN A **banner** is a long strip of cloth or paper with a message written on it.

bar bars

NOUN **1** A **bar** is a long piece of something hard, like metal or wood.

NOUN **2** A **bar** can also be a counter where people can buy something to drink.

barbecue barbecues

NOUN **1** A **barbecue** is a grill on which food is cooked outdoors over hot charcoal.

VERB **2** To **barbecue** hot dogs, you cook them over hot coals.

barber barbers

NOUN A **barber** is someone who cuts men's hair.

bar chart bar charts

NOUN A **bar chart** is a graph where information is shown in bars.

bar code bar codes

NOUN A **bar code** is a pattern of numbers and lines printed on something that is for sale, so that the price can be read by a machine.

bare barer, barest

ADJECTIVE **1** If part of your body is **bare**, it is not covered by clothes.

ADJECTIVE **2** If something is **bare**, it has nothing in it or on it. *It was winter and the trees were **bare**.*

bargain bargains

NOUN A **bargain** is something which is sold at a low price, and which you think is good value.

bark barks, barking, barked

VERB **1** When a dog **barks**, it makes a sudden rough, loud noise.

NOUN **2** **Bark** is the outside covering of a tree.

Bb

barn barns
NOUN A **barn** is a large building where a farmer stores hay and other crops.

barometer barometers
NOUN **1** A **barometer** measures the pressure of the air surrounding us.
NOUN **2** **Barometer** is also used to describe changes in public opinion. *The poll is a good barometer of students' opinions.*

barrel barrels
NOUN A **barrel** is a large wooden, metal, or plastic container for holding liquids.

barrier barriers
NOUN A **barrier** is something like a fence or wall that stops people getting past.

base bases
NOUN **1** The **base** is the bottom of something.
NOUN **2** Number **bases** are a whole pattern of counting. A base ten counting system uses ones, tens, and hundreds.

basement basements
NOUN The **basement** of a building is a floor below ground level.

basic
ADJECTIVE **1** **Basic** is used to describe things like the food and equipment that people really need in their lives.
ADJECTIVE **2** **Basic** also means the simplest things you need to know about a subject. *I'm not good at this yet, but I've got the basic idea.*
basically ADVERB

basin basins
NOUN A **basin** is a wide round container which is open at the top.

basket baskets
NOUN A **basket** is used for holding or carrying things. It is usually made from strips of thin wood or cane.

bat bats, batting, batted
NOUN **1** In some games, like baseball, you use a wooden **bat** to hit the ball.
NOUN **2** A **bat** is also a small animal like a mouse with leathery wings. Bats fly at night, and sleep hanging upside down.
VERB **3** If you are **batting**, you are having a turn at hitting the ball with a bat in baseball.

bath baths
NOUN A **bath** is a container for water. It is big enough to sit or lie in, so that you can wash yourself all over.

bathroom bathrooms
NOUN The **bathroom** is the room where the bath or shower is.

battery batteries
NOUN A **battery** is an object which stores electric power. There are tiny batteries for things like watches, and larger batteries for flashlights.

battle battles
NOUN A **battle** is a fight between enemy forces, on land, at sea, or in the air.

bawl bawls, bawling, bawled
VERB If a child is **bawling**, that child is crying very loudly and angrily.

bay bays
NOUN A **bay** is a deep curve in a coastline.

beach beaches
NOUN The **beach** is the land covered with sand or pebbles that is next to the sea.

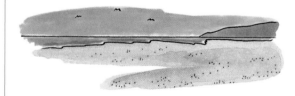

bead beads
NOUN A **bead** is a small piece of glass or plastic with a hole through it. Beads can be threaded together to make a necklace or bracelet.

beak beaks
NOUN A **beak** is the hard outside part of a bird's mouth.

beam beams, beaming, beamed

NOUN **1** A **beam** is a long thick bar of wood, metal, or concrete, used to support part of a building.

NOUN **2** A **beam** is also a line of light from an object such as a flashlight or the sun.

VERB **3** If you **beam**, you give a big smile.

bean beans

NOUN A **bean** is a vegetable. Its outer covering is called a pod, and inside it has large seeds, also called beans. See *Vegetables* on page 256.

bear bears, bearing, bore

NOUN **1** A **bear** is a large, strong animal with thick fur and sharp claws.

VERB **2** If you **bear** something, you put up with it. *I can't bear all this homework.*

beard beards

NOUN A **beard** is the hair which grows on the lower part of a man's face.

beat beats, beating, beat, beaten

VERB **1** If you **beat** someone in a race or competition, you do better than they do.

VERB **2** If someone **beats** another person or an animal, they hit them hard.

VERB **3** If you **beat** eggs, you stir them very fast.

VERB **4** Your heart **beats** with a regular rhythm all the time.

beautiful

ADJECTIVE **1** You say something is **beautiful** if it gives you great pleasure to look at it or listen to it.

ADJECTIVE **2** You say someone is **beautiful** if they are lovely to look at.

beaver beavers

NOUN A **beaver** is a furry animal which lives in or near water.

because

CONJUNCTION You say **because** when you are going to give a reason for something. *I left the party because they were playing silly games.*

become becomes, becoming, became, become

VERB To **become** means to start being different in some way. *The smell became stronger.*

bed beds

NOUN **1** A **bed** is a piece of furniture to lie down on when you rest or sleep.

NOUN **2** The **bed** of the sea or of a river is the ground beneath it.

bedroom bedrooms

NOUN Your **bedroom** is the room where you sleep.

bedtime

NOUN Your **bedtime** is the time when you usually go to bed.

bee bees

NOUN A **bee** is a flying insect. People keep bees for the honey that they make. See **beehive**.

See also *Insects* on page 259.

beech beeches

NOUN A **beech** is a large tree.

beef

NOUN **Beef** is the meat from a cow.

beehive beehives

NOUN A **beehive** is a house for bees, where a beekeeper collects the honey.

beer beers

NOUN **Beer** is a drink made from grain.

beet **beets**

NOUN A **beet** is a dark red root vegetable.
See *Vegetables* on page 256.

beetle **beetles**

NOUN A **beetle** is an insect with four wings. The front two act as hard covers to the body when the beetle is not flying. See *Insects* on page 259.

before

PREPOSITION **1** If something happens **before** something else, it happens earlier. *Can I see you **before** lunch?*
ADVERB **2** If you have done something **before**, it is not the first time.

beg **begs, begging, begged**

VERB If you **beg** someone to do something, you ask them very anxiously to do it. *Tom **begged** his dad to take him to the football game.*

begin **begins, beginning, began, begun**

VERB When you **begin**, you start. *I **began** school on Thursday.*

beginner **beginners**

NOUN A **beginner** is someone who has just started to learn something.

beginning **beginnings**

NOUN The **beginning** of something is the first part of it.

begun

VERB **Begun** is the past participle of **begin**.

behave **behaves, behaving, behaved**

VERB The way you **behave** is the way you act.
behavior NOUN

behind

PREPOSITION **1 Behind** means on the other side of something. *She was **behind** the counter.*
PREPOSITION **2** If you are **behind** someone, you are in back of them.

beige

ADJECTIVE Something that is **beige** is a pale creamy-brown color.
See *Colors* on page 271.

believe **believes, believing, believed**

VERB If you **believe** something or someone, you think what is said is true.

bell **bells**

NOUN A **bell** is a piece of metal shaped like a cup, which rings when something hits it.

belong **belongs, belonging, belonged**

VERB **1** If something **belongs** to you, it is your own.
VERB **2** If you **belong** to something, like a club, you are a member of it.

below

PREPOSITION If something is **below** something else, it is underneath it.

belt **belts**

NOUN A **belt** is a strip of leather or other material that you put around your waist.

bench **benches**

NOUN A **bench** is a long seat, usually made of wood.

bend **bends, bending, bent**

VERB When something **bends**, it becomes curved or crooked.

beneath

PREPOSITION If something is **beneath** something else, it is below it.

bent

ADJECTIVE If something is **bent**, it has become curved or crooked. See **bend**.

berry **berries**

NOUN A **berry** is a small, round, soft fruit that grows on a bush or a tree.

beside

PREPOSITION If something is **beside** something else, it is next to it.

best

ADJECTIVE **Best** means the "most good," or better than anything else. *That's the best program I've seen.*

better

ADJECTIVE **1** Something that is **better** than something else is of a higher standard or quality. *Your bicycle is better than mine.*

ADJECTIVE **2 Better** can also mean more sensible. *It would be better to go home.*

ADJECTIVE **3** If you are feeling **better** after an illness, you are not feeling so ill.

between

PREPOSITION If something is **between** two other things, it is in the space or time that separates them. *The toy store is between the bank and the library.*

beware

VERB You tell people to **beware** if there is danger of some kind. *Beware of the bull.*

bicycle **bicycles**

NOUN A **bicycle** is a vehicle with two wheels. You sit on it and turn pedals with your feet to make it go.

big **bigger, biggest**

ADJECTIVE Something or somebody **big** is large in size or importance.

bike **bikes**

NOUN **Bike** is an abbreviation of **bicycle**.

bill **bills**

NOUN **1** A **bill** is a piece of paper saying how much money you owe. *Mom just got the electricity bill.*

NOUN **2** A bird's **bill** is its beak.

bin **bins**

NOUN A **bin** is a container, usually with a lid, for putting garbage in.

bind **binds, binding, bound**

VERB If you **bind** something, you tie something like string or cloth tightly around it so that it is held in place.

biology

NOUN **Biology** is the study of living things.

birch **birches**

NOUN A **birch** is a tall tree that has thin peeling bark.

bird **birds**

NOUN A **bird** is an animal with two legs, two wings, and feathers.

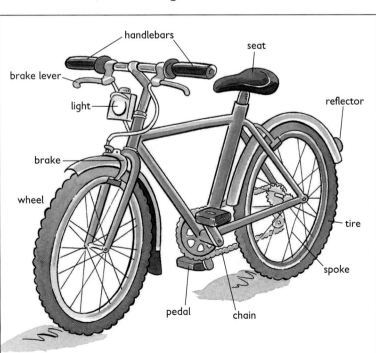

Bb

birth **births**

NOUN The **birth** of a baby is when it comes out of its mother's body.

birthday **birthdays**

NOUN Your **birthday** is a special date that is remembered every year, because it was the day you were born.

biscuit **biscuits**

NOUN A **biscuit** is a small, dry kind of cake.

bit **bits**

NOUN **1** A **bit** of something is a small piece of it.

NOUN **2** A **bit** is a piece of metal that goes in a horse's mouth.

VERB **3** Bit is also the past tense of **bite**.

bite **bites, biting, bit, bitten**

VERB If you **bite** something, you use your teeth to hold, cut, or tear it.

bitter

ADJECTIVE **1** If something has a **bitter** taste, it tastes sharp and unpleasant.

ADJECTIVE **2** Someone who is **bitter** feels angry and disappointed.

black **blacker, blackest**

ADJECTIVE If the color of something is **black**, it is the color of these letters. *See Colors on page 271.*

blackberry **blackberries**

NOUN **Blackberries** are small, soft, dark purple fruits that grow on brambles.

blackbird **blackbirds**

NOUN A **blackbird** is a European songbird.

blackboard **blackboards**

NOUN A **blackboard** is a dark board that people can write on in chalk.

blacksmith **blacksmiths**

NOUN A **blacksmith** works with iron to make things, like horseshoes.

blade **blades**

NOUN **1** A **blade** is the sharp edge of a knife or sword.

NOUN **2** A single piece of grass is a **blade**.

blame **blames, blaming, blamed**

VERB If somebody **blames** a person for something bad that happened, they say that person made it happen.

blank **blanker, blankest**

ADJECTIVE If something is **blank**, it has nothing written or drawn on it.

blanket **blankets**

NOUN A **blanket** is a large, warm cloth, often used to cover people in bed.

blaze **blazes**

NOUN A **blaze** is a strong bright fire.

blazer **blazers**

NOUN A **blazer** is a kind of jacket, often in the colors of a school or sports team.

bleed **bleeds, bleeding, bled**

VERB If part of your body **bleeds**, blood comes out of it.

blend **blends, blending, blended**

VERB When you **blend** two or more things together, they become a smooth mixture.

blew

VERB **Blew** is the past tense of **blow**.

blind **blinds**

NOUN **1** A **blind** is rolled material that you pull down to cover a window.

ADJECTIVE **2** Someone who is **blind** cannot see.

blindness NOUN

blindfold **blindfolds**

NOUN A **blindfold** is a strip of cloth tied over someone's eyes so that they cannot see.

blink **blinks, blinking, blinked**

VERB When you **blink**, you shut your eyes and open them again quickly.

blister **blisters**

NOUN A **blister** is a small bubble on your skin, containing watery liquid. Blisters are caused by a burn or rubbing.

blizzard **blizzards**

NOUN A **blizzard** is a bad snowstorm with strong winds.

block **blocks, blocking, blocked**

NOUN **1** A **block** is the distance from one street to the next.

NOUN **2** A **block** of something like stone or wood is a large rectangular piece of it.

VERB **3** To **block** means to get in the way.

block graph **block graphs**

NOUN A **block graph** is used to show information clearly, by using blocks to make columns.

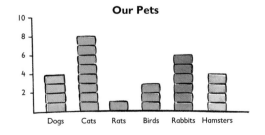

blood

NOUN **Blood** is the red liquid that your heart pumps around inside your body.

bloom **blooms, blooming, bloomed**

VERB When a plant **blooms**, its flowers open.

blossom

NOUN **Blossom** is the flowers that appear on a tree before the fruit.

blot **blots**

NOUN A **blot** is a mark made by a drop of liquid, especially ink.

blouse **blouses**

NOUN A **blouse** is a kind of shirt worn by a girl or a woman.

blow **blows, blowing, blew, blown**

VERB **1** When the wind **blows**, the air moves faster.

VERB **2** If you **blow**, you send out a stream of air from your mouth.

NOUN **3** A **blow** is a hard hit.

blue **bluer, bluest**

ADJECTIVE Something that is **blue** is the color of the sky on a sunny day.
See Colors on page 271.

bluebell **bluebells**

NOUN A **bluebell** is a flower that often grows wild in the woods.

blunt

ADJECTIVE **1** A **blunt** knife is not sharp.

ADJECTIVE **2** Something that is **blunt** has a rounded, rather than pointed, end. *My pencil's **blunt**.*

blur **blurs**

NOUN A **blur** is a shape that you cannot see clearly. *The car went past so fast it was just a **blur**.*

blurred ADJECTIVE   **blurry** ADJECTIVE

blurb **blurbs**

NOUN A **blurb** is a short piece written to attract people's interest. There is usually a blurb on the back of a book. *The **blurb** says this book is exciting.*

blush **blushes, blushing, blushed**
VERB When you **blush** you become red in the face, usually because you are embarrassed.

boar **boars**
NOUN A **boar** is a male pig.

board **boards**
NOUN A **board** is a flat, thin piece of wood.

boast **boasts, boasting, boasted**
VERB If you **boast**, you talk too proudly about something.

boat **boats**
NOUN A **boat** is a small vessel for traveling on water. See **ship**.

body **bodies**
NOUN **1** Your **body** is every part of you. Some animals, like elephants, have very large bodies.
See *Your body* on page 258.
NOUN **2** You can say **body** when you mean just the main part of a person, not counting head, arms, and legs.
NOUN **3** A **body** is a dead person.

bog **bogs**
NOUN A **bog** is an area of land that is always wet and spongy.

boil **boils, boiling, boiled**
VERB **1** When liquid **boils** it gets very hot. It bubbles and steam rises from it.
VERB **2** If you **boil** food, you cook it in boiling water.
NOUN **3** A **boil** is a painful red swelling on the skin.

bold **bolder, boldest**
ADJECTIVE **1** Someone who is **bold** is not afraid of risk or danger.
ADJECTIVE **2** Letters that are in **bold** type are thicker than ordinary printed letters.

bolt **bolts, bolting, bolted**
NOUN **1** A **bolt** is a long, round, metal pin with a flat end. It screws into a nut to fasten things.

NOUN **2** A **bolt** is a metal bar that you can slide across to keep a door shut.
VERB **3** If you **bolt** a door or window, you lock it with a bolt.
VERB **4** When a person or animal **bolts**, they suddenly run very fast.

bomb **bombs**
NOUN A **bomb** is a weapon which explodes and damages a large area.

bone **bones**
NOUN Your **bones** are the hard parts inside your body which make up your skeleton.

bonfire **bonfires**
NOUN A **bonfire** is a fire lit outdoors, often at colleges.

bonnet **bonnets**
NOUN A **bonnet** is a baby's or woman's hat tied under the chin.

book **books, booking, booked**
NOUN A **book** is a number of pages held together inside a cover.
VERB If you **book** something, you ask someone to keep it for you. *We booked seats at the theater.*

bookkeeper **bookkeepers**
NOUN A **bookkeeper** is someone who keeps the records of a company.

boot **boots**
NOUN **Boots** are strong shoes that cover your ankle and sometimes your calf.

border **borders**
NOUN **1** A **border** is the line dividing two countries.
NOUN **2** A **border** is a strip along the edge of something, usually as a decoration.

bore **bores, boring, bored**
VERB **1** If somebody **bores** you, you do not find them interesting.
VERB **2** If you **bore** a hole in something, you make a hole with a drill.
VERB **3** **Bore** is the past tense of **bear**.

bored

ADJECTIVE When you are **bored**, you feel tired and impatient because you have nothing interesting to do.
boredom NOUN

boring

ADJECTIVE Something **boring** is so dull that you have no interest in it.

born

VERB When a baby is **born**, it comes out of its mother's body.

borrow **borrows, borrowing, borrowed**

VERB When you **borrow** something, someone lets you have it for a while but they expect you to give it back later.

boss **bosses**

NOUN Someone's **boss** is the head of the place where they work.

bossy

ADJECTIVE A **bossy** person likes to tell others what to do.

both

ADJECTIVE OR PRONOUN You use **both** when you are talking about two things or people. *She wanted **both** pairs of jeans.*

bother **bothers, bothering, bothered**

VERB **1** If something **bothers** you, it annoys you or makes you feel worried.
VERB **2** If you **bother** about something, you care about it and take trouble over it.

bottle **bottles**

NOUN A **bottle** is a container for keeping liquids in. Bottles are usually made of glass or plastic.

bottom **bottoms**

NOUN **1** The **bottom** of something is the lowest part of it.
NOUN **2** Your **bottom** is the part of your body that you sit on.

bought

VERB **Bought** is the past tense of **buy**.

boulder **boulders**

NOUN A **boulder** is a big rounded rock.

bounce **bounces, bouncing, bounced**

VERB When something **bounces**, it springs back in the opposite direction as soon as it hits something hard.

bound **bounds, bounding, bounded**

VERB **1** When animals or people **bound**, they move quickly with large leaps.
ADJECTIVE **2** If something is **bound to** happen, it is sure to happen.

boundary **boundaries**

NOUN The **boundary** of an area of land is its outer limit.

bow **bows, bowing, bowed**
(*rhymes with* **low**)

NOUN **1** A **bow** is a kind of knot with two loops used to tie laces and ribbons.
NOUN **2** A **bow** is also a weapon used for shooting arrows.
NOUN **3** The **bow** for a stringed musical instrument is a long piece of wood with horsehair stretched along it.
(*rhymes with* **now**) VERB **4** When you **bow**, you bend your body forward.

bowl **bowls**

NOUN A **bowl** is an open container used for holding liquid or serving food.

box **boxes**

NOUN A **box** is a container with straight sides, made from something stiff, like cardboard, wood, or plastic.

boy **boys**

NOUN A **boy** is a male child.

bracelet **bracelets**

NOUN A **bracelet** is a band or chain which is worn around the wrist or arm as an ornament.

bracket **brackets**

NOUN **Brackets** are a pair of written marks [ ] placed around words that are not part of the main text.
See *Punctuation* on page 264.

Braille

NOUN **Braille** is a form of writing using raised dots that blind people can read by touching the dots with their fingers.

brain **brains**

NOUN Your **brain** is inside your head and controls your whole body. It lets you think, feel, and remember.

brainstorm **brainstorms, brainstorming, brainstormed**

VERB When people **brainstorm**, they get together to develop ideas. *This morning we are **brainstorming** words about dogs.*

brake **brakes**

NOUN The **brake** is the part of a vehicle that slows it down or stops it.

bramble **brambles**

NOUN A **bramble** is a wild bush with thorns.

branch **branches**

NOUN A **branch** is part of a tree that grows out from the trunk.

brass

NOUN **Brass** is a yellow metal made from copper and zinc. It is used for making things like ornaments and some musical instruments.

brave **braver, bravest**

ADJECTIVE If you are **brave**, you show you can do something even if it is frightening.

bravely ADVERB **bravery** NOUN

bread

NOUN **Bread** is a very common food, made with flour and baked in an oven.

breadth

NOUN The **breadth** of something is the distance that it measures from one side to the other.

break **breaks, breaking, broke, broken**

VERB **1** If you **break** something, it splits into pieces or stops working.
VERB **2** If you **break** a rule or a promise, you fail to keep it.

breakdown **breakdowns**

NOUN If someone's car has a **breakdown**, it stops working during a journey.

breakfast **breakfasts**

NOUN **Breakfast** is the first meal of the day.

breast **breasts**

NOUN **Breasts** are the two round parts on the front of a woman's body, which can produce milk to feed a baby.

breath

NOUN Your **breath** is the air that you take into and let out of your lungs.

breathe **breathes, breathing, breathed**

VERB When you **breathe**, you take air into your lungs through your nose or mouth, and then let it out again.

breed **breeds**

NOUN A **breed** of an animal is a particular kind. For example, a labrador is a breed of dog.

breeze **breezes**

NOUN A **breeze** is a gentle wind.

brick **bricks**

NOUN A **brick** is a block used for building. It is made of baked clay.

bride **brides**

NOUN A **bride** is a woman on or near her wedding day.

bridegroom **bridegrooms**

NOUN A **bridegroom** is a man on or near his wedding day.

bridesmaid **bridesmaids**

NOUN A **bridesmaid** is a woman or girl who helps a bride on her wedding day.

bridge **bridges**

NOUN A **bridge** is something built over things like rivers, railways, or roads, so that people or vehicles can get across.

brief **briefer, briefest**

ADJECTIVE Something that is **brief** lasts only a short time.

briefly ADVERB

briefcase **briefcases**

NOUN A **briefcase** is a flat case used for carrying papers.

bright **brighter, brightest**

ADJECTIVE **1** **Bright** colors are clear and easy to see.

ADJECTIVE **2** A light that is **bright** shines strongly.

ADJECTIVE **3** Someone who is **bright** is quick at learning or noticing things.

brilliant

ADJECTIVE **1** A **brilliant** color or light is extremely bright.

ADJECTIVE **2** Someone who is **brilliant** is extremely smart or clever.

brim **brims**

NOUN **1** If you fill a cup to the **brim**, you fill it right up to the top.

NOUN **2** The **brim** of a hat is the part that sticks outward from the head.

bring **brings, bringing, brought**

VERB **1** If you **bring** someone on a visit, they come with you.

VERB **2** If you **bring** something, you have it with you when you arrive.

bristle **bristles**

NOUN The **bristles** of a brush are the thick hairs or thin pieces of plastic which are fixed to the main part of it.

brittle

ADJECTIVE If something is **brittle**, it is hard but easily broken.

broad **broader, broadest**

ADJECTIVE Something such as a road or river that is **broad** is very wide.

broadcast **broadcasts**

NOUN A **broadcast** is a program or announcement on radio or television.

broke

VERB **Broke** is the past tense of **break**.

broken

VERB **Broken** is the past participle of **break**.

brooch **brooches**

NOUN A **brooch** is a small piece of jewelry which is worn pinned to a dress, blouse, or coat.

broom **brooms**

NOUN A **broom** is a kind of brush with a long handle.

brother **brothers**

NOUN Someone's **brother** is a boy or man who has the same parents as they have.

brought

VERB **Brought** is the past tense of **bring**.

brown **browner, brownest**

ADJECTIVE Something that is **brown** is the color of earth or of wood.

See *Colors* on page 271.

bruise **bruises**

NOUN A **bruise** is a purple mark on your skin where something has hit it.

a
b
Bb
c
d
e
f
g
h
i
j
k
l
m
n
o
p
q
r
s
t
u
v
w
x
y
z

brush brushes

NOUN A **brush** is a lot of bristles fixed to a handle. Different brushes are used for jobs like cleaning your teeth or painting.

bubble bubbles

NOUN A **bubble** is a ball of air or gas. You can make bubbles with soapy water. Soda has bubbles, too.

bucket buckets

NOUN A **bucket** is a container with a handle, often used for carrying water.

buckle buckles

NOUN A **buckle** is a fastening on the end of a belt or strap.

bud buds

NOUN A **bud** is a small lump on a plant which will open into a leaf or flower.

Buddhist Buddhists

NOUN A **Buddhist** is someone who follows the teachings of Buddha.

buffalo buffaloes

NOUN A **buffalo** is an animal like a large cow with long curved horns.

bug bugs

NOUN **1** A **bug** is an insect.
NOUN **2** A **bug** is also an illness, such as a flu bug or a stomach bug.
VERB **3** To **bug** someone is to annoy or bother them.

build builds, building, built

VERB If you **build** something, you make it by joining things together.

builder builders

NOUN A **builder** is a person whose job is to build houses and other buildings.

building buildings

NOUN A **building** is a place like a house that has walls and a roof.

bulb bulbs

NOUN **1** A **bulb** is the glass part of a lamp that gives out light.
NOUN **2** A **bulb** is also a root shaped like an onion. Many spring flowers such as daffodils and tulips grow from bulbs.

bulge bulges, bulging, bulged

VERB If something **bulges**, it sticks out in a lump. *His pockets **bulged** with money.*

bull bulls

NOUN A **bull** is a male cow, elephant, or whale.

bulldozer bulldozers

NOUN A **bulldozer** is a tractor with a steel blade on the front. It is used for moving large amounts of earth or stone.

bullet bullets

NOUN **1** A **bullet** is a small piece of metal fired from a gun.
NOUN **2** A **bullet point** is a heavy dot used to draw attention to a piece of text.

bully bullies

NOUN A **bully** is someone who hurts or frightens other people.

bump bumps, bumping, bumped

VERB **1** If you **bump** into something, you hit it while you are moving.
NOUN **2** If you hear a **bump**, it sounds like something falling to the ground.
NOUN **3** A **bump** is a raised uneven part on a surface such as a road.

bumper bumpers

NOUN **Bumpers** are bars on the front and back of a vehicle that protect it if there is an accident.

bun buns

NOUN A **bun** is a small, round bread.

bunch bunches

NOUN A **bunch** is a group of things together, like flowers or grapes.
*See **Collective nouns** on page 262.*

bundle **bundles**

NOUN A **bundle** is a number of small things that have been tied together.

bungalow **bungalows**

NOUN A **bungalow** is a house with all its rooms on one floor.

bunk beds

NOUN **Bunk beds** are two single beds fixed one above the other.

burger **burgers**

NOUN A **burger** is a flat piece of ground meat. It is often served on a bun.

burglar **burglars**

NOUN A **burglar** is someone who breaks into buildings to steal things.

burn **burns, burning, burned** or **burnt**

VERB **1** If something is **burning**, it is being spoiled or destroyed by fire.

VERB **2** People often **burn** logs to keep warm.

NOUN **3** A **burn** is an injury caused by heat or fire.

burrow **burrows**

NOUN A **burrow** is a hole in the ground that an animal lives in.

burst **bursts, bursting, burst**

VERB When something like a balloon or tire **bursts**, it splits open suddenly.

bury **buries, burying, buried**

VERB If you **bury** something, you put it in a hole in the ground and cover it.

bus **buses**

NOUN A **bus** is a large motor vehicle. People pay to go on buses.

bush **bushes**

NOUN A **bush** is a large woody plant with lots of branches. It is smaller than a tree.

business **businesses**

NOUN **1 Business** is the work of making, buying, and selling things or services.

NOUN **2** A **business** is a group of people who make and sell things.

bus stop **bus stops**

NOUN A **bus stop** is a place where people can get on or off buses.

busy **busier, busiest**

ADJECTIVE **1** When you are **busy**, you are working hard on something.

ADJECTIVE **2** A place that is **busy** is full of people doing things or moving about.

but

CONJUNCTION You use **but** to join two parts of a sentence when the second part is unexpected. *Megan likes most green vegetables,* **but** *she won't eat broccoli.*

butcher **butchers**

NOUN A **butcher** is a shopkeeper who cuts up meat and sells it.

butter

NOUN **Butter** is a yellow substance made from cream. You spread it on bread or use it for cooking.

butterfly **butterflies**

NOUN A **butterfly** is an insect with four large wings which flies during the day. See *Insects* on page 259.

button **buttons**

NOUN **1** A **button** is a small disk used to fasten clothes.

NOUN **2** A **button** is also a part of a machine that you press to make it work.

buy **buys, buying, bought**

VERB When you **buy** something, you get it by paying money for it.

buzz **buzzes, buzzing, buzzed**

VERB If something **buzzes**, it makes a "zzz" sound like a bee.

a

Bb

c
d
e
f
g
h
i
j
k
l
m
n
o
p
q
r
s
t
u
v
w
x
y
z

Cc

cab **cabs**
NOUN **1** The **cab** is the place where the driver sits in a bus, truck, or train.
NOUN **2** A **cab** is another word for a taxi.

cabbage **cabbages**
NOUN A **cabbage** is a vegetable that looks like a large ball of leaves.
See *Vegetables* on page 256.

cabin **cabins**
NOUN **1** A **cabin** is a room in a ship, boat, or airplane for passengers or crew.
NOUN **2** A **cabin** is also a small house in the woods.

cable **cables**
NOUN **1** A **cable** is a thick rope or chain.
NOUN **2** A **cable** is also a bundle of wires with a rubber covering, which carries electricity.
NOUN **3** Cable television is a system in which the signals are sent along wires.

cactus **cactuses**
or **cacti**
NOUN A **cactus** is a plant with spines. It can grow in hot, dry places like deserts.

café **cafés**
NOUN A **café** is a place with tables and chairs where you buy drinks and snacks.

cage **cages**
NOUN A **cage** is a box or room with bars in which birds or animals are kept.

cake **cakes**
NOUN A **cake** is a sweet food made with flour, sugar, shortening, and eggs, and baked in an oven.

calculate **calculates, calculating, calculated**
VERB If you **calculate** something in math, you work it out.

calculation **calculations**
NOUN A **calculation** is something you work out in math.

calculator **calculators**
NOUN A **calculator** is a small electronic machine which you can use to give you the answer to different math problems.

calendar **calendars**
NOUN A **calendar** is a list of the months, weeks, and days in a year.

calf **calves**
NOUN **1** Calves are young cows, elephants, and whales.
See *Young animals* on page 260.
NOUN **2** Your **calf** is the part at the back of your leg between the knee and ankle.

call **calls, calling, called**
VERB **1** If you **call** someone, you shout for them, or telephone them.
VERB **2** If you **call** someone something, you give them a name.
VERB **3** If an animal or thing is **called** something, that is their name.

calm **calmer, calmest**
ADJECTIVE **1** If you are **calm**, you do not seem worried or excited.
ADJECTIVE **2** If the sea is **calm**, it is smooth and still because there is no wind.

came
VERB **Came** is the past tense of **come**.

camel **camels**
NOUN A **camel** is a large animal which carries people and things in the desert.

camera **cameras**
NOUN A **camera** is a piece of equipment you use to take pictures.

camouflage **camouflages, camouflaging, camouflaged**
VERB To **camouflage** something is to hide it by giving it the same color or appearance as its surroundings.

camp **camps**
NOUN A **camp** is a place where people stay in tents.

can **could; cans**
VERB 1 If you **can** do something, you are able to do it. *I can swim.*
NOUN 2 A **can** is a metal container for something like food, drink, or paint.

canal **canals**
NOUN A **canal** is a narrow stretch of water made for boats to travel along.

cancel **cancels, cancelling, cancelled**
VERB If you **cancel** something that has been planned, you stop it from happening.

candle **candles**
NOUN A **candle** is a wax stick with a string called a wick inside. You light the wick and it burns to give light.

cane **canes**
NOUN 1 A **cane** is the long hollow stem of a plant such as bamboo.
NOUN 2 A **cane** is a tall narrow stick used to support things.

cannot
VERB **Cannot** means unable.

canoe **canoes**
NOUN A **canoe** is a small light boat, moved with a paddle.

can't
VERB **Can't** is a contraction of **cannot**.

canvas
NOUN **Canvas** is strong cloth, used for making things like tents and sails.

canyon **canyons**
NOUN A **canyon** is a narrow valley with very steep sides, often with a river.

cap **caps**
NOUN 1 A **cap** is a soft flat hat with a peak at the front.
NOUN 2 A **cap** is also a small flat lid on a bottle or container.

capable
ADJECTIVE If a person is **capable** of doing something, they are able to do it. *He's capable of doing better.*

capacity **capacities**
NOUN The **capacity** of something is the largest amount it can hold, produce, or carry. *The capacity of this cup is 8 ounces.*

capital **capitals**
NOUN 1 The **capital** is the main city in a country. *Paris is the capital of France.*
NOUN 2 A **capital** is a big letter of the alphabet, such as A, B, and C. Capital letters are also called uppercase letters. See **lowercase**.
See *Punctuation* on page 264.

captain **captains**
NOUN 1 A **captain** is the person in charge of a ship or an airplane.
NOUN 2 A **captain** is the person who leads a team in sports like football.

caption **captions**
NOUN A **caption** is the wording printed underneath a picture which explain what the picture is about.

capture **captures, capturing, captured**
VERB If you **capture** somebody, you take them prisoner.

car **cars**
NOUN A **car** is a road vehicle with wheels and an engine. It needs a driver and has room for passengers.

a
b
Cc
d
e
f
g
h
i
j
k
l
m
n
o
p
q
r
s
t
u
v
w
x
y
z

caravan caravans

NOUN A **caravan** is a group of people or vehicles traveling together.

card cards

NOUN **1** A greeting **card** usually has a picture on the front and is sent to people on special days such as birthdays.

NOUN **2** Playing **cards** are small pieces of card with numbers or pictures on them. They are used for card games.

cardboard

NOUN **Cardboard** is thick, stiff paper.

cardigan cardigans

NOUN A **cardigan** is a knitted sweater. You fasten it at the front with buttons.

care cares, caring, cared

VERB **1** If you **care** about something or someone, you think they are important.

VERB **2** If you **care** for a person or animal, you look after them.

NOUN **3** If you do something with **care**, you take trouble over it.

career careers

NOUN Someone's **career** is the work they do, which they hope to do for a long time. *John wants a career in teaching.*

careful

ADJECTIVE If someone is **careful**, they try to do things safely and well.

careless

ADJECTIVE If you are **careless**, you do not pay attention to what you are doing.

caress caresses, caressing, caressed

VERB If you **caress** someone, you treat them with kindness and affection.

caretaker caretakers

NOUN A **caretaker** is a person who looks after a large building such as a school.

cargo cargoes

NOUN **Cargo** is the goods carried on a ship or plane.

carnival carnivals

NOUN A **carnival** is a sort of party in the streets. There is usually music and dancing, and people dress up and decorate cars and trucks.

carpenter carpenters

NOUN A **carpenter** is a person who works with wood.

carpet carpets

NOUN A **carpet** is a thick covering for a floor, often made of wool.

carriage carriages

NOUN A **carriage** is a vehicle with wheels to carry a baby. In the past, a carriage was pulled by horses.

carrot carrots

NOUN A **carrot** is a long, thin orange vegetable that grows in the ground. *See Vegetables on page 256.*

carry carries, carrying, carried

VERB When you **carry** something, you pick it up and take it with you.

cart carts

NOUN A **cart** is a heavy wooden vehicle pulled by horses or cattle on farms.

carton cartons

NOUN A **carton** is a strong cardboard or plastic box for holding food or drink.

cartoon cartoons

NOUN **1** A **cartoon** is a film where the characters are drawn instead of being real people.

NOUN **2** A **cartoon** is also a funny drawing in a magazine, newspaper, or book.

a
b
Cc
d
e
f
g
h
i
j
k
l
m
n
o
p
q
r
s
t
u
v
w
x
y
z

cartwheel **cartwheels**

NOUN A **cartwheel** is a movement. You put your hands on the floor and move your legs until you land on your feet again.

carve **carves, carving, carved**

VERB **1** If you **carve** an object, you cut it out of something like stone or wood.

VERB **2** If someone **carves** a piece of meat, they cut slices from it.

case **cases**

NOUN A **case** is a box for keeping or carrying things in.

cash

NOUN **Cash** is coins and paper money.

cassette **cassettes**

NOUN A **cassette** is a small flat container with magnetic tape inside, which is used for recording and playing back sounds.

cast **casts, casting, cast**

NOUN **1** The **cast** of a play or film is all the people who act in it.

NOUN **2** A **cast** is an object made by pouring liquid plaster or metal into a container and leaving it to harden.

VERB **3** If something **casts** a shadow onto a place, it makes a shadow fall there.

VERB **4** If someone like a witch **casts** a spell on someone or something, they do magic that affects that person or thing.

castle **castles**

NOUN A **castle** is a large building with walls or ditches around it to protect it from attack.

cat **cats**

NOUN A **cat** is a small furry animal, often kept as a pet. There are also larger, wild cats, such as lions and tigers.

catalog **catalogs**

NOUN A **catalog** is a list of things for sale or for looking at.

catch **catches, catching, caught**

VERB **1** If you **catch** something, you take hold of it while it is moving.

VERB **2** If you **catch** a bus or train, you get on it to go somewhere.

VERB **3** If you **catch** something like measles, you get that illness.

catching

ADJECTIVE An illness that is **catching** can spread very quickly.

category **categories**

NOUN A **category** is a set of things with a particular feature or quality in common.

caterpillar **caterpillars**

NOUN A **caterpillar** is a very small animal like a worm with legs, that will change into a butterfly or moth.

cathedral **cathedrals**

NOUN A **cathedral** is a large, important church.

cattle

NOUN Bulls and cows are called **cattle**.

caught

VERB **Caught** is the past tense of **catch**.

cauliflower **cauliflowers**

NOUN A **cauliflower** is a round white vegetable with green leaves on the outside.

See *Vegetables* on page 256.

cause **causes, causing, caused**

VERB To **cause** something means to make it happen.

cautious

ADJECTIVE Someone who is **cautious** acts carefully to avoid possible danger.

a b **Cc** d e f g h i j k l m n o p q r s t u v w x y z

cave

cave caves
NOUN A **cave** is a large hole in the side of a hill or cliff, or in the ground.

CD CDs
NOUN CD is an abbreviation of **compact disc**.

CD-ROM CD-ROMs
NOUN **CD-ROM** is an abbreviation of **compact disc read-only memory**. It is a disc which can be played on a computer to show sounds and pictures.

ceiling ceilings
NOUN The **ceiling** is the inside roof of a room.

celebrate celebrates, celebrating, celebrated
VERB If you **celebrate** something, you do something enjoyable like having a party, to show it is a special occasion.

celery
NOUN **Celery** is a vegetable with long, pale green stalks.
See *Vegetables* on page 256.

cell cells
NOUN 1 Animals and plants are made from tiny parts called **cells**.
NOUN 2 A **cell** is also a small room where a prisoner lives.

cellar cellars
NOUN A **cellar** is the same thing as a basement.

Celsius
ADJECTIVE You use degrees **Celsius** to measure temperature. In the Celsius scale, 0 degrees (0°C) is the freezing point of water and 100 degrees (100°C) is its boiling point.

cement
NOUN **Cement** is a gray powder which is mixed with sand and water and used to make bricks stick together.

cemetery cemeteries
NOUN A **cemetery** is a place where dead people are buried.

center centers
NOUN 1 The **center** of anything is the middle of it.
NOUN 2 A **center** is a place where people can go for a particular purpose, for example sports.

centigrade
ADJECTIVE **Centigrade** means the same as **Celsius**.

centimeter centimeters
NOUN A **centimeter** (cm) is a measure of length. It is slightly less than half an inch.

centipede centipedes
NOUN A **centipede** is a tiny animal like a worm, but with lots of legs.

central
ADJECTIVE Something that is **central** is in the middle of an object or an area.

century centuries
NOUN A **century** is a period of 100 years. The 21st century is the time between 2000 and 2099.

cereal cereals
NOUN 1 **Cereal** is a plant which has seeds called grain that can be used for food.
NOUN 2 **Cereal** is also a food made from grain that is often eaten for breakfast.

ceremony ceremonies
NOUN A **ceremony** is a set of formal actions performed at a special occasion such as a wedding.

certain

ADJECTIVE If you are **certain** of something, you are sure it is true.

certificate **certificates**

NOUN A **certificate** is a piece of paper which says that something important like a birth or marriage took place.

chain **chains**

NOUN A **chain** is made from rings of metal joined together in a line.

chair **chairs**

NOUN A **chair** is a seat with a back, for one person.

chalk

NOUN **Chalk** is a soft white rock. It can be made into sticks for writing on blackboards.

champion **champions**

NOUN A **champion** is a person who has beaten everyone else in a contest.

chance **chances**

NOUN **1** If there is a **chance** that something will happen, it might happen.
NOUN **2** If you are given a **chance** to do something, you are allowed to do it if you want to.
by chance PHRASE If something happens **by chance**, it has not been planned.

change **changes, changing, changed**

VERB **1** When something **changes**, it becomes different.
VERB **2** When you **change** your clothes, you put on different ones.
NOUN **3** If there is a **change** in something, it is different in some way.
NOUN **4** **Change** is the money you are given when you pay more than the right amount for something.

channel **channels**

NOUN **1** A **channel** is a passage for water or other liquid.
NOUN **2** Television companies use **channels** to broadcast programs.

chaos

NOUN **Chaos** is a state of complete confusion, where nothing is organized.

chapter **chapters**

NOUN A **chapter** is a part of a book.

character **characters**

NOUN **1** The **characters** of a book, film, or play are the people it is about.
NOUN **2** Someone's **character** is the sort of person they are. *She has a kind character*.

charge **charges, charging, charged**

VERB **1** If someone **charges** you money, they ask you to pay for something.
VERB **2** If something or someone **charges** toward you, they rush forward.
in charge PHRASE If you are **in charge** of something, you are the person looking after it.

charity **charities**

NOUN A **charity** is an organization which raises money for a particular cause, such as people in need.

charm **charms**

NOUN **1** A **charm** is a small ornament that is fixed to a bracelet or necklace.
NOUN **2** A **charm** is also a magical spell or an object that is supposed to bring good luck.

chart **charts**

NOUN **1** A **chart** is a sheet of paper that shows things like dates or numbers.
NOUN **2** A **chart** can also be a map of the sea or of the stars.

chase **chases, chasing, chased**

VERB If you **chase** someone, you run after them to try and catch them.

chat **chats**

NOUN A **chat** is a friendly talk about things that are not very important.

cheap

cheap **cheaper, cheapest**
ADJECTIVE Something **cheap** costs very little, or less than you might expect.

cheat **cheats, cheating, cheated**
VERB When someone **cheats**, they lie or do unfair things to get what they want.

check **checks, checking, checked**
VERB **1** If you **check** something, you make sure it is correct or safe.
NOUN **2** A **check** is a piece of paper that people use to pay for things. *She paid for her groceries with a check.*

checkout **checkouts**
NOUN A **checkout** is the place in a supermarket where you pay.

cheek **cheeks**
NOUN Your **cheeks** are the sides of your face below your eyes.

cheer **cheers, cheering, cheered**
VERB When you **cheer**, you shout to show you are pleased about something or to encourage a person or team.

cheerful
ADJECTIVE Someone who is **cheerful** shows they are feeling happy.

cheese **cheeses**
NOUN **Cheese** is a food made from milk. Some cheeses have a strong flavor.

cheetah **cheetahs**
NOUN A **cheetah** is a large wild animal of the cat family, with black spots.

chemist **chemists**
NOUN A **chemist** is a scientist trained in chemistry.

chemistry
NOUN **Chemistry** is the scientific study of how substances are made up and how they work together.

cherish **cherishes, cherishing, cherished**
VERB If you **cherish** something, you appreciate it.

cherry **cherries**
NOUN A **cherry** is a small round red or black fruit with a hard seed called a pit in the middle. See *Fruit* on page 257.

chess
NOUN **Chess** is a game for two people. It is played on a board marked in black and white squares.

chest **chests**
NOUN **1** Your **chest** is the top part of the front of your body, between your neck and your waist.
NOUN **2** A **chest** is a large heavy box, usually made of wood.

chestnut **chestnuts**
NOUN **1** A **chestnut** is a large tree.
NOUN **2** A **chestnut** is also a shiny brown nut that grows on a chestnut tree.

chew **chews, chewing, chewed**
VERB When you **chew** food, you bite it several times.

chick **chicks**
NOUN A **chick** is a baby bird. See *Young animals* on page 260.

chicken **chickens**
NOUN A **chicken** is a bird kept on a farm for its eggs and meat.

chickenpox
NOUN **Chickenpox** is an illness that gives you itchy spots.

chief chiefs
NOUN A **chief** is a person in charge of other people.

child children
NOUN A **child** is a young boy or girl.

childhood
NOUN A person's **childhood** is the time of life when they are a child.

childish
ADJECTIVE You call a person **childish** if they are not acting in an adult way.

children
PLURAL NOUN **Children** is the plural of **child**.

chilly chillier, chilliest
ADJECTIVE If you feel **chilly**, you are not quite warm enough to be comfortable.

chime chimes
NOUN A **chime** is the musical sound made by a bell or a clock.

chimney chimneys
NOUN A **chimney** is a pipe that takes smoke from a fire up into the air.

chimpanzee chimpanzees
NOUN A **chimpanzee** is a small ape with dark fur that lives in forests in Africa.

chin chins
NOUN Your **chin** is the part of your face below your mouth.

chip chips, chipping, chipped
NOUN 1 A **chip** is a long, thin fried piece of potato.
NOUN 2 A silicon **chip** is a tiny piece of special material used in computers.
VERB 3 When you **chip** something, you break a small piece off it.

chisel chisels
NOUN A **chisel** is a tool with a long thin blade and a sharp end, which is used for cutting wood or stone.

chocolate chocolates
NOUN 1 **Chocolate** is a type of candy.
ADJECTIVE 2 **Chocolate** is a brownish color.

choice choices
NOUN 1 A **choice** is the different things that you can choose from.
NOUN 2 A **choice** can also be someone or something that you choose. *If you need a captain, Jessica would be a good choice.*

choir choirs
NOUN A **choir** is a group of people who sing together.

choke chokes, choking, choked
VERB If you **choke**, you cannot breathe because not enough air can get to your lungs. *He choked on a chicken bone.*

choose chooses, choosing, chose, chosen
VERB To **choose** something is to decide which thing you want to have or do.

chop chops, chopping, chopped
VERB 1 When someone **chops** something like wood, they cut it with an ax.
NOUN 2 A **chop** is a slice of meat on a bone.

chorus choruses
NOUN A **chorus** is a part of a song which is repeated after each verse.

a
b
Cc
d
e
f
g
h
i
j
k
l
m
n
o
p
q
r
s
t
u
v
w
x
y
z

closed
ADJECTIVE If something is **closed**, it is not open.

cloth cloths
NOUN **1** Cloth is material made from something like cotton or wool.
NOUN **2** A **cloth** is a piece of cloth used for cleaning.

clothes
PLURAL NOUN **Clothes** are the things people wear, such as shirts, pants, and dresses.

cloud clouds
NOUN **1** A **cloud** is a patch of white or gray mist that floats in the sky.
NOUN **2** You can use **cloud** to describe a lot of smoke, steam, or dust.
cloudy ADJECTIVE

clover
NOUN **Clover** is a small wild plant. It has white or purple flowers, and leaves divided into three parts.

clown clowns
NOUN A **clown** is someone in a circus who wears funny clothes and does silly things to make people laugh.

club clubs
NOUN A **club** is an organization joined by people who are interested in the same thing, such as chess or riding.

clue clues
NOUN A **clue** is something that helps to solve a problem or mystery.

clump clumps
NOUN A **clump** is a small group of plants growing together.

clumsy clumsier, clumsiest
ADJECTIVE Someone who is **clumsy** moves awkwardly and carelessly.
clumsily ADVERB

clung
VERB **Clung** is the past tense of **cling**.

cluster clusters
NOUN A **cluster** is a number of things close together in a small group.

clutch clutches, clutching, clutched
VERB **1** If you **clutch** something, you hold it tightly with your hand.
NOUN **2** A **clutch** is a group of eggs laid by a bird.
See *Collective nouns* on page 262.

clutter
NOUN **Clutter** is an untidy mess.

co-
PREFIX Co- means together. For example, "coeducation" is boys and girls being taught together.
See *Prefixes* on page 264.

coach coaches
NOUN **1** A **coach** is a large carriage pulled by horses.
NOUN **2** A **coach** is also a section of a train that carries passengers.
NOUN **3** A **coach** is someone who trains you for a sport or gives you extra lessons.

coal
NOUN **Coal** is a hard black rock which is dug out of the ground and burned to give heat.

coarse coarser, coarsest
ADJECTIVE Anything that is **coarse** looks and feels rough.

coast coasts
NOUN The **coast** is the place where the land meets the sea.

coat coats
NOUN **1** A **coat** is a piece of clothing with long sleeves that you wear over other clothes when you go out.
NOUN **2** An animal's **coat** is its fur.
NOUN **3** A layer of paint is called a **coat**.

cobweb cobwebs
NOUN A **cobweb** is a net made by a spider to trap insects.

cockpit **cockpits**
NOUN A **cockpit** is where the pilot sits in a plane.

cocoa
NOUN **Cocoa** is a brown powder made from the seeds of the cacao tree, and also a hot drink made from this powder.

coconut **coconuts**
NOUN A **coconut** is a large nut with white flesh, milky juice, and a hard hairy shell.

cocoon **cocoons**
NOUN A **cocoon** is a covering of silky threads that some young insects make for themselves before they grow into adults.

cod
NOUN A **cod** is a large sea fish which is caught for food.

code **codes**
NOUN **1** A **code** is a system of changing letters in a message for other letters or symbols, so that only people who know the code can read it.
NOUN **2** A **code** is also a group of letters and numbers that identify something. *Do you know the area **code** for Miami?*
NOUN **3** A **code** is also a set of rules.

coffee
NOUN **Coffee** is a coarse powder made by grinding roasted coffee beans, and also a hot drink made from this powder.

cog **cogs**
NOUN A **cog** is a wheel with teeth which turns another part of a machine.

coil **coils**
NOUN A **coil** is a series of loops into which something has been wound.

coin **coins**
NOUN A **coin** is a small piece of metal used as money.

cold **colder, coldest; colds**
ADJECTIVE **1** If the weather is **cold**, the temperature outside is low.
NOUN **2** A **cold** is a common illness. You sneeze and your nose feels blocked.

collage **collages**
NOUN A **collage** is a picture made by sticking pieces of paper or cloth onto a surface.

collapse **collapses, collapsing, collapsed**
VERB If someone or something **collapses**, they suddenly fall down.

collar **collars**
NOUN **1** The **collar** of a shirt or jacket is the part that fits around your neck.
NOUN **2** A **collar** is also a leather band around the neck of a dog or cat.

collect **collects, collecting, collected**
VERB **1** If you **collect** a number of things, you bring them together for a special reason. *She **collected** sticks for firewood.*
VERB **2** If you **collect** someone or something from a place, you gather them together. *We had to **collect** the band members from school.*

collection **collections**
NOUN A **collection** is a group of things brought together over a period of time. *My dad's got a huge stamp **collection**.*

collective noun **collective nouns**
NOUN In grammar, a **collective noun** refers to a group of things. For example, a group of sheep is called a "flock." *See Collective nouns on page 262.*

college **colleges**
NOUN A **college** is where people go to study after they have left high school.

a
b
Cc
d
e
f
g
h
i
j
k
l
m
n
o
p
q
r
s
t
u
v
w
x
y
z

collide **collides, colliding, collided**
VERB If a moving object **collides** with something, it hits it.
collision NOUN

colon **colons**
NOUN The punctuation mark : is a **colon**. You can use it in several ways, for example in front of a list of things.
See *Punctuation* on page 264.

color **colors**
NOUN The **color** of something is the way it looks in daylight. *The color of grass is green.*
See *Colors* on page 271.

colt **colts**
NOUN A **colt** is a young male horse.

column **columns**
NOUN **1** A **column** is a tall post which supports part of a building.

NOUN **2** A **column** is also a vertical strip of print in a newspaper or magazine.
NOUN **3** If numbers are arranged in vertical lists, these are called **columns**.

comb **combs**
NOUN A **comb** is a flat piece of plastic or metal with narrow teeth on one edge. You use it to tidy your hair.

come **comes, coming, came, come**
VERB **1** To **come** to a place is to move there or arrive there.
VERB **2** If you **come** from a place, you were born there, or it is your home.

comedy **comedies**
NOUN A **comedy** is a play or film that makes people laugh.

comet **comets**
NOUN A **comet** is an object which travels around the sun, leaving a long bright trail behind it.

comfort **comforts, comforting, comforted**
VERB If you **comfort** someone, you make them feel less worried or unhappy.

comfortable
ADJECTIVE If something is **comfortable**, it is easy to wear or use.

comic **comics**
NOUN A **comic** is a magazine that tells stories in pictures.

comma **commas**
NOUN A **comma** is a punctuation mark (,) which is used to separate parts of a sentence or items on a list.
See *Punctuation* on page 264.

command **commands, commanding, commanded**
VERB If you **command** someone to do something, you order them to do it.

commercial **commercials**
NOUN A **commercial** is an advertisement on television or radio.

common
ADJECTIVE If something is **common**, you often see it or it often happens.

common noun **common nouns**
NOUN **Common nouns** name things in general. For example, "boy," "dog," and "computer" are all common nouns.
See *Noun* on page 262.

common sense
NOUN If you have **common sense**, you usually act sensibly and do the right thing.

commotion

NOUN A **commotion** is a lot of noise, confusion, and excitement.

communicate **communicates, communicating, communicated**

VERB If you **communicate** with someone, you give them information by talking or writing to them.

compact disc **compact discs**

NOUN A **compact disc** is a round flat silver-colored object which can store information. It is called a **CD** for short.

company **companies**

NOUN **1 Company** is being with others so you are not lonely.

NOUN **2** A **company** is a group of people who work together to make or sell things.

comparative **comparatives**

NOUN In grammar, the **comparative** is the form of an adjective which has "more" of that adjective. For example, "happier" is the comparative of "happy."

See *Adjective on page 263*.

compare **compares, comparing, compared**

VERB When you **compare** two or more things, you look at them to see in what ways they are the same or different.

compass **compasses**

NOUN **1** A **compass** is an instrument with a needle that always points north.

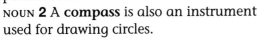

NOUN **2** A **compass** is also an instrument used for drawing circles.

compass point **compass points**

NOUN The main **compass points** are north, south, east, and west.

competition **competitions**

NOUN A **competition** is an event to find out who is best at doing something.

complain **complains, complaining, complained**

VERB If you **complain**, you say that you are not happy about something.

complete

ADJECTIVE **1** If something is **complete**, it has been finished.

ADJECTIVE **2** If you talk about a **complete** thing, you mean all of it. *I need a complete change of clothes.*

complicated

ADJECTIVE Something **complicated** is made up of so many parts that it is difficult to understand or deal with.

compose **composes, composing, composed**

VERB If you **compose** something, like a poem or a piece of music, you write it.

compound **compounds**

NOUN In language, a **compound** is a word that is made up of two or more words. "Playground," "armchair," and "toothache" are all compounds.

computer **computers**

NOUN A **computer** is a machine that stores information and works things out according to instructions in a program.

concave

ADJECTIVE A **concave** surface curves inward.

conceal **conceals, concealing, concealed**

VERB If you **conceal** something, you hide it carefully.

concentrate **concentrates, concentrating, concentrated**

VERB If you **concentrate** on something, you give it all your attention.

concerned

ADJECTIVE If you are **concerned** about something, it worries you.

concert concerts

NOUN A **concert** is a performance by musicians, usually in a big hall.

conclusion conclusions

NOUN 1 A **conclusion** is something you decide is true after you have thought carefully.

NOUN 2 The **conclusion** of something is its ending.

concrete

NOUN **Concrete** is a building material made of cement, sand, and water, which goes hard when it is set.

condition conditions

NOUN 1 The **condition** of something is the state it is in.

NOUN 2 A **condition** is a rule you must agree to before you are allowed to do something. *You can go out on one condition – you must be home by five.*

conductor conductors

NOUN A **conductor** is someone who controls the way musicians play together.

cone cones

NOUN A **cone** is a solid curved shape with a flat circular base and a pointed top.

See *Solid shapes* on page 271.

confess confesses, confessing, confessed

VERB If you **confess**, you say that you have done something wrong.

confident

ADJECTIVE 1 If you are **confident** about something, you are sure about it.

ADJECTIVE 2 People who are **confident** know that they can do something well.

confuse confuses, confusing, confused

VERB 1 To **confuse** someone means to make them unsure what to do. *The new road layout confused everyone.*

VERB 2 If you **confuse** two things, you mix them up by mistake. *I always confuse the twins because they are so alike.*

congratulate congratulates, congratulating, congratulated

VERB If you **congratulate** someone, you say you are pleased that something special has happened to them.

conjunction conjunctions

NOUN In grammar, a **conjunction** is a word that joins two other words or parts of a sentence. "And," "but," "while" and "although" are all conjunctions.

connect connects, connecting, connected

VERB If you **connect** two things, you join them together.

connective connectives

NOUN In grammar, a **connective** is a word or phrase that joins parts of a text. For example, "at last" and "because" are connectives.

connoisseur connoisseurs

NOUN A **connoisseur** is an expert in something, like food or wine.

conquer conquers, conquering, conquered

VERB To **conquer** people is to take control of their country by force.

conscious

ADJECTIVE If you are **conscious**, you are awake and know what is happening.

consecutive

ADJECTIVE If things are **consecutive**, they happen one after the other. *October, November, and December are consecutive months.*

consider **considers, considering, considered**

VERB If you **consider** something, you think about it carefully.

consist **consists, consisting, consisted**

VERB Something that **consists** of particular things is made up of them.

consonant **consonants**

NOUN A **consonant** is any letter of the alphabet except a, e, i, o, and u. See **vowel**.

constant

ADJECTIVE Something that is **constant** happens all the time. *She complained of a constant headache.*

construct **constructs, constructing, constructed**

VERB If you **construct** something, you build it or make it.

consume **consumes, consuming, consumed**

VERB If you **consume** something, you eat or drink it, or use it up.

contain **contains, containing, contained**

VERB The things that something **contains** are the things in it.

container **containers**

NOUN A **container** is something you put things in.

content

ADJECTIVE If you are **content**, you are happy and satisfied with your life.

contents

PLURAL NOUN The **contents** of something like a box or cake are the things in it. The **contents page** of a book tells you what is in it.

contest **contests**

NOUN A **contest** is a competition or game which you try to win.

continent **continents**

NOUN A **continent** is a very large area of land, such as Africa or Asia.

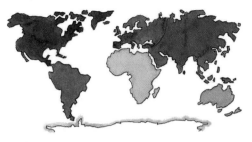

continue **continues, continuing, continued**

VERB If you **continue** to do something, you go on doing it.

continuous

ADJECTIVE Something that is **continuous** goes on without stopping.

contraction **contractions**

NOUN A **contraction** is a shortened form of word or words. For example, "I'm" is a contraction of "I am."

contradict **contradicts, contradicting, contradicted**

VERB If you **contradict** someone, you say the opposite of what they have just said.

control **controls, controlling, controlled**

VERB **1** If you **control** something, you make it behave exactly as you want it to. NOUN **2** The **controls** on a machine are knobs or other things used to work it.

convenient

ADJECTIVE If something is **convenient**, it is easy to use or do.

conversation **conversations**

NOUN If you have a **conversation** with someone, you talk to each other.

convex

ADJECTIVE A **convex** surface curves outward.

convince convinces, convincing, convinced

VERB If someone or something **convinces** you, they make you believe that something is true.

cook cooks, cooking, cooked

VERB When you **cook** food, you prepare it for eating by heating it.

cool cooler, coolest

ADJECTIVE If something is **cool**, its temperature is low but it is not cold.

coolheaded

ADJECTIVE A **coolheaded** person is not easily excited.

coordinates

NOUN **Coordinates** are two numbers or letters which help you find the exact position of something. They are often used on maps, graphs, and charts.

cope copes, coping, coped

VERB If you **cope** with a task or problem, you deal with it successfully.

copper

NOUN **Copper** is a reddish-brown metal.

copy copies, copying, copied

NOUN **1** A **copy** is something made to look exactly like something else.
VERB **2** If you **copy** something, you make a copy of it.
VERB **3** If you **copy** what someone does, you do the same thing.

coral corals

NOUN **Coral** is a hard substance that forms in the sea from the skeletons of tiny animals called corals.

cord cords

NOUN **Cord** is thick, strong string.

core cores

NOUN The **core** of a fruit is the hard part in the middle that contains seeds.

cork corks

NOUN **1** **Cork** is the light bark of the cork oak tree.
NOUN **2** A **cork** is a piece of cork used to block the open end of a bottle.

corn

NOUN **Corn** is a sweet, yellow vegetable, often eaten on the cob.

corner corners

NOUN A **corner** is the place where two edges or roads join.

correct corrects, correcting, corrected

ADJECTIVE **1** Something that is **correct** is true and has no mistakes.
VERB **2** If you **correct** your work, you put right any mistakes you made.

corridor corridors

NOUN A **corridor** is a long passage in a building or train.

cost costs, costing, cost

VERB If something **costs** an amount of money, you can buy it for that amount.

costume costumes

NOUN **1** A **costume** is the clothes worn by an actor, or that people wear for special events.
NOUN **2** **Costume jewelry** is inexpensive rings, necklaces, and bracelets.

cot cots

NOUN A **cot** is a collapsible bed.

cottage cottages
NOUN A **cottage** is a small house, usually in the country.

cotton
NOUN **1** Cotton is a cloth made from the soft fibers of the cotton plant.
NOUN **2** Cotton thread is used for sewing.
NOUN **3** Cotton balls are soft fluffy cotton, often used for cleaning the skin.

cough coughs
NOUN A **cough** is a noise made by someone forcing air out of their throat.

could
VERB **1** Could is part of the verb **can**. You use **could** to say that something might happen. *It could rain tomorrow.*
VERB **2** You also say **could** when you are asking for something politely. *Could you please tell me the way to the school?*

council councils
NOUN The **council** is a group of people who look after the affairs of a town, district, or county.

count counts, counting, counted
VERB **1** When you **count**, you say numbers in order. *Count up to a hundred.*
VERB **2** If you **count** a number of things, you are finding out how many there are.

counter counters
NOUN **1** A **counter** is a long narrow table in a shop, where things are sold.
NOUN **2** A **counter** is also a small round flat object, usually made of plastic, that is used in board games.

country countries
NOUN **1** A **country** is a land that has its own government and language.
NOUN **2** The **country** is land away from towns and cities.

couple couples
NOUN **1** A **couple** of things or people means two of them. *It should only take a couple of days.*
NOUN **2** Two people are sometimes called a **couple**, especially if they are married or having a relationship.

coupon coupons
NOUN A **coupon** is a piece of printed paper that allows you to pay less than usual for something.

courage
NOUN **Courage** is not showing that you are afraid of something.

course courses
NOUN **1** A **course** is a series of lessons.
NOUN **2** A **course** can also be one part of a meal.
of course PHRASE You use **of course** to make something you are saying stronger. *Of course I still want to go.*

court courts
NOUN **1** A **court** is an area marked out for a game like tennis or badminton.
NOUN **2** A **court** is also a place where things to do with the law are decided.
NOUN **3** The **court** of a king or queen is where they live with their family.

courtyard courtyards
NOUN A **courtyard** is an open flat area of ground with walls all around it.

cousin cousins
NOUN Your **cousin** is a child of your uncle or aunt.

cover covers, covering, covered
VERB **1** If you **cover** something, you put something over it to protect or hide it.
NOUN **2** The **covers** on a bed are the blankets or duvet that you have over you to keep you warm.
NOUN **3** The **cover** of a book or magazine is the outside of it.

cow cows
NOUN A **cow** is a large farm animal that gives milk.

coward cowards
NOUN A **coward** is someone who avoids anything dangerous, painful, or difficult.

cowboy cowboys
NOUN A **cowboy** is a man whose job is to look after cattle.

crab crabs
NOUN A **crab** is a sea animal. It has four pairs of legs, two pincers, and a flat round body covered by a shell.

crack cracks, cracking, cracked
VERB **1** If you **crack** something, or it cracks, it has a small split in it but does not quite break.
NOUN **2** A **crack** is the line on something that shows it is nearly broken.
NOUN **3** A **crack** is also a sudden loud noise.

cracker crackers
NOUN **1** A **cracker** is a thin crisp wafer, often slightly salty.
NOUN **2** A **cracker** can be a cardboard tube covered in colored paper, that people have at parties. It makes a sharp sound when you pull the ends apart.

cradle cradles
NOUN A **cradle** is a small box-shaped bed for a baby.

crane cranes
NOUN **1** A **crane** is a machine that moves heavy things by lifting them.

NOUN **2** A **crane** is also a large water bird with long legs and a long neck.

crash crashes, crashing, crashed
NOUN **1** A **crash** is a traffic accident.
NOUN **2** A **crash** is also a sudden loud noise like something breaking.
VERB **3** If something **crashes**, it hits something else and makes a loud noise.

crate crates
NOUN A **crate** is a large box used for transporting or storing things.

crawl crawls, crawling, crawled
VERB When you **crawl**, you move forward on your hands and knees.

crayon crayons
NOUN A **crayon** is a colored wax.

craze crazes
NOUN A **craze** is something that is very popular for a short time.

crazy crazier, craziest
ADJECTIVE **1** Someone or something **crazy** is very strange or foolish.
ADJECTIVE **2** If you are **crazy** about something, you are enthused about it.

creak creaks, creaking, creaked
VERB If something **creaks**, it makes an odd squeaking sound.

cream
ADJECTIVE **1** Something that is **cream** in color is yellowish-white.
NOUN **2** **Cream** is the pale yellow part of milk.

crease creases, creasing, creased
NOUN **1** A **crease** is a line made by folding or wrinkling something.
VERB **2** If you **crease** something, you make lines appear on it.

create creates, creating, created
VERB To **create** something means to cause it to happen, or exist.

creature creatures
NOUN A **creature** is any animal, such as a bird, fish, or insect.

creep **creeps, creeping, crept**
VERB If you **creep** somewhere, you move quietly and slowly.

crescent **crescents**
NOUN A **crescent** is a curved shape that is wider in the middle than at the ends, like the moon.

crew **crews**
NOUN A **crew** is the people who work on a ship, aircraft, or spacecraft.

cricket **crickets**
NOUN **1** Cricket is an outdoor game between two teams of 11 players.
NOUN **2** A **cricket** is a small jumping insect that makes a chirping sound by rubbing its wings together.

cried
VERB **Cried** is the past tense of **cry**.

cries
VERB **Cries** is a present tense form of **cry**.

crime **crimes**
NOUN A **crime** is something which is against the law.

criminal **criminals**
NOUN A **criminal** is someone who has done something that is against the law.

crimson
ADJECTIVE **Crimson** is dark red.

crinkle **crinkles, crinkling, crinkled**
VERB When something **crinkles**, it becomes slightly creased.

crisp
ADJECTIVE **1** Things like fruit and lettuce that are **crisp** are fresh and firm.
NOUN **2** A **crisp** is a baked dessert of fruit with a crumb topping.

criticize **criticizes, criticizing, criticized**
VERB If you **criticize** someone, you say what you think is wrong with them.

crocodile **crocodiles**
NOUN A **crocodile** is a large reptile, about 15 feet long.
See *Reptiles* on page 259.

crocus **crocuses**
NOUN **Crocuses** are small yellow, purple, or white spring flowers.

crooked
ADJECTIVE Something that is **crooked** is bent or twisted.

crop **crops**
NOUN A **crop** is plants grown for food.

cross **crosser, crossest; crosses, crossing, crossed**
ADJECTIVE **1** Someone who is **cross** is angry about something.
NOUN **2** A **cross** is a mark like + or ×.
VERB **3** If you **cross** something like a road, you go from one side to the other.

crossing **crossings**
NOUN A **crossing** is a place where you can cross the road safely.

crouch **crouches, crouching, crouched**
VERB If you **crouch** down, you bend your legs under you so that you are close to the ground.

a
b
Cc
d
e
f
g
h
i
j
k
l
m
n
o
p
q
r
s
t
u
v
w
x
y
z

crow crows
NOUN A **crow** is a large black bird.

crowd crowds
NOUN A **crowd** is a large number of people together in one place.

crowded
ADJECTIVE A place that is **crowded** is full of people.

crown crowns
NOUN A **crown** is an ornament that kings and queens sometimes wear on their heads.

cruel crueler, cruelest
ADJECTIVE Someone who is **cruel** hurts people or animals without caring.

cruise cruises
NOUN A **cruise** is a vacation on a ship that travels to different places.

crumb crumbs
NOUN A **crumb** is a very small piece of food such as bread or cookies.

crumble crumbles, crumbling, crumbled
VERB If you **crumble** something that is soft, it breaks into lots of little pieces.

crumple crumples, crumpling, crumpled
VERB If you **crumple** paper or cloth, you squash it so that it is full of creases.

crunch crunches, crunching, crunched
VERB If you **crunch** something, you crush it noisily, for example between your teeth or under your feet.

crush crushes, crushing, crushed
VERB To **crush** something is to destroy its shape by squeezing it.

crust crusts
NOUN The **crust** is a hard layer on the outside of something such as bread.

cry cries, crying, cried
VERB **1** When you **cry**, tears come from your eyes.
NOUN **2** A **cry** is a sudden sound that you make when you are surprised or hurt.

crystal crystals
NOUN A **crystal** is a mineral that has formed into a regular shape.

cub cubs
NOUN A **cub** is a young wild animal such as a lion, fox, or bear.
See *Young animals* on page 260.

cube cubes
NOUN A **cube** is a solid shape with six square faces all the same size.
See *Solid shapes* on page 271.

cuboid cuboids
NOUN A **cuboid** is a rectangular box shape with six faces. All the faces are rectangles.
See *Solid shapes* on page 271.

cuckoo cuckoos
NOUN A **cuckoo** is a gray bird. Cuckoos lay their eggs in other birds' nests.

cucumber cucumbers
NOUN A **cucumber** is a long, thin, dark green vegetable, eaten raw.
See *Vegetables* on page 256.

cuddle cuddles, cuddling, cuddled
VERB When you **cuddle** someone, you put your arms around them.

culprit culprits
NOUN A **culprit** is someone who has done something harmful or wrong.

cunning
ADJECTIVE Someone who is **cunning** plans to get what they want, often by tricking other people.

cup cups
NOUN **1** A **cup** is a small container with a handle which you drink out of.
NOUN **2** A **cup** is also a prize for the winner of a game or competition.

cupboard cupboards
NOUN A **cupboard** is a piece of furniture with doors and shelves.

cure cures, curing, cured
NOUN **1** A **cure** is something that makes people better when they have been ill.
VERB **2** If someone or something **cures** a person, they make them well again.

curiosity
NOUN **Curiosity** is wanting to know about things.

curious
ADJECTIVE **1** Someone who is **curious** wants to know more about something.
ADJECTIVE **2** Something that is **curious** is unusual and hard to explain.

curl curls, curling, curled
VERB **1** If an animal **curls** up, it makes itself into a rounded shape.
NOUN **2** Curls are pieces of hair shaped in curves and circles.
curly ADJECTIVE

currant currants
NOUN **Currants** are small dried grapes.

current currents
NOUN **1** A **current** is a steady movement of water or air.
ADJECTIVE **2** Something that is **current** is happening now.

curriculum curriculums or curricula
NOUN A **curriculum** is the different courses taught at a school or college.

curry curries
NOUN **Curry** is an Indian dish made with spices.

cursor cursors
NOUN A **cursor** is a small sign on a computer screen that shows where the next letter or number will appear.

curtain curtains
NOUN A **curtain** is a large piece of material that you pull across a window to cover it.

curve curves
NOUN A **curve** is a smooth, gradually bending line.
curved ADJECTIVE

cushion cushions
NOUN A **cushion** is a soft object put on a seat to make it more comfortable.

custom customs
NOUN A **custom** is something that people usually do. *It's his **custom** to take the dog for a walk after supper.*

customer customers
NOUN A **customer** is a person who buys something, especially from a store.

cut cuts, cutting, cut
VERB **1** If you **cut** yourself, you hurt yourself by accident on something sharp.
VERB **2** If you **cut** something, you use a knife or scissors to remove parts of it.

cutlery
NOUN **Cutlery** is the knives, forks, and spoons that you eat your food with.

cycle cycles, cycling, cycled
NOUN **1** A **cycle** is a bicycle.
VERB **2** If you **cycle**, you ride a bicycle.
cyclist NOUN

cygnet cygnets
NOUN A **cygnet** is a young swan.
See *Young animals* on page 260.

cylinder cylinders
NOUN A **cylinder** is a three-dimensional shape like a tube with flat circular ends.
cylindrical ADJECTIVE
See *Solid shapes* on page 271.

a b **Cc** d e f g h i j k l m n o p q r s t u v w x y z

Dd

dad **dads**
NOUN Your **dad** is your father.

daffodil **daffodils**
NOUN A **daffodil** is a yellow trumpet-shaped flower that blooms in the spring.

dagger **daggers**
NOUN A **dagger** is a weapon like a knife.

daily
ADJECTIVE Something that is **daily** happens every day.

dairy **dairies**
NOUN A **dairy** is a farm or place that sells milk and food made from milk, such as butter and cheese.

daisy **daisies**
NOUN A **daisy** is a small wild flower with white petals and a yellow center.

dam **dams**
NOUN A **dam** is a wall built across a river or stream to hold back water.

damage **damages, damaging, damaged**
VERB To **damage** something means to harm or spoil it.

damp **damper, dampest**
ADJECTIVE Something that is **damp** is slightly wet.

dance **dances, dancing, danced**
VERB When you **dance**, you move your body in time to music.

dandelion **dandelions**
NOUN A **dandelion** is a wild plant with bright yellow flowers.

danger **dangers**
NOUN A **danger** is something that could harm you.

dangerous
ADJECTIVE If something is **dangerous**, it is likely to harm you.

dare **dares, daring, dared**
VERB If you **dare** to do something, you are brave enough to do it.

dark **darker, darkest**
ADJECTIVE When it is **dark**, there is not enough light to see properly.
darkness NOUN

dart **darts, darting, darted**
VERB **1** If a person or animal **darts**, they move suddenly and quickly.
NOUN **2** A **dart** is a short arrow that you throw in the game of darts.

dash **dashes, dashing, dashed**
VERB **1** If you **dash** somewhere, you run or go there quickly.
NOUN **2** A **dash** is the punctuation mark (–) which shows a change of subject, or which may be used instead of parentheses. See *Punctuation* on page 264.

data
NOUN **Data** is information, usually in the form of facts or figures.

database **databases**
NOUN A **database** is a collection of information, often stored in a computer.

date **dates**
NOUN **1** If someone asks you the **date**, you tell them the day and the month.
NOUN **2** A **date** is a small brown sticky fruit which grows on palm trees.

daughter **daughters**
NOUN A girl is the **daughter** of her parents.

dawdle **dawdles, dawdling, dawdled**
VERB If you **dawdle**, you walk slowly, taking more time than you should.

dawn

NOUN **Dawn** is the time of day when it first begins to get light.

day days

NOUN A **day** is the 24 hours between one midnight and the next.

daylight

NOUN **Daylight** is the light that there is during the day before it gets dark.

dazzle dazzles, dazzling, dazzled

VERB If a light **dazzles** you, it is so bright that you cannot really see for a while.

de-

PREFIX When **de-** is added to a noun or verb, it means to remove. For example, "deforest" means to take away the forest.

See *Prefixes* on page 264.

dead

ADJECTIVE A person, animal, or plant that is **dead** is no longer living.

deaf

ADJECTIVE Someone who is **deaf** cannot hear very well, or cannot hear at all.

deal deals, dealing, dealt

VERB **1** When you **deal** in a card game, you give cards to the players.

VERB **2** If you **deal** with something, you do what needs to be done with it.

dear dearer, dearest

ADJECTIVE You use **Dear** at the beginning of a letter before the name of the person you are writing to.

death

NOUN **Death** is the end of life, when an animal or person dies.

decade decades

NOUN A **decade** is a period of ten years.

decay decays, decaying, decayed

VERB When something like a plant or piece of meat **decays**, it becomes rotten.

deceive deceives, deceiving, deceived

VERB If someone **deceives** you, they make you believe something untrue.

December

NOUN **December** is the 12th month of the year. It has 31 days.

decide decides, deciding, decided

VERB If you **decide** to do something, you make up your mind to do it.

decimal decimals

ADJECTIVE **1** A **decimal** system involves counting in units of ten.

NOUN **2** A **decimal** or **decimal fraction** is written with a dot followed by numbers, such as 0.2, 8.35. The numbers after the dot represent tenths, hundredths, and so on.

NOUN **3** A **decimal point** is the dot that comes between whole numbers and fractions.

NOUN **4** A **decimal place** is the position of a number after a decimal point.

decision decisions

NOUN A **decision** is a choice you make about what you think should be done.

deck decks

NOUN A **deck** is a floor on a ship or bus.

decorate decorates, decorating, decorated

VERB **1** If you **decorate** something, you add things to make it more attractive.

VERB **2** If someone **decorates** a room, they put up wallpaper or paint it.

decorations PLURAL NOUN

decrease

decrease decreases, decreasing, decreased
VERB If something **decreases**, or if you decrease it, it becomes less.

deep deeper, deepest
ADJECTIVE If something is **deep**, it goes a long way down. *The river is very deep.*

deer
NOUN A **deer** is a large hoofed animal. Male deer have horns called antlers.

defeat defeats, defeating, defeated
VERB If you **defeat** someone, you beat them in a game or contest.

defend defends, defending, defended
VERB If you **defend** someone or something, you do something to protect them against danger.
defense NOUN

define defines, defining, defined
VERB If you **define** something, you say what it is or what it means.

definite
ADJECTIVE **1** Something that is **definite** is unlikely to be changed. *We have a definite date for the outing.*
ADJECTIVE **2** Definite can also mean certain or true. *Lots of stories were going around, but they heard nothing definite.*
definitely ADVERB

definition definitions
NOUN A **definition** explains the meaning of a word.

degree degrees
NOUN **1** A **degree** is a unit of measurement of temperature, for example, 70°F.
NOUN **2** In math, a **degree** is a unit of measurement of angles. For example, a right angle is 90°.

delay delays, delaying, delayed
VERB If something **delays** you, it causes you to slow down or be late.

delete deletes, deleting, deleted
VERB If you **delete** some writing, you cross it out or remove it.

deliberate
ADJECTIVE If you do something that is **deliberate**, you do it on purpose.
deliberately ADVERB

delicate
ADJECTIVE **1** Something that is **delicate** is small and graceful.
ADJECTIVE **2** Someone who is **delicate** becomes ill easily.

delicious
ADJECTIVE Food that is **delicious** tastes or smells very nice.

delight delights, delighting, delighted
VERB If something **delights** you, it gives you a lot of pleasure.
delighted ADJECTIVE

deliver delivers, delivering, delivered
VERB If you **deliver** something, you take it to someone and hand it to them.

demand demands, demanding, demanded
VERB If you **demand** something, you say strongly that is what you want.

demonstrate **demonstrates, demonstrating, demonstrated**
VERB **1** If someone **demonstrates** something, they show you how to do it.
VERB **2** If people **demonstrate**, they hold a public meeting, or march, to show they are strongly for or against something.
demonstration NOUN

den **dens**
NOUN A **den** is the home of some wild animals, such as lions or foxes.

dense **denser, densest**
ADJECTIVE Something **dense** is hard to see through. *They were in a **dense** forest.*

dent **dents, denting, dented**
VERB If somebody **dents** something, they make a hollow in it by hitting it.

dentist **dentists**
NOUN A **dentist** is someone who examines and treats people's teeth.

deny **denies, denying, denied**
VERB If you **deny** something, you say that it is untrue.

depart **departs, departing, departed**
VERB When someone or something **departs** from a place, they leave it.
departure NOUN

depend **depends, depending, depended**
VERB **1** If you **depend** on someone, you need them.
VERB **2** If you can **depend** on someone, you know you can trust them.

depth
NOUN The **depth** of something is how deep it is.

descend **descends, descending, descended**
VERB To **descend** means to go down.

descending
ADJECTIVE When things are in **descending** order, each thing is lower than the one before it. *The numbers 10, 9, 8, and 7 are in **descending** order.*

describe **describes, describing, described**
VERB If you **describe** a person or thing, you say what they are like.
description NOUN

desert **deserts**
NOUN A **desert** is very dry land with very little plant life.

deserted
ADJECTIVE If a place is **deserted**, there are no people there.

deserve **deserves, deserving, deserved**
VERB If you **deserve** something, you have earned it by what you have done.

design **designs, designing, designed**
NOUN **1** A **design** is a pattern that is used to decorate something.
VERB **2** If you **design** something, you plan it and make a drawing of it.

desk **desks**
NOUN A **desk** is a special table that you use for writing or reading.

dessert **desserts**
NOUN A **dessert** is a sweet food served after the main course of a meal.

destroy **destroys, destroying, destroyed**
VERB To **destroy** something means to damage it so much it cannot be mended.

detail **details**
NOUN A **detail** is a small part or thing that you notice when you look at something carefully.

a
b
c
Dd
e
f
g
h
i
j
k
l
m
n
o
p
q
r
s
t
u
v
w
x
y
z

detective

detective detectives
NOUN A **detective** is a person whose job is to find out who did a crime.

determined
ADJECTIVE If you are **determined** to do something, nothing will stop you.

develop develops, developing, developed
VERB When something **develops**, it grows or becomes more advanced.

dew
NOUN **Dew** is the small drops of water that form on surfaces outdoors at night.

diagonal
ADJECTIVE A **diagonal** line slants from one corner of something to the opposite corner.

diagram diagrams
NOUN A **diagram** is a drawing that explains something.

dial dials
NOUN A **dial** is a numbered disk on an instrument like a clock.

dialogue dialogues
NOUN In a story, play, or film, **dialogue** is conversation.

diameter diameters
NOUN A **diameter** is a straight line drawn right through the center of a circle.

diamond diamonds
NOUN **1** A **diamond** is a very hard, clear jewel which sparkles.
NOUN **2** A **diamond** is also a shape with four straight sides, like a square, but slightly flattened.
See *Colors and flat shapes* on page 271.

diary diaries
NOUN A **diary** is a book in which you write about what you have done.

dice
NOUN **Dice** are small cubes with spots on each of their six sides.

dictionary dictionaries
NOUN A **dictionary** is a book in which words are listed alphabetically and explained.

did
VERB **Did** is the past tense of **do**.

didn't
VERB **Didn't** is a contraction of **did not**.

die dies, dying, died
VERB When a person, animal, or plant **dies**, they stop living.

diesel diesels
NOUN A **diesel** is a kind of engine that burns a special oil instead of gasoline.

diet diets
NOUN **1** A **diet** is the food that a person or animal normally eats.
NOUN **2** A **diet** is also a special range of foods that a doctor tells someone to eat if they have a health or weight problem.

difference differences
NOUN **1** The **difference** between two things is the way in which they are unlike each other.
NOUN **2** In math, you can work out the **difference** between two numbers by taking the smaller number away from the larger number.

different
ADJECTIVE Something that is **different** from something else is not like it in one or more ways.

difficult
ADJECTIVE Something that is **difficult** is not easy to do or understand.
difficulty NOUN

dig digs, digging, dug
VERB When people **dig**, they break up soil or sand with a spade or shovel.

digest digests, digesting, digested
VERB When you **digest** food, your body breaks it down so that it can be used.
digestion NOUN

digit digits
NOUN A **digit** is a written symbol for any of the numbers from 0 to 9. For example, 384 is a three-digit number.

digital
ADJECTIVE **1 Digital** instruments, such as watches, have changing numbers instead of a dial with hands. See **analog**.
NOUN **2 Digital television** is television in which the picture is sent in digital form.

dim dimmer, dimmest
ADJECTIVE If the light is **dim**, it is rather dark and it is hard to see things.

din
NOUN A **din** is a loud, annoying noise.

dinghy dinghies
NOUN A **dinghy** is a small open boat that you sail or row.

dining room dining rooms
NOUN A **dining room** is the room where people have their meals.

dinner dinners
NOUN **Dinner** is the main meal of the day.

dinosaur dinosaurs
NOUN A **dinosaur** was a large reptile which lived in prehistoric times and became extinct.

Triceratops
Stegosaurus

dip dips, dipping, dipped
VERB If you **dip** something into a liquid, you put it in quickly.

direct directs, directing, directed
VERB **1** If you **direct** someone, you show them the way to go.
VERB **2** A person who **directs** something, like a film, is in charge of it.
ADJECTIVE **3 Direct** means in a straight line without stopping, for example on a journey. *Is there a **direct** flight to Paris?*

direction directions
NOUN **1** A **direction** is the way in which someone or something is moving or pointing.
NOUN **2 Directions** are instructions that tell you what to do or which way to go.

dirt
NOUN **Dirt** is dust, mud, or stains on a surface or fabric.

dirty dirtier, dirtiest
ADJECTIVE Something that is **dirty** is marked or covered with mud or stains.

dis-
PREFIX **Dis-** is added to the beginning of words to form a word that means the opposite, for example "agree" → "disagree."
See *Prefixes* on page 264.

disabled
ADJECTIVE A **disabled** person has a condition or injury that makes it hard or impossible to do some things.
disability NOUN

disagree disagrees, disagreeing, disagreed
VERB If you **disagree** with someone, you think what they are saying is wrong.

disappear disappears, disappearing, disappeared
VERB If someone **disappears**, they go out of sight.

disappoint disappoints, disappointing, disappointed
VERB If something **disappoints** you, it is not as good as you thought it would be.
disappointment NOUN

a
b
c
Dd
e
f
g
h
i
j
k
l
m
n
o
p
q
r
s
t
u
v
w
x
y
z

disapprove

disapprove
VERB If you **disapprove** of something, you think it is wrong or bad.

disaster disasters
NOUN A **disaster** is something very bad that happens, such as an airplane crash.
disastrous ADJECTIVE

disc discs
NOUN A **disc** is a flat round object.

disco discos
NOUN A **disco** is a place where people go to dance to pop music.

discover discovers, discovering, discovered
VERB When you **discover** something, you find it or find out about it.
discovery NOUN

discuss discusses, discussing, discussed
VERB When you **discuss** something, you talk about it with someone else.
discussion NOUN

disease diseases
NOUN A **disease** is an illness in people, animals, or plants.

disguise disguises
NOUN A **disguise** is something that changes the way you look, so that people do not recognize you.

disgust
NOUN **Disgust** is a feeling of strong dislike for someone or something.

dish dishes
NOUN A **dish** is a shallow container for serving meals in.

dishonest
ADJECTIVE If someone is **dishonest**, they are not truthful.

dishwasher dishwashers
NOUN A **dishwasher** is a machine that washes things like plates.

disk disks
NOUN A **disk** is used for storing information in a computer.

dislike dislikes, disliking, disliked
VERB If you **dislike** someone or something, you do not like them.

dismiss dismisses, dismissing, dismissed
VERB When someone in authority **dismisses** you, they tell you to leave.

display displays
NOUN A **display** is an arrangement of things which is done to show to people.

dissolve dissolves, dissolving, dissolved
VERB If something **dissolves** in a liquid, it becomes mixed in with it. See **solution**.

distance distances
NOUN The **distance** between two things is the amount of space between them.

distant
ADJECTIVE **Distant** means far away.

distinct
ADJECTIVE If something is **distinct**, you can hear or see it clearly.

distribute distributes, distributing, distributed
VERB If you **distribute** things like leaflets, you hand them out to several people.

district districts
NOUN A **district** is the area around a place. *He's the only doctor in this **district**.*

disturb disturbs, disturbing, disturbed
VERB If you **disturb** someone, you interrupt them or spoil their peace and quiet.

disturbance **disturbances**

NOUN A **disturbance** is something that spoils people's peace and quiet.

ditch **ditches**

NOUN A **ditch** is a trench dug at the side of a road or field, to drain water.

dive **dives, diving, dived**

VERB To **dive** is to jump head first into water with your arms above your head.

diver NOUN

divide **divides, dividing, divided**

VERB **1** When something is **divided**, it is separated into smaller parts.

VERB **2** When you **divide** numbers, you share them into equal groups. For example, 15 can be divided into 3 groups of 5, or 5 groups of 3. $15 \div 3 = 5$ or $15 \div 5 = 3$.

divisible

ADJECTIVE A number that is **divisible** can be divided by another number without leaving a remainder. 27 is divisible by 3.

division **divisions**

NOUN **1** **Division** is separating something into two or more parts.

NOUN **2** In math, **division** is the process of dividing one number by another. The sign $\div$ is used for division.

divorce **divorces**

NOUN A **divorce** is the legal ending of a marriage.

Diwali

NOUN **Diwali** is a Hindu festival of light that is celebrated in the autumn.

dizzy **dizzier, dizziest**

ADJECTIVE If you feel **dizzy**, your head feels funny, as if you are going to fall over.

do **does, doing, did, done**

VERB **1** If you **do** something, you get on and finish it. *Have you **done** your work?*

VERB **2** **Do** can be used with other verbs. *Do you want some more?*

doctor **doctors**

NOUN A **doctor** is a person who treats people when they are ill.

document **documents**

NOUN **1** A **document** is a piece of paper which is an official record of something.

NOUN **2** A **document** is also a piece of text stored as a file in a computer.

dodge **dodges, dodging, dodged**

VERB If you **dodge**, you move suddenly out of the way.

does

VERB **Does** is a present tense form of **do**.

doesn't

VERB **Doesn't** is a contraction of **does not**.

dog **dogs**

NOUN A **dog** is an animal. Dogs bark and are often kept as pets, or used to guard things.

doll **dolls**

NOUN A **doll** is a child's toy that looks like a baby or a small person.

dollar **dollars**

NOUN A **dollar** is a unit of money in the United States.

dolphin **dolphins**

NOUN A **dolphin** is a mammal which lives in the sea.

dome

dome domes
NOUN A **dome** is a round roof.

domino dominoes
NOUN A **domino** is a small black rectangular block, marked with spots. Dominoes are used for playing games.

done
VERB **Done** is the past participle of **do**.

donkey donkeys
NOUN A **donkey** is an animal like a small horse, with longer ears.

don't
VERB **Don't** is a contraction of **do not**.

door doors
NOUN A **door** swings or slides to open and close the entrance to something.

dose doses
NOUN A **dose** is the amount of a medicine that you have to take.

dot dots
NOUN A **dot** is a small round mark.

double
ADJECTIVE If something is **double** the size or amount of something else, it is twice as big.

doubt doubts
NOUN If you have a **doubt** about something, you are not sure about it.

doubtful
ADJECTIVE **1** If you are **doubtful** about something, you are not sure about it.
ADJECTIVE **2** Something that is **doubtful** seems unlikely or uncertain.

dough
NOUN **Dough** is the floury mixture used to make things like pastry or bread.

doughnut doughnuts
NOUN A **doughnut** is a ring of sweet dough cooked in hot fat.

dove doves
NOUN A **dove** is a bird like a small pigeon.

down
PREPOSITION **1** If you go **down** a hill, you go to a lower level.
ADVERB **2** If you put something **down**, you put it on a surface.
ADVERB **3** If an amount of something goes **down**, it gets less. *My spending money's gone **down**.*
NOUN **4** **Down** is soft feathers.

downstairs
ADVERB If you go **downstairs**, you go toward the ground floor.

doze dozes, dozing, dozed
VERB When you **doze**, you sleep lightly.

dozen dozens
NOUN If you have a **dozen** things, you have 12 of them.

draft drafts
NOUN A **draft** is an early rough version of something you are writing.

drag drags, dragging, dragged
VERB If you **drag** a heavy object, you pull it along the ground.

dragon dragons
NOUN In stories, a **dragon** is a fierce animal like a big lizard. It has wings and claws and breathes fire.

dragonfly dragonflies
NOUN A **dragonfly** is a brightly colored insect, usually found near water.

See *Insects* on page 259.

drain drains, draining, drained
NOUN **1** A **drain** is a pipe that carries water away.
VERB **2** If a liquid **drains** away, it flows slowly to somewhere else.

drake **drakes**

NOUN A **drake** is a male duck.

drama **dramas**

NOUN **1** A **drama** is a serious play for the theater, television, or radio.

NOUN **2** **Drama** is something that affects people seriously.

dramatic

ADJECTIVE Something **dramatic** is very exciting and interesting.

dramatically ADVERB

drank

VERB **Drank** is the past tense of **drink**.

drastic

ADJECTIVE If you do something **drastic**, you take sudden, severe, or violent action.

drastically ADVERB

draw **draws, drawing, drew, drawn**

VERB **1** When you **draw**, you use something like a pencil or crayon to make a picture or a pattern.

VERB **2** When you **draw** the curtains, you pull them across a window.

NOUN **3** A **draw** is the result in a game or competition in which nobody wins.

drawbridge **drawbridges**

NOUN A **drawbridge** is a bridge that can be pulled up to stop people from getting into a castle.

drawer **drawers**

NOUN A **drawer** is a box that slides in and out of a piece of furniture.

drawing **drawings**

NOUN A **drawing** is a picture made with a pencil, pen, or crayon.

dread **dreads, dreading, dreaded**

VERB If you **dread** something, you feel worried and frightened about it.

dreadful

ADJECTIVE Something that is **dreadful** is very bad or unpleasant.

dream **dreams, dreaming, dreamed** or **dreamt**

VERB **1** When you **dream**, you see events in your mind while you are asleep.

VERB **2** If you **dream** while you are awake, you think about things you would like to happen.

dream NOUN

dress **dresses, dressing, dressed**

VERB **1** When you **dress**, you put on your clothes.

NOUN **2** A **dress** is a piece of clothing for women or girls made up of a skirt and top joined together.

drew

VERB **Drew** is the past tense of **draw**.

dribble **dribbles, dribbling, dribbled**

VERB **1** When babies **dribble**, water trickles from their mouth.

VERB **2** When players **dribble** the ball in a game like basketball, they bounce it while running.

drift **drifts, drifting, drifted**

VERB **1** When something **drifts**, it is carried along slowly by wind or water.

NOUN **2** A **drift** is a pile of snow heaped up by the wind.

drill **drills**

NOUN A **drill** is a tool for making holes.

drink **drinks, drinking, drank, drunk**

VERB **1** When you **drink**, you take liquid into your mouth and swallow it.

NOUN **2** A **drink** is a liquid which you swallow to stop you from being thirsty.

a
b
c
Dd
e
f
g
h
i
j
k
l
m
n
o
p
q
r
s
t
u
v
w
x
y
z

drip **drips, dripping, dripped**
VERB When something **drips**, drops of liquid fall from it one after the other.

drive **drives, driving, drove, driven**
VERB If someone **drives** a vehicle, they make it move and control it.

drizzle
NOUN **Drizzle** is light rain.

drop **drops, dropping, dropped**
VERB **1** If you **drop** something, you let it fall.
NOUN **2** A **drop** is a tiny amount of liquid.

drought **droughts**
NOUN A **drought** is a long period of time when no rain falls.

drove
VERB **Drove** is the past tense of **drive**.

drown **drowns, drowning, drowned**
VERB If someone **drowns**, they die because they have gone under water and cannot breathe.

drug **drugs**
NOUN A **drug** is a substance that is used to treat or prevent disease, or stop pain. Some drugs can be dangerous.

drum **drums**
NOUN A **drum** is a musical instrument which you hit to make a noise. It has skin stretched tightly over the end.

drunk
VERB **Drunk** is the past participle of **drink**.

dry **drier** or **dryer, driest**
ADJECTIVE Something that is **dry** has no water in it at all.
dry VERB

duck **ducks**
NOUN A **duck** is a common water bird with short legs and webbed feet.

due
ADJECTIVE If something is **due** at a particular time, it should happen then.

dug
VERB **Dug** is the past tense of **dig**.

dull **duller, dullest**
ADJECTIVE **1** Something that is **dull** is not interesting.
ADJECTIVE **2** Dull means not bright.
ADJECTIVE **3** A **dull** pain is not sharp.

dumpling **dumplings**
NOUN A **dumpling** is dough that is cooked by boiling or steaming.

dungeon **dungeons**
NOUN A **dungeon** is a dark underground prison in a castle.

during
PREPOSITION Something that happens **during** a period of time happens in that period. *I worked **during** the holidays.*

dusk
NOUN **Dusk** is the part of the day when it is beginning to get dark.

dust
NOUN **Dust** is dry fine powdery material, such as particles of earth, dirt, or pollen.
dusty ADJECTIVE

Dutch oven **Dutch ovens**
NOUN A **Dutch oven** is a heavy pot with a lid.

duty **duties**
NOUN A **duty** is something you feel you should do. *He only went to see his aunt because he felt it was his **duty**.*

duvet **duvets**
NOUN A **duvet** is a comforter for a bed.

dye **dyes, dyeing, dyed**
VERB If you **dye** something, such as hair or cloth, you change its color by soaking it in a special liquid.

dying
VERB See **die**.

Ee

each
ADJECTIVE **Each** means every one taken separately. *She gave **each** child a pencil.*

eager
ADJECTIVE If you are **eager**, you very much want to do or have something.

eagle eagles
NOUN An **eagle** is a large strong bird with a sharp curved beak and claws.

ear ears
NOUN Your **ears** are the parts of your body that you use for hearing.

early earlier, earliest
ADJECTIVE **1 Early** means near the beginning of a period of time. *We took the **early** train to school.*
ADVERB **2** You also use **early** to mean sooner than expected. *I arrived at the party **early**.*

earn earns, earning, earned
VERB If you **earn** something, such as money, you get it by working for it.

earring earrings
NOUN An **earring** is a piece of jewelry worn on or through the ear for decoration.

earth

NOUN **1** The **Earth** is the planet we live on.
NOUN **2** The soil that plants grow in is also called **earth**.

earthquake earthquakes
NOUN An **earthquake** is when the ground shakes because of movement beneath the surface.

east
NOUN **East** is one of the four main points of the compass. It is the direction in which the sun rises. See **compass point**.
eastern ADJECTIVE

Easter
NOUN **Easter** is a Christian festival that celebrates Christ's resurrection.

easy easier, easiest
ADJECTIVE Something that is **easy** can be done without difficulty.
easily ADVERB

eat eats, eating, ate, eaten
VERB When you **eat**, you chew and swallow food.

echo echoes
NOUN An **echo** is a sound that bounces back from something, like the walls of a cave or building.

eclipse eclipses

NOUN An **eclipse** of the sun is when the moon comes in front of the sun and hides it for a short time.

edge edges
NOUN **1** An **edge** is the end or side of something.
NOUN **2** An **edge** is where two faces of a three-dimensional shape meet.

edible
ADJECTIVE Something that is **edible** is safe to eat.

edit edits, editing, edited
VERB **1** If you **edit** a piece of writing, you correct it so that it is ready for printing.
VERB **2** When someone **edits** a film or television program, they select different parts and arrange them in a particular order.

educate educates, educating, educated
VERB To **educate** someone means to teach them over a long period, so that they learn about many different things.

education

NOUN **Education** is the teaching you receive at a school, college, or university.

eel **eels**

NOUN An **eel** is a long thin fish that looks like a snake.

effect **effects**

NOUN An **effect** is a change made by something. *I'm still suffering from the effects of my cold.*

effort **efforts**

NOUN **Effort** is the physical or mental energy needed to do something.

egg **eggs**

NOUN **1** An **egg** is an oval object laid by female birds. Reptiles, fish, and insects also lay eggs. A baby animal develops inside the egg until it is ready to be born.

NOUN **2** In a female mammal, an **egg** is a cell produced in its body which can develop into a baby.

elastic

ADJECTIVE **1** Something **elastic** is able to stretch easily.

NOUN **2** **Elastic** is a material, like rubber, which stretches and can then return to its original size.

elbow **elbows**

NOUN Your **elbow** is the joint in the middle of your arm where it bends.

electric

ADJECTIVE A machine or other object that is **electric** works by using electricity.
electrical ADJECTIVE

electricity

NOUN **Electricity** is a form of energy that is used for heating and lighting, and to work machines. It flows along wires.

electronic

ADJECTIVE Something **electronic** has transistors or silicon chips, which control an electric current.
electronically ADVERB

elephant **elephants**

NOUN An **elephant** is a large four-legged mammal with a long trunk, large ears, and ivory tusks.

elf **elves**

NOUN In fairy stories, an **elf** is a tiny child who can do magic things.

else

ADVERB You can use **else** to mean other than this or more than this. *Can you think of anything else?*

e-mail or **email**

NOUN **E-mail** is the sending of electronic messages from one computer to another.

embarrass **embarrasses, embarrassing, embarrassed**

VERB To **embarrass** someone means to make them feel shy, ashamed, or guilty about something.

embryo **embryos**

NOUN An **embryo** is a human being, or animal, which has just begun to develop inside its mother's body.

emerald **emeralds**

NOUN An **emerald** is a bright green precious stone.

emerge **emerges, emerging, emerged**

VERB If someone **emerges** from a place, they come out so that they can be seen.

emergency **emergencies**

NOUN An **emergency** is an unexpected and serious event which needs immediate action to deal with it.

emotion **emotions**

NOUN **Emotion** is a strong feeling, such as love or fear.

employ employs, employing, employed

VERB If someone **employs** you, they pay you to work for them.

employer employers

NOUN **Employers** are people who pay other people to work for them.

empty emptier, emptiest; empties, emptying, emptied

ADJECTIVE **1** Something that is **empty** has no people or things in it.

VERB **2** If you **empty** a container, you pour or take everything out of it.

enchanted

ADJECTIVE In stories, something that is **enchanted** is under a magic spell.

encourage encourages, encouraging, encouraged

VERB If you **encourage** someone, you tell them that what they are doing is good and they should go on doing it.

encyclopedia encyclopedias

NOUN An **encyclopedia** is a book, or set of books, giving information about many different subjects.

end ends, ending, ended

NOUN **1** The **end** of a period of time, or an event, is the last part.

NOUN **2** The **end** of something is the farthest point of it. *The bathroom is at the **end** of the hall.*

VERB **3** If something **ends**, it finishes.

ending endings

NOUN An **ending** is the last part of a word, story, play, or film.

enemy enemies

NOUN Your **enemy** is someone who fights or works against you.

energetic

ADJECTIVE Someone who is **energetic** is active and lively.

energetically ADVERB

energy

NOUN **1** **Energy** is the strength you need to do things. You get energy from food.

NOUN **2** **Energy** is also the power that makes things heat up, make a sound, give light, or move. Electricity is one kind of energy.

engine engines

NOUN **1** An **engine** is a machine that makes things move.

NOUN **2** An **engine** is also a large vehicle that pulls a train.

engineer engineers

NOUN An **engineer** is a person who designs or builds things such as machinery, instruments, or bridges.

enjoy enjoys, enjoying, enjoyed

VERB If you **enjoy** doing something, you like doing it very much.

enjoyable ADJECTIVE   **enjoyment** NOUN

enormous

ADJECTIVE Something that is **enormous** is extremely large.

enough

ADJECTIVE **Enough** means as much as you need. *Have you had **enough** to eat?*

enter enters, entering, entered

VERB **1** If you **enter** a place, you go into it.

VERB **2** If you **enter** a competition or examination, you take part in it.

entertain entertains, entertaining, entertained

VERB If you **entertain** somebody, you do something that they enjoy and find amusing.

entertainment

NOUN **Entertainment** is things that people watch for pleasure, such as shows and movies.

enthusiastic

ADJECTIVE If you are **enthusiastic** about something, you are very interested in it, or excited about it.

entire

ADJECTIVE **Entire** means the whole of something. *The **entire** class came to my party.*

entrance **entrances**

NOUN An **entrance** is the way into a place.

envelope **envelopes**

NOUN An **envelope** is a folded, flat paper container for a letter or card.

envious

ADJECTIVE If you are **envious** of somebody, you wish you could have the same things that they have.

environment **environments**

NOUN The **environment** is the natural world around us.

envy **envies, envying, envied**

VERB If you **envy** somebody, you wish you could have the same things that they have.

episode **episodes**

NOUN An **episode** is one of several parts of a story or drama.

equal

ADJECTIVE If two things are **equal**, they are the same as each other in size, number, or amount.

equals

VERB In math, the symbol = stands for **equals**. The numbers on each side of it have the same value: 2 + 2 = 4.

equation **equations**

NOUN **Equations** are sometimes called number sentences. The numbers on the left equal the numbers on the right. For example, $3 + 3 = 2 \times 3$ is an equation.

equator

NOUN The **equator** is an imaginary line drawn around the center of the Earth, lying halfway between the North and South Poles.

equipment

NOUN **Equipment** is the things that you need to do something. *We need some new kitchen **equipment** – especially a stove.*

erupt **erupts, erupting, erupted**

VERB When a volcano **erupts**, it throws out hot molten lava, ash, and steam.

escape **escapes, escaping, escaped**

VERB If a person or animal **escapes**, they get away from somebody or something.

especially

ADVERB You say **especially** to mean most of all. *I like cats, **especially** black ones.*

essay **essays**

NOUN An **essay** is a short piece of writing on a particular subject.

essential

ADJECTIVE Something that is **essential** is absolutely necessary.

estate **estates**

NOUN **1** An **estate** is a large area of land in the country, belonging to one person or group.

NOUN **2** An **estate** is also an area of land with lots of houses on it.

estimate estimates, estimating, estimated

VERB If you **estimate** something, you guess the size or amount of it.

evaporate evaporates, evaporating, evaporated

VERB When a liquid **evaporates**, it becomes less because it is changing from a liquid into a gas.
evaporation NOUN

even

ADVERB **1** You say **even** when something is surprising. *I like to play outside even when it is raining.*
ADJECTIVE **2** If something like a path is **even**, it is smooth and flat.
ADJECTIVE **3** An **even** number can be divided by two, with no remainder. *2, 18, and 36 are all even numbers.*

evening evenings

NOUN The **evening** is the part of the day between late afternoon and the time you usually go to bed.

event events

NOUN An **event** is something important that happens.

eventually

ADVERB **Eventually** means in the end, after a lot of delays or problems.

ever

ADVERB **Ever** means at any time in the past or future. *Have you ever seen such a big dog?*

evergreen evergreens

NOUN An **evergreen** is a tree or other bush which keeps its leaves all year round.

every

ADJECTIVE **Every** means each one. *I spoke to every child in that class.*
every other PHRASE **Every other** means one in every two. *I see my friend every other week.*

everybody

PRONOUN **Everybody** means every person. *Everybody has to eat.*

everyone

PRONOUN You can use **everyone** instead of **everybody**.

everything

PRONOUN **Everything** means all of something.

everywhere

ADVERB **Everywhere** means in all places. *Children everywhere love stories.*

evidence

NOUN **Evidence** is anything you see, read, or are told which gives you reason to believe something.

evil

ADJECTIVE An **evil** person is extremely wicked.

ewe ewes

NOUN A **ewe** is a female sheep.

ex-

PREFIX **Ex-** means former, for example, "husband" → "ex-husband."
See *Prefixes* on page 264.

exact

ADJECTIVE Something that is **exact** is accurate in every detail.

exactly

ADVERB You say **exactly** when you mean no more and no less. *My father is exactly six feet tall.*

exaggerate exaggerates, exaggerating, exaggerated

VERB If you **exaggerate**, you say something is better or worse than it really is.

examination

examination examinations

NOUN **1** An **examination**, called an **exam** for short, is a test people take to find out how much they have learned.

NOUN **2** A doctor does a medical **examination** to find out how healthy you are.

examine examines, examining, examined

VERB If you **examine** something, you look at it carefully or closely.

example examples

NOUN An **example** is one thing which shows what the rest of a set is like. *This is an example of my work.*

excellent

ADJECTIVE Something that is **excellent** is extremely good.

except

PREPOSITION **Except** means apart from. *Everyone went outside except David.*

exception exceptions

NOUN An **exception** is something that does not fit in with a general rule. *With the exception of bats, mammals cannot fly.*

exchange exchanges, exchanging, exchanged

VERB If you **exchange** something, you trade it for something else.

excite excites, exciting, excited

VERB If something **excites** you, it makes you feel happy and interested.

exciting ADJECTIVE   **excitement** NOUN

excited

ADJECTIVE If you feel **excited**, you feel happy and unable to rest.

exclaim exclaims, exclaiming, exclaimed

VERB When you **exclaim**, you speak suddenly or loudly, because you are excited or angry.

exclamation NOUN

exclamation mark exclamation marks

NOUN An **exclamation mark** is a punctuation mark (!) used in writing to express a strong feeling.

See Punctuation *on page 264.*

excuse excuses

NOUN An **excuse** is a reason you give for doing something, or not doing it.

exercise exercises

NOUN **1** **Exercise** is regular physical movements you do to keep fit.

NOUN **2** An **exercise** is a piece of work that you do to help you learn something.

exhausted

ADJECTIVE When you are **exhausted**, you are so tired you have no energy left.

exhibition exhibitions

NOUN An **exhibition** is a collection of pictures, or other things, in a public place where people can come to see them.

exist exists, existing, existed

VERB Things that **exist** are present in the world or universe now.

existence NOUN

exit exits

NOUN An **exit** is the way out of a place.

expand expands, expanding, expanded

VERB When something **expands**, it gets bigger.

expect expects, expecting, expected

VERB If you **expect** something, you think it will happen.

expedition expeditions

NOUN An **expedition** is a journey made for a special reason.

expel **expels, expelling, expelled**
VERB If someone is **expelled** from school, they are told not to come back because their behavior has been so bad.

expensive
ADJECTIVE Something that is **expensive** costs a lot of money.

experience **experiences**
NOUN **1** An **experience** is something that happens to you.
NOUN **2** Experience is knowing about something because you have been doing it for a long time.

experiment **experiments**
NOUN An **experiment** is the testing of something, either to find out its effect, or to prove something.

expert **experts**
NOUN An **expert** is someone who is very skilled at doing something or who knows a lot about something.

explain **explains, explaining, explained**
VERB **1** To explain means to say things to help people understand.
VERB **2** When you **explain**, you give reasons for something that happened.

explanation **explanations**
NOUN **1** An **explanation** is something that helps people understand something. *She gave us a clear explanation of the way the machine works.*
NOUN **2** An **explanation** is something that tells you why something happened.

explode **explodes, exploding, exploded**
VERB If something such as a firework **explodes**, it bursts with a loud bang.
explosion NOUN

explore **explores, exploring, explored**
VERB If you **explore** a place, you travel in it to find out what it is like.
exploration NOUN   explorer NOUN

explosive **explosives**
NOUN An **explosive** is a substance that can explode.

express **expresses, expressing, expressed**
VERB If you **express** an idea or feeling, you put it into words or show it by the way you act. *He could only express the way he felt by bursting into tears.*

expression **expressions**
NOUN Your **expression** is the look on your face that lets people know what you are thinking or feeling.

extinct
ADJECTIVE If an animal or plant family is **extinct**, it no longer has any living members. *The dodo has been extinct for more than 300 years.*

extra
ADJECTIVE You use **extra** to mean more than usual. *You'd better take an extra sweater – it's going to be cold.*

extraordinary
ADJECTIVE Someone or something that is **extraordinary** is very special or unusual.

extreme
ADJECTIVE Extreme means very great. *Extreme cold can cause many problems.*
extremely ADVERB

eye **eyes**
NOUN **1** Your **eyes** are the part of your body that you use for seeing.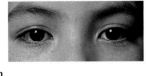
NOUN **2** The **eye** of a needle is the small hole at one end.

eyesight
NOUN **Eyesight** is the ability to see.

a
b
c
d
Ee
f
g
h
i
j
k
l
m
n
o
p
q
r
s
t
u
v
w
x
y
z

a
b
c
d
e
Ff
g
h
i
j
k
l
m
n
o
p
q
r
s
t
u
v
w
x
y
z

Ff

fable **fables**
NOUN A **fable** is a story that is meant to teach you something. Fables often have animals as the main characters.

fabric **fabrics**
NOUN **Fabric** is material made in some way, such as by weaving or knitting.

face **faces, facing, faced**
NOUN **1** Your **face** is the front part of your head from your chin to your forehead. See *Your face* on page 258.
VERB **2** If you **face** something, you have your face toward it.
NOUN **3** The **face** of a clock or watch is the part with the numbers on it that shows the time.
NOUN **4** A **face** is a surface of a three-dimensional shape.

fact **facts**
NOUN A **fact** is something that is true.
factual ADJECTIVE

factor **factors**
NOUN A **factor** is a whole number which will divide exactly into another whole number. For example, 3 is a factor of 12.

factory **factories**
NOUN A **factory** is a large building where a lot of things are made.

fade **fades, fading, faded**
VERB **1** If a color **fades**, it gets paler.
VERB **2** If the light **fades**, it gets darker.

fail **fails, failing, failed**
VERB **1** If someone **fails** when they try to do something, they cannot do it.
VERB **2** If something **fails**, it stops working. *The brakes **failed**, and the car hit a wall.*

failure **failures**
NOUN If something is a **failure**, it does not work as planned. *The picnic was a **failure** because it rained all day.*

faint **faints, fainting, fainted; fainter, faintest**
VERB **1** If someone **faints**, they become unconscious for a short time.
ADJECTIVE **2** Something like a sound or mark that is **faint** is not easy to hear or see.

fair **fairer, fairest; fairs**
ADJECTIVE **1** Something that is **fair** seems reasonable to most people.
ADJECTIVE **2** People who are **fair** have light-colored hair.
NOUN **3** A **fair** is a form of entertainment that takes place outside with amusements, sideshows, and rides.

fairly
ADVERB **Fairly** means impartially.

fairy **fairies**
NOUN In stories, **fairies** are tiny people with wings, who have magical powers.

fairy tale **fairy tales**
NOUN A **fairy tale** is a story in which magical things happen.

faithful
ADJECTIVE If you are **faithful** to someone, you can be trusted and relied on.

fake **fakes**
NOUN A **fake** is a copy of something made to trick people into thinking that it is genuine.

fall falls, falling, fell, fallen
VERB **1** When someone or something **falls**, they drop toward the ground.
VERB **2** If someone's face **falls**, they suddenly look upset or disappointed.

false
ADJECTIVE **1** If something is **false**, it is not the real thing. *My uncle has a **false** tooth.*
ADJECTIVE **2** If something you say is **false**, it is not true.

familiar
ADJECTIVE Something **familiar** is well-known or easy to recognize. *It was good to see a **familiar** face.*

family families
NOUN **1** A **family** is a group of people made up of parents and their children.
NOUN **2** A **family** is also a group of animals or plants of the same kind. *Lions and tigers belong to the cat **family**.*

famine famines
NOUN A **famine** is a shortage of food which may cause many people to die.

famous
ADJECTIVE Someone or something **famous** is very well known.

fan fans
NOUN **1** A **fan** is an object which creates a draft of cool air when it moves.

NOUN **2** If you are a **fan** of something or of someone famous, you are very interested in them.

fantastic
ADJECTIVE Something **fantastic** is wonderful and very pleasing.

fantasy fantasies
NOUN **1** A **fantasy** is a story about things that do not exist in the real world.
NOUN **2** **Fantasy** is imagining things.

far farther, farthest
ADVERB **1** **Far** means a long way away. *Are you going **far**?*
ADVERB **2** You use **far** to ask questions about distance. *How **far** is the town?*

fare fares
NOUN A **fare** is the money that you pay to travel on something like a plane or a bus.

farm farms
NOUN A **farm** is a large area of land, together with buildings, used for growing crops or raising animals.

farmer farmers
NOUN A **farmer** is a person who owns or manages a farm.

fascinate fascinates, fascinating, fascinated
VERB If something **fascinates** you, it interests you very much.

fashion fashions
NOUN A **fashion** is the style of things, like clothes, that are popular for a time.
fashionable ADJECTIVE

fast faster, fastest; fasts, fasting, fasted
ADJECTIVE **1** Someone or something that is **fast** can move very quickly.
ADJECTIVE **2** If a clock is **fast**, it shows a time that is later than the real time.
VERB **3** If someone **fasts**, they eat no food for a period of time.

fasten fastens, fastening, fastened
VERB When you **fasten** something, you close, tie, or attach it. *Remember to **fasten** your seat belt.*

fat fatter, fattest; fats
ADJECTIVE **1** A **fat** person or animal has a heavy body.
NOUN **2** **Fat** is a solid or liquid substance used in cooking. It comes from animals or vegetables.

father **fathers**

NOUN Your **father** is your male parent.

fault **faults**

NOUN **1** If people say something is your **fault**, they are blaming you for something bad that has happened.

NOUN **2** A **fault** is something wrong with the way something was made.

faulty ADJECTIVE

favor **favors**

NOUN A **favor** is something helpful you do for someone.

favorite **favorites**

NOUN Your **favorite** person or thing is the one you like better than all the others. *This teddy is my **favorite** toy.*

fax **faxes**

NOUN A **fax** is a copy of a document that can be sent along a telephone line.

fear **fears, fearing, feared**

NOUN **1** **Fear** is the worried feeling you have when you think you are in danger.

VERB **2** If you **fear** someone or something, you are frightened of them.

feast **feasts**

NOUN A **feast** is a large and special meal for many people.

feat **feats**

NOUN A **feat** is a brave or impressive act.

feather **feathers**

NOUN A **feather** is one of the very light pieces that make up a bird's coat.

February

NOUN **February** is the second month of the year. It has 28 days except in a leap year, when it has 29.

fed

VERB **Fed** is the past tense of **feed**.

feed **feeds, feeding, fed**

VERB If you **feed** a person or animal, you give them food.

feel **feels, feeling, felt**

VERB **1** If you **feel** something, like happy or sad, that is how you are at that time.

VERB **2** If you **feel** an object, you touch it to find out what it is like.

feeling **feelings**

NOUN A **feeling** is an emotion you have, like anger or happiness.

feet

PLURAL NOUN **Feet** is the plural of **foot**.

felt

VERB **1** **Felt** is the past tense of **feel**.

NOUN **2** **Felt** is a thick cloth made by pressing short threads together.

female **females**

NOUN A **female** is a person or animal that belongs to the sex that can have babies or young.

female ADJECTIVE

feminine

ADJECTIVE Someone who is **feminine** has the qualities generally expected of a woman, such as gentleness.

fence **fences**

NOUN A **fence** is a wooden or wire barrier between two areas of land.

ferocious

ADJECTIVE A **ferocious** animal or person is violent and fierce.

ferry **ferries**

NOUN A **ferry** is a boat that takes passengers, and sometimes vehicles, across a short stretch of water.

festival **festivals**

NOUN **1** A **festival** is an organized series of events and performances.

NOUN **2** A **festival** can also be a special day or period of religious celebration.

fetch fetches, fetching, fetched
VERB If you **fetch** something, you go and get it and bring it back.

fete fetes
NOUN A **fete** is an outdoor event with competitions and stalls which sell things.

fever fevers
NOUN If you have a **fever** when you are ill, you have a high temperature.

few fewer, fewest
ADJECTIVE **Few** means a small number of things. *I saw him a few minutes ago.*

fiber fibers
NOUN A **fiber** is a thin thread of something such as wool or cotton.

fiction
NOUN **Fiction** is books or stories about people and events which are made up by the author. See **nonfiction**.

fidget fidgets, fidgeting, fidgeted
VERB If you **fidget**, you keep moving about because you are nervous or bored.

field fields
NOUN A **field** is a piece of land with a fence around, used to grow crops or keep animals in.

fierce fiercer, fiercest
ADJECTIVE An animal that is **fierce** is dangerous.

fight fights, fighting, fought
VERB If you **fight** someone, you try to hurt them.

figure figures
NOUN **1** A **figure** is any of the numbers from 0 to 9. See **digit**.
NOUN **2** A **figure** is also the shape of a person. *It was just getting dark when I saw a small figure coming toward me.*

file files
NOUN **1** A **file** is a box or folded piece of card that you keep papers in.
NOUN **2** A **file** is also a set of data in a computer, which is stored under a name.
NOUN **3** A **file** is also a metal tool with rough surfaces which is used to smooth things like wood or metal.

fill fills, filling, filled
VERB If you **fill** something, you put so much into it there is no room for any more.

film films
NOUN **1** A **film** is moving pictures shown on a screen.
NOUN **2** **Film** is a long narrow piece of plastic that is used in a camera to take photographs.

filthy filthier, filthiest
ADJECTIVE Something **filthy** is very dirty.

fin fins
NOUN A fish's **fins** are like small wings that stick out of its body. They help the fish to swim and to keep its balance.

final
ADJECTIVE In a series of any kind, the **final** one is the last one.
finally ADVERB

find finds, finding, found
VERB When you **find** someone or something, you see the person or thing you have been looking for.

fine

fine **finer, finest; fines**

ADJECTIVE **1** Something that is **fine** is extremely good.

ADJECTIVE **2** Something like a thread or nib that is **fine** is very thin.

ADJECTIVE **3** If you say you are **fine**, you mean you are well and happy.

ADJECTIVE **4** When the weather is **fine**, it is dry and sunny.

NOUN **5** A **fine** is money that is paid as a punishment.

finger **fingers**

NOUN Your **fingers** are the five jointed parts at the end of your hand.

fingernail **fingernails**

NOUN Your **fingernails** are the thin hard areas that cover the ends of your fingers.

fingerprint **fingerprints**

NOUN A **fingerprint** is a mark that shows the skin pattern at the tip of a finger.

finish **finishes, finishing, finished**

VERB When you **finish** something, like a meal or a book, you reach the end of it.

fir **firs**

NOUN A **fir** is a tall pointed evergreen tree with cones, and leaves like needles.

fire **fires, firing, fired**

NOUN **1** **Fire** is the flames produced when something burns.

NOUN **2** A **fire** is also something powered by coal, gas, or electricity that gives out heat.

VERB **3** If someone **fires** a gun, a bullet is sent from the gun they are using.

fire engine **fire engines**

NOUN A **fire engine** is a large vehicle that carries firefighters and equipment for putting out fires.

firefighter **firefighters**

NOUN A **firefighter** is a person whose job is to put out fires and rescue trapped people and animals.

fireplace **fireplaces**

NOUN A **fireplace** is the opening beneath a chimney where a fire can be lit.

firework **fireworks**

NOUN A **firework** is a thing that burns with colored sparks when you light it. Some fireworks make a loud noise.

firm **firmer, firmest**

ADJECTIVE **1** Something that is **firm** does not move easily when you press or push it. *This pear isn't ripe – it is too firm!*

ADJECTIVE **2** If someone is **firm** with you about something, you know they will not change their mind.

first

ADJECTIVE OR ADVERB If something is **first** or happens first, it is number one and comes before anything else.

first aid

NOUN **First aid** is simple treatment given as soon as possible to a person who is injured or who suddenly becomes ill.

first person

NOUN The **first person** refers to yourself when you are speaking or writing. It is expressed as "I" or "we."

fish **fishes, fishing, fished**

NOUN **1** A **fish** is an animal that lives in water. It has gills, fins, and a scaly skin.

VERB **2** To **fish** is to try and catch fish for food or sport.

fisherman **fishermen**

NOUN A **fisherman** is a person who catches fish as a job or for sport.

forward

ADVERB If you move **forward**, you move the way you are facing.

look forward **PHRASE** If you **look forward** to something, you want it to happen.

fossil **fossils**

NOUN A **fossil** is the hardened remains of a prehistoric animal or plant that are found inside a rock.

fought

VERB **Fought** is the past tense of **fight**.

foul **fouler, foulest**

ADJECTIVE If something is **foul**, it is extremely unpleasant.

found

VERB **Found** is the past tense of **find**.

foundation **foundations**

NOUN The **foundations** of a building are the solid layers of material put below the ground to support it.

fountain **fountains**

NOUN A **fountain** is a jet or spray of water forced up into the air by a pump.

fox **foxes**

NOUN A **fox** is a wild animal like a dog, with reddish-brown fur and a thick tail.

fraction **fractions**

NOUN **1** In math, a **fraction** is a part of a whole number, for example $\frac{1}{4}$. *See Fractions on page 272.*

NOUN **2** A **fraction** is also a tiny part of something.

fracture **fractures**

NOUN A **fracture** is a crack or break in something, especially a bone.

fragile

ADJECTIVE Something that is **fragile** is easily broken or damaged.

fragment **fragments**

NOUN A **fragment** of something is a small piece or part of it.

frame **frames**

NOUN A **frame** is the part surrounding something, like a window or picture, or the lenses of a pair of glasses.

freckle **freckles**

NOUN **Freckles** are small, light brown spots on someone's skin.

free

ADJECTIVE **1** If a person or animal is **free**, they can go where they want. *Tom opened the cage and set the bird free.*

ADJECTIVE **2** If something is **free**, it does not cost anything.

freedom **NOUN**

freeze **freezes, freezing, froze, frozen**

VERB **1** If a liquid **freezes**, it becomes solid because the temperature is low.

VERB **2** If you **freeze** something, you store it at a very low temperature.

freezer **freezers**

NOUN A **freezer** is a part of a refrigerator for freezing and storing food.

frequent

ADJECTIVE If something is **frequent**, it happens often.

frequency **NOUN** **frequently** **ADVERB**

a
b
c
d
e
Ff
g
h
i
j
k
l
m
n
o
p
q
r
s
t
u
v
w
x
y
z

a
b
c
d
e

Ff

g
h
i
j
k
l
m
n
o
p
q
r
s
t
u
v
w
x
y
z

fresh fresher, freshest
ADJECTIVE **1** If food is **fresh**, it has been picked or made recently.
ADJECTIVE **2** Fresh water is water that is not salty.
ADJECTIVE **3** If you feel **fresh**, you feel rested and full of energy.
ADJECTIVE **4** Fresh air is the air outside.

friction
NOUN **Friction** is the force which is produced when two surfaces rub against each other.

Friday Fridays
NOUN **Friday** is the day between Thursday and Saturday.

fridge fridges
NOUN A **fridge** is a large metal container. It is kept cool so that the food in it stays fresh longer. Fridge is an abbreviation of **refrigerator**.

friend friends
NOUN A **friend** is someone you know well and like very much.

friendly friendlier, friendliest
ADJECTIVE If you are **friendly** to someone, you behave in a kind and pleasant way to them.

fright
NOUN **Fright** is a sudden feeling of fear.

frighten frightens, frightening, frightened
VERB If something **frightens** you, it makes you afraid.

frightening
ADJECTIVE Something that is **frightening** makes you feel afraid.

frog frogs
NOUN A **frog** is a small amphibious animal with smooth skin, big eyes, and long back legs which it uses for jumping.
See *Amphibians* on page 259.

front fronts
NOUN **1** The **front** of something is the part that faces forward.
NOUN **2** If you put up a **front**, you pretend to feel or think something.
in front PHRASE **In front** means ahead or farther forward.
in front of PHRASE If you do something **in front of** someone, you do it while they are there.

frost frosts
NOUN When there is a **frost**, the weather is very cold and the ground becomes covered with tiny ice crystals.

frown frowns, frowning, frowned
VERB If you **frown**, your eyebrows are drawn together. People frown when they are angry, worried, or thinking hard.

froze
VERB **Froze** is the past tense of **freeze**.

frozen
VERB **1** Frozen is the past participle of **freeze**.
ADJECTIVE **2** If something like a lake or river is **frozen**, its surface has turned to ice.
ADJECTIVE **3** If you say you are **frozen**, you mean you are very cold.

fruit fruits
NOUN A **fruit** is the part of a plant that develops from the flower and contains the seeds. Many fruits are good to eat.
See *Fruit* on page 257.

fry fries, frying, fried
VERB When you **fry** food, you cook it in a pan that contains hot fat or oil.

fuel **fuels**

NOUN **Fuel** is something like gasoline or coal that is burned to provide heat or power.

full **fuller, fullest**

ADJECTIVE If something is **full**, there is no room for anything more.

fumble **fumbles, fumbling, fumbled**

VERB If you **fumble** a ball, you drop it or handle it clumsily.

fun

NOUN **Fun** is something enjoyable that makes you feel happy.

funeral **funerals**

NOUN A **funeral** is a ceremony held when a person has died.

fungus **fungi** or **funguses**

NOUN A **fungus** is a plant such as a mushroom or mold that does not have flowers or leaves.

funnel **funnels**

NOUN **1** A **funnel** is an open cone which narrows to a tube. You use a funnel to pour liquid into containers.
VERB **2** **Funnel** means to direct. *The treasurer **funneled** the contributions into a special account.*

funny **funnier, funniest**

ADJECTIVE **1** **Funny** people or things make you laugh.
ADJECTIVE **2** Something that is **funny** is rather strange or surprising.
funnily ADVERB

fur

NOUN **Fur** is the soft thick body hair of many animals.
furry ADJECTIVE

furious

ADJECTIVE Someone who is **furious** is extremely angry.

furniture

NOUN **Furniture** is large objects such as tables, beds, and chairs, that people have in rooms.

further **furthest**

VERB **1** **Further** means to promote. *She wants to **further** her education by going to college.*
ADJECTIVE **2** **Further** also means more. *Write for **further** details.*

fury

NOUN **Fury** is violent or extreme anger.

fuss **fusses, fussing, fussed**

NOUN **1** A **fuss** is worried or anxious behavior that is unnecessary and often not welcome. *I don't know why you're making such a **fuss** about it.*
VERB **2** If someone **fusses**, they worry about unimportant things.

future **futures**

NOUN **1** The **future** is the time that is to come. *My family plans to move out of state sometime in the **future**.*
ADJECTIVE **2** **Future** is to do with time that is to come. *We need to look after the environment for **future** generations.*
NOUN **3** The **future tense** of a verb is the form used to talk about something that will happen in the future. For example, the sentence "Ben will be at school tomorrow" is in the future tense.

a
b
c
d
e
Ff
g
h
i
j
k
l
m
n
o
p
q
r
s
t
u
v
w
x
y
z

a
b
c
d
e
f

Gg

h
i
j
k
l
m
n
o
p
q
r
s
t
u
v
w
x
y
z

Gg

gain **gains, gaining, gained**
NOUN **1** A **gain** is an increase in the amount of something.
VERB **2** If you **gain** from something, you get something good out of it.
VERB **3** If a clock or watch **gains**, it moves too fast.

galaxy **galaxies**
NOUN **1** A **galaxy** is a large group of stars and planets in space.
NOUN **2** The **galaxy** is the group of stars and planets that the Earth belongs to.
galactic ADJECTIVE

gale **gales**
NOUN A **gale** is a strong wind.

galleon **galleons**
NOUN A **galleon** is a large sailing ship used hundreds of years ago.

gallery **galleries**
NOUN **1** A **gallery** is a place that shows paintings or sculptures.
NOUN **2** In a hall or theater, a **gallery** is a raised area at the back where people can sit and get a good view of what is happening.

gallon **gallons**
NOUN A **gallon** is a measure of volume equal to four quarts.

gallop **gallops, galloping, galloped**
VERB When a horse **gallops**, it runs fast.

game **games**
NOUN A **game** is something you play for sport or fun. Most games have rules.

gander **ganders**
NOUN A **gander** is a male goose.

gang **gangs**
NOUN A **gang** is a group of people who do things together.

gangster **gangsters**
NOUN A **gangster** is a member of a criminal gang.

gap **gaps**
NOUN A **gap** is a space between two things, or a hole in something solid.

garage **garages**
NOUN **1** A **garage** is a building in which someone can keep a car.
NOUN **2** A **garage** is also a place that sells gasoline or repairs cars.

garden **gardens**
NOUN A **garden** is land next to a house where people can grow things like vegetables, flowers, or grass.

garlic
NOUN **Garlic** is the small white bulb of an onion-like plant which has a strong taste and smell. It is used in cooking.

garment **garments**
NOUN A **garment** is a piece of clothing.

gas **gases**
NOUN **Gas** is a substance that is not liquid or solid. Air is a mixture of gases. Another type of gas is used as a fuel for cooking and central heating.

gasp **gasps, gasping, gasped**
VERB When you **gasp**, you take a short quick breath through your mouth, especially when you are surprised or in pain.

gate gates

NOUN A **gate** is a type of door that is used at the entrance to a garden or field.

gather gathers, gathering, gathered

VERB **1** If people or animals **gather**, they come together in a group.

VERB **2** If you **gather** things, you collect them from different places. *Early people used to gather berries for food.*

gave

VERB **Gave** is the past tense of **give**.

gaze gazes, gazing, gazed

VERB If you **gaze** at something, you look steadily at it for a long time.

general generals

ADJECTIVE **1** You use **general** when you are talking about most of the people in a group. *There was a general rush for the door when the bell rang.*

NOUN **2** A **general** is an army officer of very high rank.

generally ADVERB

generous

ADJECTIVE Someone who is **generous** is kind and willing to help others by giving them money or time.

gentle gentler, gentlest

ADJECTIVE Someone who is **gentle** is kind, calm, and sensitive.

gently ADVERB

gentleman gentlemen

NOUN A **gentleman** is a polite name for a man.

genuine

ADJECTIVE Something **genuine** is real and not false or pretend.

geography

NOUN **Geography** is the study of the countries of the world, and of things like their rivers, mountains, and people.

geographical ADJECTIVE

gerbil gerbils

NOUN A **gerbil** is a small furry animal with long back legs, often kept as a pet.

germ germs

NOUN A **germ** is a tiny living thing that can make people ill. You cannot see germs without using a microscope.

get gets, getting, got

VERB **1** **Get** often means the same as become. *It gets dark earlier in winter.*

VERB **2** If you **get** into a particular situation, you put yourself in that situation. *We got into a muddle.*

VERB **3** If you **get** something done, you do it or you persuade someone to do it.

VERB **4** If you **get** something, you fetch it or are given it. *I'll get us all a cup of tea.*

VERB **5** If you **get**, a train, bus, or plane, you travel on it.

ghost ghosts

NOUN A **ghost** is a shadowy figure of someone no longer living that some people believe they see.

giant giants

NOUN **1** In fairy stories, a **giant** is someone who is huge and strong.

ADJECTIVE **2** Anything that is much larger than usual can be called **giant**. *A giant wave was coming toward us.*

giddy giddier, giddiest

ADJECTIVE If you feel **giddy**, you feel silly.

gift gifts
NOUN A **gift** is a present.

gigantic
ADJECTIVE Something **gigantic** is extremely large.

giggle giggles, giggling, giggled
VERB If you **giggle**, you make quiet little laughing noises.

gill gills
NOUN The **gills** of a fish are the organs on its sides which it uses for breathing.

ginger
NOUN **Ginger** is a plant root with a hot spicy flavor, used in cooking.

giraffe giraffes
NOUN A **giraffe** is a large African mammal with a very long neck.

girl girls
NOUN A **girl** is a female child.

give gives, giving, gave, given
VERB If you **give** someone something, you hand it to them or provide it for them. *Dad **gave** me a job cleaning the car.*
give way PHRASE If something **gives way**, it collapses.

glacier glaciers
NOUN A **glacier** is a huge frozen river of slow-moving ice.

glad gladder, gladdest
ADJECTIVE If you are **glad**, you are happy and pleased.

glance glances, glancing, glanced
VERB **1** If you **glance** at something, you look at it quickly.
NOUN **2** A **glance** is a quick look.

glare glares, glaring, glared
VERB **1** If you **glare** at someone, you look at them angrily.
VERB **2** If the sun or a light **glares**, it shines with a very bright light.

glass glasses
NOUN **1** Glass is a hard transparent material that is easily broken. It is used to make windows and bottles.
NOUN **2** A **glass** is a container that you can drink from, made of glass.

glasses
PLURAL NOUN **Glasses** are two lenses in a frame, which some people wear over their eyes to help them see better.

gleam gleams, gleaming, gleamed
VERB If something **gleams**, it shines and reflects light.

glide glides, gliding, glided
VERB When something **glides**, it moves silently and smoothly.

glider gliders
NOUN A **glider** is an aircraft that does not have an engine, but flies by floating on air currents.

glimpse glimpses, glimpsing, glimpsed
VERB If you **glimpse** something, you see it very briefly.

glisten glistens, glistening, glistened
VERB If something **glistens**, it shines or sparkles. *Her eyes **glistened** with tears.*

glitter glitters, glittering, glittered
VERB If something **glitters**, it shines in a sparkling way. *Her diamond necklace **glittered** under the lights.*

gloat gloats, gloating, gloated
VERB If you **gloat**, you show great pleasure in your own success or in other people's failure.

globe globes
NOUN A **globe** is a round model of the Earth with a map of the world drawn on it.

gloomy gloomier, gloomiest
ADJECTIVE **1** If a place is **gloomy**, it is dark and dull.
ADJECTIVE **2** If people are **gloomy**, they are unhappy and not at all hopeful.
gloomily ADVERB

glossary glossaries
NOUN A **glossary** is a list of explanations of special words, usually found at the back of a book.

glossy glossier, glossiest
ADJECTIVE Something that is **glossy** is smooth and shiny.

glove gloves
NOUN A **glove** is a piece of clothing which covers your hand, with separate places for each finger.

glow glows, glowing, glowed
VERB If something **glows**, it shines with a steady dull light.

glue
NOUN **Glue** is a thick, sticky liquid used for joining things together.

gnarled
ADJECTIVE Something that is **gnarled** is old, twisted, and rough. *The old gardener's hands were **gnarled**.*

gnat gnats
NOUN A **gnat** is a very small flying insect that bites people.

gnaw gnaws, gnawing, gnawed
VERB If people or animals **gnaw** something hard, they keep biting on it.

gnome gnomes
NOUN In fairy stories, a **gnome** is a tiny old man.

go goes, going, went, gone
VERB **1** If you **go** somewhere, you move or travel there.
VERB **2** If something **goes** well, it is successful.
VERB **3** If you are **going** to do something, you will do it.
VERB **4** If a clock or watch **goes**, it works.

goal goals
NOUN **1** A **goal** in games such as soccer or hockey is the space into which players try to get the ball so that they can score.
NOUN **2** It is also called a **goal** when a player gets the ball into the goal.
NOUN **3** If something is your **goal**, you hope to succeed in doing it one day.

goat goats
NOUN A **goat** is an animal with short coarse hair, horns, and a short tail.

goblin goblins
NOUN In fairy stories, a **goblin** is a small ugly creature who likes to make trouble.

god gods
NOUN **1** A **god** is a person or thing that people worship.
NOUN **2** The name **God** is given to the Supreme Being who is worshipped by some people, such as Christians or Jews.

goddess goddesses
NOUN A **goddess** is a female god.

a b c d e f **Gg** h i j k l m n o p q r s t u v w x y z

goggles

goggles
PLURAL NOUN **Goggles** are special glasses that fit closely around your eyes to protect them.

go-kart go-karts
A **go-kart** is a very small motor vehicle with four wheels, used for racing.

gold
NOUN **1 Gold** is a valuable, yellow-colored metal that is used for making things like jewelry.
ADJECTIVE **2** Something that is **gold** in color is warm yellow.

golden
ADJECTIVE Something that is **golden** is made of gold or is a gold color.

goldfish
NOUN A **goldfish** is a gold or orange-colored fish which is often kept as a pet.

golf
NOUN **Golf** is a game in which players use long sticks called clubs to hit a small ball into special holes.

gone
VERB **Gone** is the past participle of **go**.

good better, best
ADJECTIVE **1** Someone who is **good** is kind and caring, and can be trusted.
ADJECTIVE **2** A child or animal that is **good** is well-behaved and obedient.
ADJECTIVE **3** If something like a movie or book is **good**, people like it.
ADJECTIVE **4** Someone who is **good** at something is skillful and successful at it.

goodbye
You say **goodbye** to someone when you or they are leaving.

good night
You say **good night** to someone when you or they are going to bed.

goods
PLURAL NOUN **Goods** are things that can be bought or sold.

goose geese
NOUN A **goose** is a large bird with a long neck and webbed feet. Its cry is a loud honking noise.

gorilla gorillas
NOUN The **gorilla** is the largest of the apes. It lives in African forests.

got
VERB **1 Got** is the past tense of **get**.
VERB **2** You can use **have got** instead of **have**. *We **have got** a map.*
VERB **3** You can use **have got to** instead of **have to**, when talking about something you must do. *We **have got to** win.*

government governments
NOUN A **government** is the group of people who run a country and decide about important things such as medical care and old age pensions.

grab grabs, grabbing, grabbed
VERB If you **grab** something, you take hold of it suddenly and roughly.

graceful
ADJECTIVE Someone or something that is **graceful** moves in a smooth way which is pleasant to watch.

gradual
ADJECTIVE Something that is **gradual** happens slowly.
gradually ADVERB

graffiti
NOUN **Graffiti** is words or pictures that are scribbled on walls in public places.

grain grains

NOUN **1** Grain is the seeds of plants like wheat or corn, that we use for food.

NOUN **2** A **grain** of something, such as sand or salt, is a tiny hard piece of it.

gram grams

NOUN A **gram** (g) is a small unit of mass and weight. One sheet of paper weighs about four grams. There are 1000 grams in a kilogram.

grammar

NOUN **Grammar** is the rules of a language.

grand grander, grandest

ADJECTIVE Buildings that are **grand** are large and look important.

grandad grandads

NOUN Your **grandad** is your grandfather.

grandchild grandchildren

NOUN Someone's **grandchild** is the child of their son or daughter.

grandfather grandfathers

NOUN Your **grandfather** is the father of one of your parents.

grandmother grandmothers

NOUN Your **grandmother** is the mother of one of your parents.

grandparent grandparents

NOUN Your **grandparents** are your parents' parents.

granny grannies

NOUN; INFORMAL Your **granny** is your grandmother.

grape grapes

NOUN A **grape** is a small green or purple fruit. Grapes grow in bunches on vines. They can be eaten raw, used for making wine, or dried to make raisins, or currants.

See *Fruit* on page 257.

grapefruit grapefruits

NOUN A **grapefruit** is a large round fruit. It is like an orange, but it is larger and has a pale yellow skin.

See *Fruit* on page 257.

graph graphs

NOUN A **graph** is a diagram which shows how two sets of information are related.

grasp grasps, grasping, grasped

VERB **1** If you **grasp** something, you hold it firmly.

VERB **2** If you **grasp** an idea, you understand it.

grass grasses

NOUN **Grass** is a common green plant with long thin leaves. It grows on lawns and in parks.

grasshopper grasshoppers

NOUN A **grasshopper** is an insect. It has long back legs and can jump well. The male makes a chirping sound by rubbing its back legs against its wings.

See *Insects* on page 259.

grate grates, grating, grated

NOUN **1** A **grate** is a framework of metal bars in a fireplace.

VERB **2** If you **grate** food, you shred it into small pieces.

grateful

ADJECTIVE If you are **grateful** for something nice that someone has done, you have warm feelings toward them and want to thank them.

grave graver, gravest; graves

ADJECTIVE **1** Something that is **grave** is important, serious, and worrying.

NOUN **2** A **grave** is a place where a dead person is buried.

gravel

NOUN **Gravel** is small stones used for making roads and paths.

gravity

NOUN **Gravity** is the force that makes things fall when you drop them.

gravy

NOUN **Gravy** is a brown sauce made from meat juices.

gray **grayer, grayest**

ADJECTIVE Something that is **gray** is the color of clouds on a rainy day.
See *Colors* on page 271.

graze **grazes, grazing, grazed**

VERB **1** When animals **graze**, they eat grass.
VERB **2** If you **graze** your skin, you scrape it against something and hurt yourself.

grease

NOUN **1** **Grease** is a thick oil which is put on the moving parts of cars and other machines to make them work smoothly.
NOUN **2** **Grease** is also an oily substance produced by your skin and found in your hair.
greasy ADJECTIVE

great **greater, greatest**

ADJECTIVE **1** You say something is **great** when it is large in size, number, or amount. *The waves threw a great number of shells onto the shore.*
ADJECTIVE **2** **Great** also means important. *I like to hear about great scientists.*
ADJECTIVE **3** INFORMAL **Great** can mean wonderful. *Paul had a great time.*

greedy **greedier, greediest**

ADJECTIVE Someone who is **greedy** wants more than they need of something.
greedily ADVERB

green **greener, greenest**

ADJECTIVE **1** Something that is **green** is the color of grass.
See *Colors* on page 271.
ADJECTIVE **2** **Green** is used to describe someone who is inexperienced at something.

greengrocer **greengrocers**

NOUN A **greengrocer** is a shopkeeper who sells fruit and vegetables.

greenhouse **greenhouses**

NOUN A **greenhouse** is a building which has glass walls and a glass roof. It is used to grow plants in.

greet **greets, greeting, greeted**

VERB When you **greet** someone, you look pleased to see them, and say something friendly.

greeting **greetings**

NOUN A **greeting** is something friendly that you say or do when you meet someone.

grew

VERB **Grew** is the past tense of **grow**.

grid **grids**

NOUN A **grid** is a pattern of lines crossing each other to form squares.

grief

NOUN Someone who feels **grief** is very sad, often because a person or animal they love has died.

grill **grills, grilling, grilled**

VERB If you **grill** food, you cook it on metal bars under or over heat.

grim **grimmer, grimmest**

ADJECTIVE **1** If a situation or piece of news is **grim**, it is unpleasant and worrying.
ADJECTIVE **2** If someone looks **grim**, they are serious because they are worried or angry about something.

grin grins, grinning, grinned
VERB If you **grin**, you give a broad smile.

grind grinds, grinding, ground
VERB **1** If you **grind** something, such as pepper, you crush it into a fine powder.
VERB **2** If you **grind** your teeth, you rub your upper and lower teeth together.

grip grips, gripping, gripped
VERB **1** If you **grip** something, you take hold of it firmly.
VERB **2** If something **grips** you, you find it very interesting.

groan groans, groaning, groaned
VERB If you **groan**, you make a long, low sound of pain or unhappiness.

groceries
PLURAL NOUN **Groceries** are foods such as flour, sugar, and canned foods.

groove grooves
NOUN A **groove** is a deep line cut into a surface.

ground grounds
NOUN **1** The **ground** is the surface of the Earth or the floor of a room.
NOUN **2** A **ground** is an area of land used for a certain activity, as in a parade ground.
PLURAL NOUN **3** The **grounds** of a large house are the land around it which belongs to it.
VERB **4** Ground is the past tense of **grind**.

group groups
NOUN **1** A **group** of things or people is a number of them that are linked together in some way.
NOUN **2** A **group** is also a number of musicians who perform music together.

grow grows, growing, grew, grown
VERB **1** When a person **grows**, they get bigger. All living things can grow.
VERB **2** If you **grow** plants, you put seeds or young plants in the ground and look after them.
VERB **3** When someone **grows up**, they gradually change from being a child into being an adult.

growl growls, growling, growled
VERB When an animal **growls**, it makes a low, rumbling sound, usually because it is angry.

grown
VERB **Grown** is the past participle of **grow**.

grown-up grown-ups
NOUN; INFORMAL A **grown-up** is an adult.

growth
NOUN **Growth** means getting bigger.

grub grubs
NOUN A **grub** is a wormlike insect that has just hatched from its egg.

grumble grumbles, grumbling, grumbled
VERB If you **grumble**, you complain in a bad-tempered way.

grunt grunts, grunting, grunted
VERB When a pig **grunts**, it makes a low rough noise.

guarantee guarantees, guaranteeing, guaranteed
VERB **1** If someone or something **guarantees** something, they make certain that it will happen.
NOUN **2** A **guarantee** is a written promise that if something you have bought goes wrong, it will be replaced or repaired free.

a
b
c
d
e
f
Gg
h
i
j
k
l
m
n
o
p
q
r
s
t
u
v
w
x
y
z

guard **guards, guarding, guarded**
VERB **1** If you **guard** a person or object, you stay near to them to keep them safe, or to make sure they do not escape.
NOUN **2** A **guard** is a person who protects something or someone.

guess **guesses, guessing, guessed**
VERB If you **guess** something, you give an answer without knowing if it is right.

guest **guests**
NOUN A **guest** is someone who stays at your home or who goes to an event because they have been invited.

guide **guides, guiding, guided**
VERB **1** If you **guide** someone, you show them where to go or what to do.
NOUN **2** A **guide** is someone who shows you around places.

guidebook **guidebooks**
NOUN A **guidebook** is a book that gives information about a place.

guilty **guiltier, guiltiest**
ADJECTIVE **1** If you are **guilty** of doing something wrong, you did it.
ADJECTIVE **2** If you feel **guilty**, you are unhappy because you have done something wrong.

guinea pig **guinea pigs**
NOUN A **guinea pig** is a small furry animal without a tail, often kept as a pet.

guitar **guitars**
NOUN A **guitar** is a musical instrument with strings that you play with your fingers.

gulf **gulfs**
NOUN A **gulf** is a large area of sea that stretches a long way into the land.

gulp **gulps, gulping, gulped**
VERB **1** If you **gulp** food or drink, you swallow large amounts of it.
VERB **2** If you **gulp**, you swallow air because you are nervous.

gum **gums**
NOUN **1** Your **gums** are the firm flesh your teeth are set in.
NOUN **2** Gum is a soft sweet substance that people chew but do not swallow.
NOUN **3** Gum is also a sticky substance from a plant.

gumbo
NOUN A **gumbo** is a soup that is thickened with okra and other vegetables as well as meat or seafood.

gun **guns**
NOUN A **gun** is a weapon which fires bullets or shells.

gunpowder
NOUN Gunpowder is a powder that explodes when it is lit. It is used for making things such as fireworks.

gust **gusts**
NOUN A **gust** is a sudden rush of wind.

gutter **gutters**
NOUN **1** A **gutter** is the edge of a road next to the pavement, where rain collects and flows away.
NOUN **2** A **gutter** is also an open pipe at the edge of a roof, where rain collects and flows away.

gym **gyms**
NOUN A **gym** is a room with special equipment for physical exercises. Gym here is an abbreviation of **gymnasium**.

gymnastics
NOUN Gymnastics is physical exercises, especially ones using equipment such as bars and ropes.

Hh

habit habits
NOUN A **habit** is something that you do often or regularly, sometimes without thinking about it.

habitat habitats
NOUN The **habitat** of an animal or plant is its natural home.

had
VERB **Had** is the past tense of **have**.

haddock
NOUN A **haddock** is an edible fish.

haiku
NOUN **Haiku** is a Japanese poem of 17 syllables in three lines.

hail hails, hailing, hailed
NOUN **1 Hail** is frozen rain. It falls in small balls of ice called hailstones.
VERB **2** When it is **hailing**, frozen rain is falling.

hair hairs
NOUN Your **hair** is made up of a large number of fine threads that grow on your head. Hair also grows on other parts of the body and on the bodies of some other animals.

hairdresser hairdressers
NOUN A **hairdresser** is trained to cut and style people's hair.

hairy hairier, hairiest
ADJECTIVE Someone or something that is **hairy** is covered with hair.

hajj
NOUN The **hajj** is the journey to Mecca that every Muslim must make at least once in their life if they are healthy and wealthy enough to do so.

half halves
NOUN **1** A **half** is one of two equal parts of something.
See *Fractions* on page 272.

ADVERB **2** When you are talking about time, you can use **half** to mean 30 minutes after a particular hour. *She was home by **half** past three.*

halfway
ADVERB **Halfway** is the middle of the distance between two points. *He stopped **halfway** down the stairs.*

hall halls
NOUN **1** A **hall** is the room just inside the front door of a home which leads into other rooms.
NOUN **2** A **hall** is also a large room or building used for public events.

Halloween
NOUN **Halloween** is October 31. Children celebrate it by dressing up, often as ghosts and witches.

halve halves, halving, halved
VERB If you **halve** something, you divide it into two equal parts.

ham
NOUN **Ham** is meat from the back leg of a pig. It is specially treated so that it can be kept for a long time.

hamburger hamburgers
NOUN A **hamburger** is a piece of ground meat shaped into a flat disk. Hamburgers are often eaten on a bun.

a b c d e f g **Hh** i j k l m n o p q r s t u v w x y z

hammer

hammer **hammers**

NOUN A **hammer** is a tool that is used for hitting things, such as nails into wood.

hammock **hammocks**

NOUN A **hammock** is a piece of strong cloth or netting which is hung between two supports and used as a bed.

hamster **hamsters**

NOUN A **hamster** is a small furry rodent which is often kept as a pet. Hamsters have very short tails, and large cheek pouches for carrying food.

hand **hands, handing, handed**

NOUN **1** Your **hand** is the part of your body which is at the end of your arm. It has five fingers.

NOUN **2** The **hands** of a clock point to the numbers to tell you the time.

VERB **3** When you **hand** something to someone, you pass it to them.

handbag **handbags**

NOUN A **handbag** is a small bag that women use to carry things such as money and keys.

handkerchief **handkerchiefs**

NOUN A **handkerchief** is a small square of fabric that you use for wiping your nose.

handle **handles, handling, handled**

NOUN **1** The **handle** of an object is the part you hold to pick it up and carry it.

NOUN **2** The **handle** of a door or window is the knob or lever that is used for opening or closing it.

VERB **3** If you **handle** something, you touch or feel it with your hands.

handlebar **handlebars**

NOUN **Handlebars** are the bar and handles at the front of a bicycle, used for steering.

handsome

ADJECTIVE A **handsome** man has a very attractive face.

handwriting

NOUN Someone's **handwriting** is the way in which they write with a pen or pencil.

handy **handier, handiest**

ADJECTIVE **1** If something is **handy**, it is near. *I like to keep my glasses **handy**.*

ADJECTIVE **2** If an object is **handy**, it is easy to handle or use.

hang **hangs, hanging, hung**

VERB If you **hang** something up, you fix it there so that it does not touch the ground. ***Hang** your coat on the hook.*

hangar **hangars**

NOUN A **hangar** is a large building where aircraft are kept.

hanger **hangers**

NOUN A **hanger** is a curved piece of metal, wood, or plastic that you hang clothes on.

hang-glider **hang-gliders**

NOUN A **hang-glider** is an aircraft without an engine. The pilot hangs in a harness from the frame.

Hanukkah or **Chanukah**

NOUN **Hanukkah** is the eight-day Jewish festival of lights.

happen **happens, happening, happened**

VERB **1** If something **happens**, it takes place. *What **happens** if I press this button?*

VERB **2** If you **happen** to do something, you do it by chance. *I **happened** to be near the phone when it rang.*

happiness

NOUN **Happiness** is a feeling of great pleasure.

happy **happier, happiest**

ADJECTIVE If you are **happy**, you feel good because something nice has happened or because most things are the way you want.

happily ADVERB

harbor **harbors**

NOUN A **harbor** is an area of deep water where boats can stay safely.

hard **harder, hardest**

ADJECTIVE **1** An object that is **hard** is very firm and stiff.

ADJECTIVE **2** If something is **hard** to do, you can only do it with a lot of effort.

hard disk **hard disks**

NOUN A **hard disk** is a permanent part of a computer. It is used to store large amounts of data.

harden **hardens, hardening, hardened**

VERB If something **hardens**, it becomes hard or gets harder.

hardly

ADVERB If you can **hardly** do something, you can only just do it. *The box was so heavy I could **hardly** lift it.*

hardware

NOUN **1** Hardware is tools and equipment made of metal.

NOUN **2** Hardware is also computer machinery.

hare **hares**

NOUN A **hare** is an animal like a large rabbit, but with longer ears and legs. It does not live in a burrow, but rests in grass or in a field.

harm

NOUN **Harm** is injury to a person or animal.

harmful ADJECTIVE   **harmless** ADJECTIVE

harness **harnesses**

NOUN **1** A **harness** is a set of straps which fit around a person's body to hold the person firmly in place.

NOUN **2** A horse's **harness** is a set of straps fastened around its head or body.

harsh **harsher, harshest**

ADJECTIVE **1** A person who is **harsh** is unkind.

ADJECTIVE **2** Weather that is **harsh** is cold and unpleasant.

ADJECTIVE **3** A voice or other sound that is **harsh** sounds rough and unpleasant.

harvest **harvests**

NOUN **Harvest** is the time when farmers cut and gather their ripe crop.

has

VERB **Has** is a present tense form of **have**.

hat **hats**

NOUN A **hat** is a head covering for wearing outside.

hatch **hatches, hatching, hatched**

VERB When a baby bird, insect, or other animal **hatches**, it comes out of its egg by breaking the shell.

hate **hates, hating, hated**

VERB If you **hate** something, you have a strong feeling of dislike for it.

haul **hauls, hauling, hauled**

VERB To **haul** something means to move it with a long steady pull.

haunted

ADJECTIVE A place that is **haunted** is thought to be visited by a ghost.

have **has, having, had**

VERB **1** Have can be used with other verbs to form the past tense. *I **have** already seen that film.*

VERB **2** If you **have** something, you own or possess it. *We **have** two tickets for the football game.*

VERB **3** If you **have** to do something, you must do it.

haven't

VERB **Haven't** is a contraction of **have not**.

hawk hawks

NOUN A **hawk** is a large bird of prey that eats small animals.

hay

NOUN **Hay** is grass which has been cut and dried to feed animals.

head heads, heading, headed

NOUN **1** Your **head** is the part of your body which has your brain, eyes, and mouth in it.

NOUN **2** The **head** of something is the top, start, or most important end. *Our teacher sat at the **head** of the table.*

NOUN **3** The **head** of a group or organization is the person in charge.

VERB **4** If you **head** in a particular direction, you move that way.

headache headaches

NOUN A **headache** is a pain in your head.

heading headings

NOUN A **heading** is a title at the top of a piece of writing.

headlight headlights

NOUN The **headlights** on a motor vehicle are the large powerful lights at the front.

headline headlines

NOUN **1** A **headline** is the title of a newspaper article printed in large type.

NOUN **2** The **headlines** are the main points of the radio or television news.

headphones

PLURAL NOUN **Headphones** are a pair of small speakers that you wear over or in your ears to listen to a recording without other people hearing.

headquarters

NOUN The **headquarters** of an organization is the place where the leaders of the organization work.

headstrong

ADJECTIVE If you are **headstrong**, you are determined to have your own way.

heal heals, healing, healed

VERB If something **heals**, it becomes healthy or normal again.

health

NOUN A person's **health** is how their body is, and whether they are well or ill.

healthy healthier, healthiest

ADJECTIVE **1** Someone who is **healthy** is well and not suffering from any illness.

ADJECTIVE **2** Something that is **healthy** is good for your health.

heap heaps

NOUN A **heap** is a lot of things piled up, usually untidily.

hear hears, hearing, heard

VERB When you **hear** sounds, you notice them by using your ears.

hearing

NOUN **Hearing** is the sense which makes it possible for you to be aware of sounds.

heart hearts

NOUN **1** Your **heart** is the organ that pumps the blood around inside your body.

NOUN **2** A **heart** is also a shape, used especially as a symbol of love.

heat heats, heating, heated

NOUN **1** Heat is warmth.

VERB **2** To **heat** something means to raise its temperature.

heather
NOUN **Heather** is a white bush with pink, purple, or white flowers.

heaven
NOUN **Heaven** is a place of happiness where God is believed to live.

heavy **heavier, heaviest**
ADJECTIVE Something that is **heavy** weighs a lot or weighs more than usual.

Hebrew
NOUN **Hebrew** is an ancient language now spoken in Israel, where it is the official language.

hedge **hedges**
NOUN A **hedge** is a row of bushes growing close together.

hedgehog **hedgehogs**
NOUN A **hedgehog** is a small animal with sharp spikes all over its back. It defends itself by rolling up into a ball.

heel **heels**
NOUN **1** Your **heel** is the back part of your foot.
NOUN **2** The **heel** of a shoe is the raised part underneath, at the back.

height **heights**
NOUN **1** The **height** of a person is how tall they are.
NOUN **2** The **height** of an object is its measurement from bottom to top.

held
VERB **Held** is the past tense of **hold**.

helicopter **helicopters**
NOUN A **helicopter** is an aircraft with large blades which turn very quickly. It can take off vertically, hover, and fly.

helmet **helmets**
NOUN A **helmet** is a hard hat that you wear to protect your head.

help **helps, helping, helped**
VERB **1** To **help** someone means to make something better or easier for them.
VERB **2** If you **help yourself** to something, you take it. *Help yourself to sandwiches.*
VERB **3** If you can't **help** something, you cannot control it or change it. *I can't help feeling sorry for him.*
helpful ADJECTIVE

helping **helpings**
NOUN A **helping** of food is the amount of it that you get in a single serving.

helpless
ADJECTIVE Someone who is **helpless** cannot cope on their own.

hem **hems**
NOUN The **hem** of a piece of material is the part that is folded over and sewn.

hemisphere **hemispheres**
NOUN A **hemisphere** is one half of a sphere. It can also be half of the Earth. *See Solid shapes on page 271.*

hen **hens**
NOUN **1** A **hen** is a female chicken.
NOUN **2** A **hen** can also be any female bird.

heptagon **heptagons**
NOUN A **heptagon** is a flat shape with seven straight sides. *See Colors and flat shapes on page 271.*

her
PRONOUN **1** You use **her** to refer to a woman, girl, or any female animal that has already been mentioned. *I like Katherine. I often play with her.*
ADJECTIVE **2** You also use **her** to show that something belongs to a particular female. *My dog Fluff won't eat her food.*

herd **herds**
NOUN A **herd** is a large group of animals of one kind that live together. *See Collective nouns on page 262.*

a
b
c
d
e
f
g
Hh
i
j
k
l
m
n
o
p
q
r
s
t
u
v
w
x
y
z

here

ADVERB You say **here** to mean the place where you are. *I'll stand **here** and wait.*

here and there PHRASE **Here and there** means in various places. *Bits of paper were lying **here and there** on the floor.*

hero heroes

NOUN **1** A **hero** is a man or boy who has done something brave and good.

NOUN **2** The **hero** of a story is the man or boy that the story is about. See **heroine**.

heroine heroines

NOUN **1** A **heroine** is a woman or girl who has done something brave and good.

NOUN **2** The **heroine** of a story is the woman or girl that the story is about. See **hero**.

heron herons

NOUN A **heron** is a bird that lives near water and eats fish.

herring herrings

NOUN A **herring** is a silvery fish that lives in large schools in northern seas.

herself

PRONOUN If a girl or woman does something **herself**, no one else does it. *The baby pulled **herself** up.*

hesitate hesitates, hesitating, hesitated

VERB If you **hesitate**, you pause while you are doing something, or just before you do it.

hexagon hexagons

NOUN A **hexagon** is a flat shape with six straight sides.

hexagonal ADJECTIVE

See Colors and flat shapes on page 271.

hibernate hibernates, hibernating, hibernated

VERB When certain animals, such as bears, **hibernate**, they spend the winter in a sleep-like state.

hide hides, hiding, hid, hidden

VERB **1** If you **hide** somewhere, you go where you cannot be seen.

VERB **2** If you **hide** something, you put it in a place where it cannot be seen.

hidden ADJECTIVE

high higher, highest

ADJECTIVE **1** Something that is **high** is a long way from the bottom to the top. *The wall around the garden is **high**.*

ADJECTIVE or ADVERB **2** If something is **high**, it is a long way up. *There was an airplane **high** above her.*

hill hills

NOUN A **hill** is a rounded area of land which is higher than the land surrounding it.

him

PRONOUN You use **him** to refer to a man, boy, or any male animal that has already been mentioned. *James asked me to call **him** back.*

himself

PRONOUN If a boy or man does something **himself**, no one else does it. *Ben hurt **himself** quite badly.*

Hindu **Hindus**

NOUN A **Hindu** is a person who believes in Hinduism, an Indian religion which has many gods. Hindus believe that people have another life on earth after death.

hinge **hinges**

NOUN **Hinges** are pieces of metal, wood, or plastic that are used to hold a door or lid so that it can swing freely.

hint **hints, hinting, hinted**

NOUN **1** A **hint** is a suggestion, clue, or helpful piece of advice.
VERB **2** If you **hint**, or **hint at** something, you suggest it in a way that is not obvious. *I hinted that I would like a bicycle for my birthday.*

hip **hips**

NOUN Your **hips** are the two parts at the sides of your body, between your waist and your upper legs.

hippopotamus **hippopotamuses** or **hippopotami**

NOUN A **hippopotamus** is a large African animal with thick skin and short legs. It lives in herds on the banks of large rivers, and spends a lot of time in the water. It is often called a **hippo** for short.

hire **hires, hiring, hired**

VERB If you **hire** someone, you pay them money to work for you.

his

ADJECTIVE OR PRONOUN You use **his** to show that something belongs to a man, boy, or any male animal. *Robert combed his hair.*

hiss **hisses, hissing, hissed**

VERB To **hiss** means to make a long "sss" sound.

historical

ADJECTIVE **Historical** stories are stories about things that happened in the past.

history **histories**

NOUN **History** is a study or record of the past.

hit **hits, hitting, hit**

VERB If you **hit** something, you touch it quickly and hard.

hive **hives**

NOUN A **hive** is a house for bees, made so that the beekeeper can collect the honey. See **beehive**.

hoard **hoards, hoarding, hoarded**

VERB **1** If you **hoard** things, you save or store them even though they may no longer be useful.
NOUN **2** A **hoard** is a store of things that has been saved or hidden.

hoarse **hoarser, hoarsest**

ADJECTIVE A **hoarse** voice sounds rough.

hobby **hobbies**

NOUN A **hobby** is something you enjoy doing in your spare time, such as collecting stamps or bird-watching.

hockey

NOUN **Hockey** is a game in which two teams use long sticks with curved ends to try and hit a small ball or puck into the other team's goal.

hold **holds, holding, held**

VERB **1** When you **hold** something, you keep it in your hand or arms.
VERB **2** If something **holds** a particular amount of something, it can contain that amount. *This bottle holds one quart.*

hole **holes**

NOUN A **hole** is an opening or space in something. *The dog buried his bone in a **hole** in the garden.*

holiday **holidays**

NOUN A **holiday** is a day when school or work is officially suspended.

hollow

ADJECTIVE Something that is **hollow** has a space inside it. *The owl lived in a **hollow** tree trunk.*

holly

NOUN **Holly** is an evergreen tree with prickly leaves. It often has bright red berries in winter.

home **homes**

NOUN Your **home** is the place where you live and feel you belong.

homesick

ADJECTIVE If you are **homesick**, you are sad because you are away from home.

homework

NOUN **Homework** is school work that children do at home.

homograph **homographs**

NOUN **Homographs** are words which are spelled the same, but have different meanings, for example "calf" (part of your leg) and "calf" (a young cow).

homonym **homonyms**

NOUN **Homonyms** are words which are pronounced or spelled in the same way, but which mean different things. Homographs and homophones are homonyms.

homophone **homophones**

NOUN **Homophones** are words which sound the same, but have different meanings or spellings, for example "right" and "write."

honest

ADJECTIVE Someone who is **honest** tells the truth and can be trusted.

honey

NOUN **Honey** is a sweet sticky food that is made by bees.

hood **hoods**

NOUN A **hood** is a part of a coat or jacket that you can pull over your head.

hoof **hooves** or **hoofs**

NOUN The **hoof** of an animal, such as a horse, is the hard bony part of its foot.

hook **hooks**

NOUN A **hook** is a curved piece of metal or plastic that is used for catching, holding, or hanging things.

hoop **hoops**

NOUN A **hoop** is a large ring, such as the rim around a basketball net.

hoopla **hooplas**

NOUN A **hoopla** is a commotion.

hoot **hoots, hooting, hooted**

VERB To **hoot** means to make a long "oo" sound like an owl.

hop **hops, hopping, hopped**

VERB **1** If you **hop**, you jump on one foot.
VERB **2** When animals or birds **hop**, they jump with two feet together.

hope **hopes, hoping, hoped**

VERB If you **hope** that something will happen, you want it to happen.

hopeful

ADJECTIVE If you are **hopeful**, you are fairly sure that something you want to happen will happen.

hopeless

ADJECTIVE **1** You say a situation is **hopeless** when it is very bad and you do not think it will get better.
ADJECTIVE **2** If somebody is **hopeless** at doing something, they cannot do it well. *I'm **hopeless** at arithmetic.*

horizon **horizons**

NOUN The **horizon** is the line in the far distance where the sky seems to touch the land or the sea.

horizontal

ADJECTIVE Something that is **horizontal** is level, like the horizon. See **vertical**.

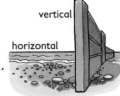

horn **horns**

NOUN **1** **Horns** are the hard pointed growths on the heads of animals such as goats.

NOUN **2** A **horn** is a musical instrument made of brass.

NOUN **3** On vehicles, a **horn** makes a loud noise as a warning.

horrible

ADJECTIVE Someone or something that is **horrible** is awful or very unpleasant.

horribly ADVERB

horror

NOUN **Horror** is a strong feeling of fear or disgust.

horse **horses**

NOUN A **horse** is a large animal which people can ride. Horses are also used for pulling things like carts.

horseshoe **horseshoes**

NOUN A **horseshoe** is a piece of metal shaped like a U. It is fixed under a horse's hoof, to protect it.

hose **hoses**

NOUN A **hose** is a long tube that sprays water.

hospital **hospitals**

NOUN A **hospital** is a place where sick and injured people are cared for.

hot **hotter, hottest**

ADJECTIVE **1** Something that is **hot** has a high temperature.

ADJECTIVE **2** If you feel **hot**, you feel too warm to be comfortable.

ADJECTIVE **3** You say food is **hot** if it has a strong taste caused by spices. *This curry is too **hot** for me.*

hotel **hotels**

NOUN A **hotel** is a building where people pay to stay, usually for a few nights.

hour **hours**

NOUN An **hour** is a period of 60 minutes. There are 24 hours in a day.

house **houses**

NOUN A **house** is a building where people live.

hover **hovers, hovering, hovered**

VERB When a bird or aircraft **hovers**, it stays in the same place in the air.

hovercraft **hovercraft or hovercrafts**

NOUN A **hovercraft** is a vehicle that travels over water or land on a cushion of air.

how

ADVERB **1** You can use **how** in questions to ask about the way something is done or known. *How did you know that?*

ADVERB **2** **How** can also be used to ask about a measurement or quantity. *How much is a ticket to New York?*

ADVERB **3** **How** is often used in greetings. *How are you?*

however

ADVERB You use **however** when you are adding a comment that is surprising after what you have just said. *I was sure I was going to win the race.* ***However**, a younger girl came first.*

howl **howls, howling, howled**

VERB To **howl** means to make a long, loud cry. *The dog **howls** when I sing.*

hug **hugs, hugging, hugged**

VERB If you **hug** someone, you put your arms around them and hold them close.

huge

ADJECTIVE Something that is **huge** is extremely big.

hum **hums, humming, hummed**

VERB If you **hum**, you sing with your lips closed.

human **humans**

NOUN A **human** is a person.

hump **humps**

NOUN A **hump** is a large lump on the back of an animal such as a camel, which is used for storing fat and water.

hundred **hundreds**

NOUN A **hundred** is the number 100.

hung

VERB **Hung** is the past tense of **hang**.

hungry **hungrier, hungriest**

ADJECTIVE When you are **hungry**, you want to eat.

hungrily ADVERB

hunt **hunts, hunting, hunted**

VERB **1** To **hunt** means to chase wild animals to kill them for food or sport.

VERB **2** If you **hunt** for something, you look for it.

hurricane **hurricanes**

NOUN A **hurricane** is a storm with very high winds.

hurry **hurries, hurrying, hurried**

VERB If you **hurry** somewhere, you go there as quickly as you can.

hurt **hurts, hurting, hurt**

VERB **1** If part of your body **hurts**, you feel pain.

VERB **2** If you have been **hurt**, you have been injured.

ADJECTIVE **3** If someone feels **hurt**, they feel unhappy because someone has been unkind to them.

husband **husbands**

NOUN A woman's **husband** is the man she is married to.

hut **huts**

NOUN A **hut** is a small, simple building with one or two rooms.

hutch **hutches**

NOUN A **hutch** is a cage made of wood and wire netting. Pets such as rabbits are kept in hutches.

hygiene

NOUN **Hygiene** is keeping yourself and your surroundings clean, especially to stop the spread of disease.

hymn **hymns**

NOUN A **hymn** is a Christian song in praise of God.

hyphen **hyphens**

NOUN A **hyphen** is a punctuation mark (-) used to join together words or parts of words, for example "left-handed." *See Punctuation on page 264.*

Ii

ice **ices, icing, iced**
NOUN **1** Ice is water that has frozen solid.
VERB **2** If you **ice** cakes, you cover them
with icing.

iceberg **icebergs**
NOUN An **iceberg** is
a large mass of ice
floating in the sea.

ice cream **ice creams**
NOUN **Ice cream** is a very cold sweet-
tasting creamy food.

ice skate **ice skates**
NOUN An **ice skate** is a boot with a metal
blade fixed underneath. You wear it
when you skate on ice.

icicle **icicles**
NOUN An **icicle** is a pointed piece of ice
which hangs from roofs, or wherever
water has been dripping and freezing.

icing
NOUN **Icing** is a mixture of powdered
sugar and water or egg whites. It is used
to cover cakes as a decoration.

icy **icier, iciest**
ADJECTIVE Something which is **icy** has
ice on it, or is very cold. *This wind is icy.*

idea **ideas**
NOUN **1** If you have an **idea**, you
suddenly think of a way of doing
something.
NOUN **2** An **idea** is a picture in your mind.

ideal
ADJECTIVE The **ideal** person or thing is
the best one possible for the situation.

identical
ADJECTIVE Things that are **identical** are
exactly the same in every detail.

idle **idler, idlest**
ADJECTIVE An **idle** person is someone
who does not do very much.

igloo **igloos**
NOUN An **igloo** is
a dome-shaped
house built out
of blocks of snow.

ignore **ignores, ignoring, ignored**
VERB If you **ignore** someone, you
deliberately take no notice of them.

ill
ADJECTIVE Someone who is **ill** has
something wrong with their health.

illness **illnesses**
NOUN An **illness** is something like a cold
or measles that people can suffer from.

illuminations
PLURAL NOUN **Illuminations** are colored
lights put up to decorate a town.

illustrate **illustrates, illustrating, illustrated**
VERB If you **illustrate** something, you
add pictures to it.

illustration **illustrations**
NOUN An **illustration** is a picture or
diagram in a book or magazine.

illustrator **illustrators**
NOUN An **illustrator** is an artist who
draws pictures for books and magazines.

I'm
I'm is a contraction of **I am**.

imaginary
ADJECTIVE Something that is **imaginary**
is not real. It is only in your mind. *She
has imaginary talks with famous people.*

a
b
c
d
e
f
g
h
Ii
j
k
l
m
n
o
p
q
r
s
t
u
v
w
x
y
z

imagination

imagination
NOUN Your **imagination** is your ability to think of ideas, or to form pictures in your mind.

imagine imagines, imagining, imagined
VERB When you **imagine** something, you form a picture of it in your mind.

imitate imitates, imitating, imitated
VERB If you **imitate** someone, you copy the way they speak or behave.

imitation imitations
NOUN An **imitation** is a copy of something else.

immediately
ADVERB If something happens **immediately**, it happens right away.

impatient
ADJECTIVE Someone who is **impatient** does not like to be kept waiting.

important
ADJECTIVE **1** If someone says something is **important**, they mean it matters a lot.
ADJECTIVE **2** Someone who is **important** has a lot of power in a particular group.

impossible
ADJECTIVE Something that is **impossible** cannot be done.

impressive
ADJECTIVE If something is **impressive**, people admire it, usually because it is large or important.

imprison imprisons, imprisoning, imprisoned
VERB If someone is **imprisoned**, they are locked up, usually in a prison.

improve improves, improving, improved
VERB If something **improves**, it gets better.

improvement improvements
NOUN An **improvement** is a change in something that makes it better.

in
PREPOSITION **1** You use **in** to say where something is, or where it is going. *Put it in the box.*
PREPOSITION **2** You also use **in** to say when something should happen. *I'll be home in 20 minutes.*
ADVERB **3** You use **in** to mean at home. *Is anybody in?*

inch inches
NOUN An **inch** is a unit of length equal to about two and a half centimeters. There are 12 inches in a foot.

include includes, including, included
VERB If you **include** something in a whole thing, you make it part of the whole thing. *Batteries are included.*

increase increases, increasing, increased
VERB **1** If something **increases**, it becomes greater.
NOUN **2** An **increase** is a rise in the number, level, or amount of something.

index indexes
NOUN An **index** is an alphabetical list at the back of a book that helps you find the things you want to read about.

indignant
ADJECTIVE If you are **indignant**, you feel angry about something that is unfair.

individual
ADJECTIVE **Individual** means having to do with one particular person, rather than a whole group.

infant infants
NOUN An **infant** is a baby or young child.

influence influences
NOUN An **influence** is the effect that someone or something has on you, that can change the way you think or behave. *That boy is a bad influence on you.*

informal

ADJECTIVE **1 Informal** means relaxed. You usually speak or behave in this way when you are with people you know well.

ADJECTIVE **2** In a dictionary, a word shown as **informal** is more suitable for everyday talk than it is for writing.

information

NOUN If someone gives you **information** about something, they tell you about it.

infuriate **infuriates, infuriating, infuriated**

VERB If someone or something **infuriates** you, they make you extremely angry.

ingredient **ingredients**

NOUN **Ingredients** are the things that are used to make something, especially in cooking.

inhabit **inhabits, inhabiting, inhabited**

VERB If you **inhabit** a place, you live there.

inhabitant **inhabitants**

NOUN The **inhabitants** of a place are the people who live there.

initial **initials**

NOUN An **initial** is the first letter of a name. *David Hunt's **initials** are D.H.*

injection **injections**

NOUN If a doctor or nurse gives you an **injection**, they put medicine into your body with a special needle.

injure **injures, injuring, injured**

VERB If something **injures** a person or animal, it damages part of their body.

injury NOUN

ink **inks**

NOUN **Ink** is the colored liquid that is used for writing and printing.

inland

ADVERB If you go **inland**, you go away from the coast toward the middle of a country.

inn **inns**

NOUN An **inn** is a small hotel.

innocent

ADJECTIVE Someone who is **innocent** has not done anything wrong.

insect **insects**

NOUN An **insect** is a small animal with six legs and usually wings. Ants, flies, butterflies, and beetles are all insects.

See *Insects* on page 259.

insert **inserts, inserting, inserted**

VERB If you **insert** an object into something, you put it into it. *She **inserted** the key in the lock.*

inside

ADVERB, PREPOSITION, OR ADJECTIVE **Inside** means in something. *It was raining, so they had to play **inside**... It was very cold **inside** the church... He hid his money in an **inside** pocket.*

insist **insists, insisting, insisted**

VERB If you **insist** on doing something, you refuse to give in.

inspect **inspects, inspecting, inspected**

VERB If you **inspect** something, you look at every part of it carefully.

inspire **inspires, inspiring, inspired**

VERB If something **inspires** you, it gives you new ideas and enthusiasm.

instant

ADJECTIVE Something **instant** happens immediately. *The new pop group was an **instant** success.*

a
b
c
d
e
f
g
h
Ii
j
k
l
m
n
o
p
q
r
s
t
u
v
w
x
y
z

instead

ADVERB **Instead** means in place of. *Take the stairs **instead** of the elevator.*

instruction **instructions**

NOUN **1** An **instruction** is something that someone tells you to do.

PLURAL NOUN **2 Instructions** are words that tell you how to do something.

instrument **instruments**

NOUN **1** An **instrument** is a tool that is used to do a particular job.

NOUN **2** An **instrument** is also an object, such as a piano or guitar, that you play to make music.

insult **insults, insulting, insulted**

VERB If you **insult** someone, you offend them by being rude to them.

integer **integers**

NOUN An **integer** is any of the whole numbers used for counting.

intelligent

ADJECTIVE A person who is **intelligent** can understand, learn, and think things out quickly and well.

intend **intends, intending, intended**

VERB If you **intend** to do something, you have decided to do it, or plan to do it.

interest **interests**

NOUN If you have an **interest** in something, you want to learn or hear more about it.

interesting

ADJECTIVE If something is **interesting**, it attracts or keeps your attention.

interfere **interferes, interfering, interfered**

VERB If something **interferes** with something else, it gets in the way. *Don't let TV **interfere** with your homework.*

interjection **interjections**

NOUN An **interjection** is a word you say suddenly to show surprise, pain, or anger, such as "Ouch!" or "Wow!"

Internet

NOUN The **Internet** is a worldwide communication system that people use through computers.

interpret **interprets, interpreting, interpreted**

VERB If you **interpret** what someone says or does, you say what it means.

interrupt **interrupts, interrupting, interrupted**

VERB **1** If you **interrupt** someone, you start talking before they have finished what they were saying.

VERB **2** If you **interrupt** what someone is doing, you make them stop doing it for a while.

interval **intervals**

NOUN An **interval** is a time between two events, or a space between two objects.

interview **interviews, interviewing, interviewed**

VERB If you **interview** someone, you ask them questions about themselves.

introduction **introductions**

NOUN An **introduction** is a piece of writing at the beginning of a book, which usually tells you what it is about.

invent **invents, inventing, invented**

VERB **1** If you **invent** a story or an excuse, you make it up.

VERB **2** If someone **invents** something, such as a machine or an instrument, they are the first person to think of it.

invention **inventions**

NOUN An **invention** is something that is a completely new idea. *She is working on an **invention** that will help people.*

Kk

kangaroo **kangaroos**
NOUN A **kangaroo** is a large Australian animal which moves forward by jumping on its back legs.

keen **keener, keenest**
ADJECTIVE Someone who is **keen** to do something wants to do it very much.

keep **keeps, keeping, kept**
VERB **1** If you **keep** something for somebody, you save it for them.
VERB **2** If you **keep** doing something, you do it over and over again.
VERB **3** If something **keeps** you a certain way, you stay that way because of it.
*That dog is **keeping** me awake.*

kennel **kennels**
NOUN A **kennel** is a small house for a dog.

kept
VERB **Kept** is the past tense of **keep**.

kerchief **kerchiefs**
NOUN A **kerchief** is a piece of cloth worn around the head or neck.

ketchup
NOUN **Ketchup** is a cold tomato sauce.

kettle **kettles**
NOUN A **kettle** is a covered container used to boil water.

key **keys**
NOUN **1** A **key** is a specially shaped piece of metal that fits into a lock.
NOUN **2** The **keys** on something like a computer keyboard, or a piano, are the buttons that you press to use it.
ADJECTIVE **3** **Key** words or sentences are an important part of a piece of text.

keyboard **keyboards**
NOUN A **keyboard** is a row of buttons called keys on a piano or computer.

kick **kicks, kicking, kicked**
VERB If you **kick** something, you hit it with your foot.

kid **kids**
NOUN **1** A **kid** is a young goat.
See Young animals on page 260.
NOUN **2** INFORMAL A **kid** is a child.

kidnap **kidnaps, kidnapping, kidnapped**
VERB If someone **kidnaps** another person, they take them away by force.

kill **kills, killing, killed**
VERB To **kill** someone or something means to cause them to die.

kilogram **kilograms**
NOUN A **kilogram** (kg) is a unit of mass and weight. One kilogram, or kilo, is equal to 1000 grams.

kilometer **kilometers**
NOUN A **kilometer** is a unit of distance equal to 1000 meters.

kilt **kilts**
NOUN A **kilt** is a pleated skirt worn by men as part of the national costume of Scotland.

kind **kinds; kinder, kindest**
NOUN **1** If you talk about a **kind** of object, you mean a sort of object.
ADJECTIVE **2** Someone who is **kind** behaves in a gentle, caring way.
kindness NOUN

king **kings**
NOUN A **king** is a man who rules a country. Kings are not chosen by the people, but are born into a royal family.

a b c d e f g h i j **Kk** l m n o p q r s t u v w x y z

kingdom kingdoms

NOUN **1** A **kingdom** is a country or region that is ruled by a king or queen.

NOUN **2** The animal **kingdom** is all the animals in the world. *This creature is the largest in the animal kingdom.*

kingfisher kingfishers

NOUN A **kingfisher** is a brightly colored bird that lives by rivers and eats fish.

kiss kisses, kissing, kissed

VERB If you **kiss** someone, you touch them with your lips.

kit kits

NOUN A **kit** is a set of things that are used for a particular purpose. *Have you seen my first aid kit?*

kitchen kitchens

NOUN A **kitchen** is a room that is used for preparing and cooking food.

kite kites

NOUN **1** A **kite** is a frame covered with paper or cloth which you fly in the sky at the end of a piece of string.

See Colors and flat shapes on page 271.

kitten kittens

NOUN A **kitten** is a young cat.

See Young animals on page 260.

kiwi kiwis

NOUN A **kiwi** is a type of bird found in New Zealand. Kiwis cannot fly.

kiwi fruit kiwi fruits

NOUN A **kiwi fruit** is a fruit with a brown hairy skin and green flesh.

See Fruit on page 257.

knead kneads, kneading, kneaded

VERB Dough is **kneaded** by pressing it again and again with the heels of your hands.

knee knees

NOUN Your **knee** is the joint where your leg bends.

kneel kneels, kneeling, kneeled or knelt

VERB When you **kneel**, you bend your legs until your knees are touching the ground.

knew

VERB **Knew** is the past tense of **know**.

knickers

PLURAL NOUN **Knickers** are loose, short pants that end just below the knee.

knife knives

NOUN A **knife** is a sharp, metal tool that you use to cut things.

knight knights

NOUN Hundreds of years ago, a **knight** was a man in armor who rode into battle for his king or queen.

knit knits, knitting, knitted

VERB If you **knit**, you make something from wool using two long needles.

knob knobs

NOUN **1** A **knob** is a round handle on a door or a drawer.

NOUN **2** A **knob** is also a round button on a piece of equipment such as a radio.

knock knocks, knocking, knocked

VERB If you **knock** on something, you hit it hard.

knot knots

NOUN A **knot** is a tie in something, such as string or cloth.

know knows, knowing, knew

VERB **1** If you **know** a fact, you have it in your mind and do not need to learn it.

VERB **2** If you **know** somebody, you have met them before.

knowledge

NOUN **Knowledge** is all the facts and information that you know.

knuckle knuckles

NOUN Your **knuckles** are the bony parts where your fingers join your hands and where your fingers bend.

koala koalas

NOUN A **koala** is an Australian animal that looks like a small bear with gray fur.

Ll

label labels
NOUN A **label** is a small notice that tells you what something is or gives you information. *Read the **label** on the medicine bottle.*

laboratory laboratories
NOUN A **laboratory** is a place where scientists work, using special equipment.

labor
NOUN **Labor** is hard work.

lace laces
NOUN **1** **Lace** is a very fine decorated cloth made with a lot of holes in it.
NOUN **2** **Laces** are cords that you use to fasten your shoes.

lack lacks, lacking, lacked
VERB If you **lack** something, you do not have it when you need it.

ladder ladders
NOUN A **ladder** is a wooden or metal frame used for climbing up things like walls or trees.

ladle ladles
NOUN A **ladle** is a big, deep spoon with a long handle, which is used to serve soup.
ladle VERB

lady ladies
NOUN **Lady** is a polite name for a woman. *I think this **lady** was in front of me.*

ladybug ladybugs
NOUN A **ladybug** is a small, round flying beetle with spots on its wings.
See *Insects on page 259.*

laid
VERB **Laid** is the past tense of **lay**.

lain
VERB **Lain** is the past participle of **lie**.

lake lakes
NOUN A **lake** is a large area of fresh water with land all around it.

lamb lambs
NOUN A **lamb** is a young sheep.
See *Young animals on page 260.*

lame
ADJECTIVE An animal which is **lame** cannot walk properly.

lamp lamps
NOUN A **lamp** is an object that gives light.

lamppost lampposts
NOUN A **lamppost** is a tall column in the street, with a light at the top.

land lands, landing, landed
NOUN **1** **Land** is the part of the world that is solid, dry ground.
VERB **2** When an aircraft **lands**, it comes down from the air onto land or water.

landlady landladies
NOUN A **landlady** is a woman who rents rooms to people.

landlord landlords
NOUN A **landlord** is a man who rents rooms to people.

landmark landmarks
NOUN A **landmark** is a building, or a feature of the land, that can be used to find out where you are.

landscape landscapes
NOUN A **landscape** is everything you can see when you look across an area of land.

lane lanes
NOUN **1** A **lane** is a narrow road, especially in the country.
NOUN **2** A **lane** is also part of a main road or highway. It is marked with lines to guide drivers.

a b c d e f g h i j k **Ll** m n o p q r s t u v w x y z

language

a
b
c
d
e
f
g
h
i
j
k
Ll
m
n
o
p
q
r
s
t
u
v
w
x
y
z

language **languages**

NOUN A **language** is the words that are used by the people of a country when they speak or write to each other.

lantern **lanterns**

NOUN A **lantern** is a light in a container. It has sides which the light can shine through and is usually made of glass, metal, or paper.

lap **laps, lapping, lapped**

NOUN **1** Your **lap** is the flat area formed by the tops of your legs when you are sitting down.

VERB **2** When an animal **laps** up liquid, it drinks using its tongue to get the liquid into its mouth.

large **larger, largest**

ADJECTIVE Something **large** is big.

larva **larvae**

NOUN A **larva** is an insect at an early stage of its life. It looks likes a short, fat worm.

laser **lasers**

NOUN A **laser** is a machine which produces a narrow beam of light. Lasers are used for many different things, including medical operations.

last **lasts, lasting, lasted**

ADJECTIVE **1** The **last** thing or event is the most recent one. *I saw him **last** week.*

ADVERB **2** If something happens **last**, it happens after everything else. *I came in **last** in the race.*

VERB **3** If something **lasts**, it continues to exist or happen. *Her speech **lasted** an hour.*

at last PHRASE If something happens **at last**, it happens after a long time.

late **later, latest**

ADJECTIVE OR ADVERB **1** If you are **late** arriving somewhere, you get there after the time you were supposed to.

ADJECTIVE OR ADVERB **2** Late means near the end of a period of time. *We had a picnic in the **late** afternoon.*

lately

ADVERB If something has happened **lately**, it happened not long ago.

laugh **laughs, laughing, laughed**

VERB When you **laugh**, you make the sound people make when they are happy or think something is funny.
laughter NOUN

launch **launches, launching, launched**

VERB **1** When a rocket or satellite is **launched**, it is sent into the sky.

VERB **2** To **launch** a ship means to send it into the water for the first time.

laundromat **laundromat**

NOUN A **laundromat** is the trademark name for a shop where people pay to use washing machines.

lava

NOUN **Lava** is a very hot, liquid rock which comes out of volcanoes.

lavender

NOUN **1** Lavender is a plant with pale purple flowers that have a pleasant smell.

ADJECTIVE **2** Lavender is a pale purple color.

law **laws**

NOUN A **law** is a rule that is made by the government.

lawn **lawns**

NOUN A **lawn** is an area of short grass in a garden or park.

lawnmower **lawnmowers**

NOUN A **lawnmower** is a machine for cutting the grass on lawns.

lawyer lawyers

NOUN A **lawyer** is a person who understands the law and can advise people about it.

lay lays, laying, laid

VERB **1** If you **lay** something somewhere, you put it there carefully.

VERB **2** When a bird **lays** an egg, it expels the egg from its body.

VERB **3** If you are **laid up**, you are in bed with an injury or illness.

layer layers

NOUN A **layer** is a single thickness of something that lies on top of, or underneath, something else.

layout layouts

NOUN The **layout** of something is the way it is arranged.

lazy lazier, laziest

ADJECTIVE Someone who is **lazy** does not want to work or do anything hard.

lazily ADVERB

lead leads, leading, led

(*rhymes with* **feed**)

VERB **1** If you **lead** someone to a particular place, you go with them to show them the way.

VERB **2** Someone who **leads** a group of people is in charge of them.

VERB **3** If you are **leading** in a race or game, you are winning at that point.

NOUN **4** A dog's **lead** is a long thin piece of leather or a chain. You fix one end to the collar and hold the other end.

(*rhymes with* **fed**) NOUN **5** Lead is a gray, heavy metal.

(*rhymes with* **fed**) NOUN **6** The **lead** in a pencil is the center part of it that makes a mark on paper.

leader leaders

NOUN The **leader** of a group of people is the person who is in charge.

leaf leaves

NOUN A **leaf** is one of the flat green parts of a plant. Different sorts of plants have differently shaped leaves.

leaflet leaflets

NOUN A **leaflet** is a piece of paper with information or advertising printed on it.

leak leaks, leaking, leaked

VERB **1** If a pipe or container **leaks**, it has a hole which lets gas or liquid escape.

VERB **2** If liquid or gas **leaks**, it escapes from a pipe or container.

lean leans, leaning, or **leaned; leaner, leanest**

VERB **1** When you **lean** somewhere, you bend your body in that direction.

VERB **2** When you **lean** on something, you rest your body against it for support.

ADJECTIVE **3** Lean meat has little or no fat.

leap leaps, leaping, leapt or leaped

VERB If you **leap** somewhere, you jump over a long distance, or high in the air.

leap year leap years

NOUN A **leap year** is a year with 366 days. There is a leap year every four years.

learn learns, learning, learned

VERB When you **learn** something, you get to know it or find out how to do it.

least

NOUN **1** The **least** is the smallest possible amount of something. *That is the **least** of my problems.*

ADJECTIVE OR ADVERB **2** Least is a superlative form of **little**, meaning very small in amount. *We bought the **least** expensive bike... She ate the **least** of all of them.*

leather

NOUN **Leather** is the specially treated skin of animals. It is used for making things like shoes and furniture.

leave leaves, leaving, left

VERB **1** When you **leave** a place, you go away from it.

VERB **2** If you **leave** someone somewhere, they stay behind after you go away.

VERB **3** In math, when you take one number from other, it **leaves** a third number.

led

VERB **Led** is the past tense of **lead**.

ledge ledges

NOUN A **ledge** is a narrow shelf on the side of a cliff or rock face, or on the outside of a building.

leek leeks

NOUN A **leek** is a long, white vegetable with green leaves. *See Vegetables on page 256.*

left

VERB **1** Left is the past tense of **leave**.

NOUN **2** The **left** is the side that you begin reading on in English.

ADJECTIVE OR ADVERB **3** Left means on or toward the left side of something. *Turn **left** at the end of the road.*

leg legs

NOUN **1** Legs are the parts of your body which stretch from the hips to the feet.

NOUN **2** The **legs** of an object, such as a table, are the parts which rest on the floor and support the object's weight.

legend legends

NOUN A **legend** is an old and popular story which may or may not be true.

lemon lemons

NOUN A **lemon** is a yellow, oval fruit. Lemons are juicy, but they taste sour. *See Fruit on page 257.*

lemonade

NOUN **Lemonade** is a drink made from lemons, sugar, and water.

lend lends, lending, lent

VERB If you **lend** something to someone, you let them have it for a while.

length lengths

NOUN **1** The **length** of something is the distance that it measures from one end to the other.

NOUN **2** The **length** of something like a vacation is the period of time that it lasts.

lens lenses

NOUN A **lens** is a curved piece of glass that makes light go in a certain way. Lenses are used in things like cameras, telescopes, and glasses.

lent

VERB **Lent** is the past tense of **lend**.

leopard leopards

NOUN A **leopard** is a large, wild cat that lives in the forests of Africa and Asia. It has yellow fur with black spots.

less

ADJECTIVE OR ADVERB **Less** is a comparative form of **little**, meaning not as much. *A shower uses **less** water than a bath.*

lesson lessons

NOUN A **lesson** is a short period of time when you are taught something.

let lets, letting, let

VERB **1** If you **let** someone do something, you allow them to do it.

VERB **2** If someone **lets** a house or apartment that they own, they rent it out.

letter letters

NOUN **1** A **letter** is a written message to someone, usually sent through the mail.

NOUN **2** Letters are written symbols which go together to make words.

lettering

NOUN **Lettering** is letters that have been drawn, painted, or printed on something, such as a sign or greeting card. *The birthday invitation had very big **lettering** on it.*

lettuce

NOUN **Lettuce** is a plant with large green leaves that you eat raw in salads.
See *Vegetables* on page 256.

level levels

ADJECTIVE **1** A surface that is **level** is smooth, flat, and parallel to the ground.
ADVERB **2** If you are **level** with someone, you are next to them.
NOUN **3** The **level** of a liquid is the height it comes up to. *After heavy rain, the river rose to a dangerous **level**.*

lever levers

NOUN **1** A **lever** is a long bar that you put under a heavy object and press down on to make the object move.
NOUN **2** A **lever** is also a handle on a machine that you pull down to make the machine work.

library libraries

NOUN A **library** is a building where books are kept for people to come and read or borrow.

lick licks, licking, licked

VERB If you **lick** something, you move your tongue across it.

lid lids

NOUN A **lid** is a cover for a box or other container.

lie lies, lying, lay, lain; lied

VERB **1** To **lie** somewhere means to rest there horizontally.
VERB **2** To **lie** means to say something that is not true.

life lives

NOUN The **life** of a person or animal is the time between their birth and death.

lifeboat lifeboats

NOUN A **lifeboat** is a boat that is used to rescue people in danger at sea.

lifetime

NOUN Your **lifetime** is the period of time during which you are alive.

lift lifts, lifting, lifted

VERB **1** If you **lift** something, you move it to a higher position.
NOUN **2** A **lift** can mean a happy feeling. A compliment gives you a **lift**.

light lights; lighter, lightest; lights, lighting, lighted or lit

NOUN **1** **Light** is the brightness from the sun, moon, fire, or lamps, that lets you see things.
NOUN **2** A **light** is a lamp or other object that gives out brightness.
ADJECTIVE **3** A place that is **light** is bright because of the sun or the use of lamps.
ADJECTIVE **4** A **light** color is pale.
ADJECTIVE **5** A **light** object does not weigh much.
VERB **6** To **light** something means to cause light to shine on it or in it.
VERB **7** To **light** a fire means to make it start burning.

lighthouse lighthouses

NOUN A **lighthouse** is a tower with a powerful flashing light at the top, which is used to guide ships or to warn them of danger.

lightning

NOUN **Lightning** is a bright flash of light in the sky produced by natural electricity during a thunderstorm.

a
b
c
d
e
f
g
h
i
j
k
Ll
m
n
o
p
q
r
s
t
u
v
w
x
y
z

like

like likes, liking, liked
PREPOSITION **1** If one thing is **like** another, it is similar to it.
VERB **2** If you **like** someone or something, you find them pleasant.

likely likelier, likeliest
ADJECTIVE Something that is **likely** will probably happen or is probably true.

limb limbs
NOUN A **limb** is an arm or leg.

limerick limericks
NOUN A **limerick** is a funny nonsense poem of five lines.

limit limits
NOUN A **limit** is a line or a point beyond which something cannot go. *There is a speed **limit** on this road.*

limp limps, limping, limped; limper, limpest
VERB **1** If you **limp**, you walk unevenly because you have hurt your leg or foot.
ADJECTIVE **2** Something that is **limp** is soft and floppy. *This lettuce is a bit **limp**.*

line lines
NOUN **1** A **line** is a long thin mark. Some writing paper has lines on it to show you where to write.
NOUN **2** A **line** of people or things is a number of them in a row.

NOUN **3** In a piece of writing, a **line** is a number of words together. *A limerick has five **lines**.*
NOUN **4** A railway **line** is one of the heavy metal rails that trains run on.

linen
NOUN **Linen** is a kind of cloth made from a plant called flax. It is used for things like sheets and tablecloths.

liner liners
NOUN A **liner** is a large passenger ship that makes long journeys.

link links
NOUN **1** A **link** is one of the rings in a chain.
NOUN **2** A **link** is also a connection between two things. *The keychain was held together by a **link**.*

lion lions
NOUN A **lion** is a large, wild cat. Lions live in parts of Africa and Asia, in groups called prides.

lioness lionesses
NOUN A **lioness** is a female lion.

lip lips
NOUN Your **lips** are the top and bottom outer edges of your mouth.

liquid liquids
NOUN A **liquid** is anything which is not a solid or a gas, and which can be poured.

list lists
NOUN A **list** is a set of things that are written one below the other.

listen listens, listening, listened
VERB If you **listen** to a sound that you can hear, you pay attention to it.
listener NOUN

lit
VERB **Lit** is the past tense of **light**.

liter liters
NOUN A **liter** is a unit used to measure volume and capacity. It roughly equals one quart.

literacy
NOUN **Literacy** is the ability to read and write.

litter litters
NOUN **1** Litter is trash left lying untidily outside.
NOUN **2** A **litter** is a group of animals born to the same mother at the same time.
See *Collective nouns* on page 262.

little less, lesser, least

ADJECTIVE **1** Something or someone that is **little** is small in size.

ADVERB **2** Little can mean not much. *Our lazy cat does very **little**.*

live lives, living, lived

(*rhymes with* **give**)

VERB **1** If you **live** in a place, that is where your home is.

VERB **2** To **live** means to be alive.

live

(*rhymes with* **hive**)

ADJECTIVE **1** A **live** animal is living.

ADJECTIVE **2** Live television or radio is broadcast as it happens.

lively livelier, liveliest

ADJECTIVE Someone who is **lively** is cheerful and full of energy.

liver livers

NOUN Your **liver** is a large organ in your body. Its job is to clean your blood.

living

ADJECTIVE **1** Living things are plants, animals, and humans that are alive. All living things need food to grow.

NOUN **2** Someone who earns a **living** earns enough money to buy all the things they need. *She earns a **living** as an artist.*

living room living rooms

NOUN The **living room** in a house is the room where the family spends most of their time.

lizard lizards

NOUN A **lizard** is a small reptile with four short legs and a long tail. It has a rough dry skin. The babies hatch from eggs.

See *Reptiles* on page 259.

llama llamas

NOUN A **llama** is a South American animal of the camel family, with long thick hair.

load loads, loading, loaded

NOUN **1** A **load** is things which are being carried somewhere.

VERB **2** When you **load** a camera, you put film into it so that it is ready to use.

VERB **3** When you **load** a computer, you put information or a program into it.

loaf loaves

NOUN A **loaf** is bread that has been baked into one shape. You cut a loaf into slices.

lobster lobsters

NOUN A **lobster** is a sea creature with a hard shell, two large claws, and eight legs.

local

ADJECTIVE **Local** means belonging to the area where you live or work. *I read about it in the **local** paper.*

locate locates, locating, located

VERB To **locate** someone or something is to find out where they are.

location locations

NOUN A **location** is a place, or the position of something. *The school is being moved to a new **location**.*

lock locks, locking, locked

VERB **1** If you **lock** something, you close it and fasten it with a key.

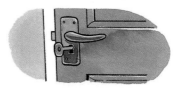

NOUN **2** A **lock** is used to keep something, such as a door or case, closed. You can only open a lock with the right key.

locomotive locomotives

NOUN A **locomotive** is the engine which pulls trains along railway tracks.

loft lofts

NOUN A **loft** is the space under the roof of a house, often used for storing things.

log logs

NOUN A **log** is a piece of a thick branch from a tree.

lollipop lollipops

NOUN A **lollipop** is a hard candy on a stick.

lone

ADJECTIVE **Lone** means alone or solitary. It also means only or single.

lonely lonelier, loneliest

ADJECTIVE Someone who is **lonely** is sad because they are on their own, or do not have any friends.

long longer, longest; longs, longing, longed

ADJECTIVE **1** Something **long** takes up more time than usual. *It was a long movie.*

ADJECTIVE **2** Something that is **long** is far from one end to the other. *It's a long way from London to New York.*

VERB **3** If you **long** for something, you want it very much.

look looks, looking, looked

VERB **1** If you **look** in a particular direction, you turn your eyes that way.

VERB **2** If you say how someone **looks**, you tell them how they seem to you.

VERB **3** If you **look after** someone, you care for them.

VERB **4** If you **look for** someone or something, you try to find them.

VERB **5** If you are **looking forward** to something, you want it to happen because you think you will enjoy it.

loop loops

NOUN A **loop** is a circular shape in something long and thin. For example, when you tie shoelaces, the bow has two loops in it.

loose looser, loosest

ADJECTIVE **1** Something that is **loose** is not firmly fixed. *I've got a loose tooth.*

ADJECTIVE **2** Things that are **loose** are not fixed together. *She had four loose sheets of paper in her bag.*

loot loots, looting, looted

VERB **1** **Loot** means to steal from stores, or houses in a riot or war.

NOUN **2** **Loot** is stolen money or valuables.

lopsided

ADJECTIVE **Lopsided** means something that is unbalanced, with one side heavier, larger, or higher than the other.

lose loses, losing, lost

VERB **1** If you **lose** something, you cannot find it.

VERB **2** If someone **loses** weight, they become thinner.

VERB **3** If you **lose** something like a game or a race, someone does better than you.

lost

ADJECTIVE **1** If you are **lost**, you cannot find your way or do not know where you are.

VERB **2** **Lost** is the past tense of **lose**.

lot lots

NOUN A **lot** of something, or **lots** of something, is a large amount of it.

lottery lotteries

NOUN A **lottery** is a way of raising money by selling tickets. The winner is chosen by chance.

loud **louder, loudest**
ADJECTIVE A **loud** sound is one that makes a lot of noise. *The firework went off with a loud bang.*

loudspeaker **loudspeakers**
NOUN A **loudspeaker** is a piece of equipment that is used so that sounds can be heard. Microphones, radios, and CD players all need loudspeakers.

lounge **lounges**
NOUN A **lounge** in a hotel is a room where people sit and relax.

love **loves, loving, loved**
VERB **1** If you **love** someone, you have strong feelings of affection for them.
VERB **2** If you **love** something, you like it very much. *I love pizza.*

lovely **lovelier, loveliest**
ADJECTIVE Something that is **lovely** is very pleasing to look at or listen to.

low **lower, lowest**
ADJECTIVE Something that is **low** measures only a short distance from the ground to the top. *He jumped over the low wall.*

lower **lowers, lowering, lowered**
VERB **1** If you **lower** something, you move it slowly downward. *As it was getting dark, she lowered the blind.*
VERB **2** If you **lower** your voice, you speak more quietly.

lowercase
ADJECTIVE **Lowercase** letters are the small letters of the alphabet, such as a, b, c, and d. *The letters down the side of this page are lowercase.* See **uppercase**.

loyal
ADJECTIVE If you are **loyal** to someone, you always support them.

luck
NOUN **Luck** is something that seems to happen without any reason. Luck can be good or bad.

lucky **luckier, luckiest**
ADJECTIVE Someone who is **lucky** seems to have good luck.
luckily ADVERB

luggage
NOUN **Luggage** is all the suitcases, bags, and things that you take with you when you travel.

lump **lumps**
NOUN **1** A **lump** is a piece of something solid. *She took a lump of modeling clay.*
NOUN **2** A **lump** on someone's body is a small swelling.

lunar
ADJECTIVE **Lunar** is used to describe something that has to do with the moon.

lunch **lunches**
NOUN **Lunch** is a meal that you have in the middle of the day.

lung **lungs**
NOUN Your **lungs** are the two parts of your body inside your chest that fill with air when you breathe.

luxury **luxuries**
NOUN A **luxury** is something quite expensive to buy, which you like very much, but do not need.
luxurious ADJECTIVE

lying
VERB **Lying** is the present participle of **lie**.

Mm

machine **machines**

NOUN A **machine** is a piece of equipment which does a particular kind of work. It is usually powered by an engine or by electricity.

machinery

NOUN **Machinery** is machines in general.

mad **madder, maddest**

ADJECTIVE **1** Someone who is **mad** has an illness in their mind.

ADJECTIVE **2** If you describe someone as **mad**, you mean they are foolish or silly.

ADJECTIVE **3** INFORMAL Someone who is **mad** is angry.

ADJECTIVE **4** INFORMAL If you are **mad** about someone or something, you like them very much.

made

VERB **Made** is the past tense of **make**.

magazine **magazines**

NOUN A **magazine** is a thin book which comes out regularly, usually once a week or once a month. It has articles, stories, and pictures.

maggot **maggots**

NOUN A **maggot** looks like a tiny worm. Maggots change into flies.

magic

NOUN **1** In stories, **magic** is the thing that makes impossible things happen.

ADJECTIVE **2** Magic tricks entertain and puzzle people.

magical ADJECTIVE

magician **magicians**

NOUN **1** In stories, a **magician** is a person who has magic powers.

NOUN **2** A **magician** is also a real person who can do magic tricks.

magnet **magnets**

NOUN A **magnet** is a special piece of metal. It pulls or attracts iron or steel toward it. Magnets can also push other magnets away.

magnetic ADJECTIVE

magnificent

ADJECTIVE Something that is **magnificent** is very grand.

magnifying glass **magnifying glasses**

NOUN A **magnifying glass** is a piece of glass that makes objects appear to be bigger than they really are.

magpie **magpies**

NOUN A **magpie** is a bird of the crow family. It has black and white markings.

mail

NOUN **Mail** is things like letters and parcels that are sent through the post office.

main

ADJECTIVE The **main** part of something is the most important part.

maize

NOUN **Maize** is a tall plant that produces sweet corn.

major

ADJECTIVE You use **major** to describe something important. *This is a **major** discovery.*

make **makes, making, made**

VERB **1** If you **make** something new, you use your skill to shape it or put it together.

VERB 2 To **make** something happen is to cause it. *My new boots **made** a loud squeak.*

VERB 3 If you **make** a mistake, you do something wrong.

VERB 4 If you **make** someone do something, you force them to do it. *My mom **makes** me eat vegetables.*

male **males**
NOUN A **male** is a person or animal that belongs to the sex that cannot have babies.
male ADJECTIVE

mammal **mammals**
NOUN A **mammal** is a warm-blooded animal. Female mammals give birth to live babies. They feed their babies with milk from their own bodies.

man **men**
NOUN A **man** is an adult male human being. See **woman**.

manage **manages, managing, managed**
VERB 1 If you **manage** to do something, you succeed in doing it. *He **managed** to get a seat on the bus.*
VERB 2 Someone who **manages** an organization is in charge of it.

mane **manes**
NOUN The **mane** of an animal, such as a horse or a male lion, is the long, thick hair that grows from its neck.

mango **mangoes or mangos**
NOUN A **mango** is a sweet yellowish fruit which grows in tropical countries. See *Fruit* on page 257.

manner **manners**
NOUN **1** The **manner** in which you do something is how you do it.
NOUN **2** Your **manner** is the way in which you behave and talk. *It is good **manners** to be polite.*

mantel **mantels**
NOUN A **mantel** is a shelf over a fireplace.

manufacture **manufactures, manufacturing, manufactured**
VERB To **manufacture** goods is to make them in a factory.

many
ADJECTIVE **1** If there are **many** people or things, there are a large number of them.
ADJECTIVE **2** You also use **many** to ask how great a quantity is or to give information about it. *How **many** tickets do you want?*

map **maps**
NOUN A **map** is a drawing of a particular area as it would look from above.

marathon **marathons**
NOUN A **marathon** is a race in which people have to run 26 miles along roads.

marble **marbles**
NOUN **1** Marble is a very hard stone which shines when it is polished. Statues and parts of buildings are sometimes made of marble.
NOUN **2** Marbles is a children's game played with small, colored glass balls. These balls are also called marbles.

march **marches, marching, marched**
VERB When you **march**, you walk with quick, regular steps like a soldier.

March
NOUN **March** is the third month of the year. It has 31 days.

mare **mares**
NOUN A **mare** is an adult female horse.

margarine

margarine

NOUN **Margarine** is a food that looks like butter but is made from vegetable oil and animal fats. You can spread it on bread and use it for cooking.

margin **margins**

NOUN The **margin** is the blank space at each side on a written or printed page.

mark **marks**

NOUN **1** A **mark** is a small stain. *I can't get that **mark** off your shirt.*

NOUN **2** A **mark** is also something that has been written or drawn. *He made little **marks** on the paper with his pencil.*

NOUN **3** At school, a **mark** is a letter or number showing how well you have done in homework or on a test.

marketplace **marketplaces**

NOUN A **marketplace** is a place with many small stalls selling different goods.

marmalade

NOUN **Marmalade** is a jam made from fruit like oranges or lemons. People often eat it spread on toast for breakfast.

marriage **marriages**

NOUN **Marriage** is the relationship between a husband and wife.

married

ADJECTIVE Someone who is **married** has a husband or wife.

marry **marries, marrying, married**

VERB A man and woman who **marry** become husband and wife.

marsh **marshes**

NOUN A **marsh** is an area of land which is always very wet and muddy.

marsupial **marsupials**

NOUN A **marsupial** is a mammal whose babies are carried in a pouch at the front of their mother's body. Kangaroos are marsupials.

marvelous

ADJECTIVE Something that is **marvelous** is wonderful.

masculine

ADJECTIVE **Masculine** refers to qualities and things that are typical of men.

mask **masks**

NOUN A **mask** is something you wear over your face to protect or disguise you.

mass **masses**

NOUN **1** A **mass** of things is a large number of them grouped together.

NOUN **2** The **mass** of something is the amount of matter it contains. Mass is measured in grams or ounces. People often say "weight" when they mean "mass." Mass and weight are different. If you were on the Moon, you would weigh less than on Earth, but your mass would not change. See **weight**.

NOUN **3** In the Roman Catholic church, a **Mass** is a religious service.

massive

ADJECTIVE Something **massive** is extremely large.

mast **masts**

NOUN A **mast** is the tall upright pole that supports the sail of a boat.

mat **mats**

NOUN **1** A **mat** is a small piece of carpet.

NOUN **2** A **mat** is also something used to protect a table from plates or glasses.

match matches, matching, matched
NOUN **1** A **match** is an organized game of something like tennis or soccer.
NOUN **2** A **match** is also a thin stick of wood that can make a flame.
VERB **3** If you **match** things, you find a connection between them. *Match the animals with the countries they come from.*

mate mates
NOUN **1** INFORMAL A **mate** is a friend.
NOUN **2** An animal's **mate** is its partner.

material materials
NOUN **1** **Material** is cloth.
NOUN **2** A **material** is anything that can be used to make something else. Wood, stone, plastic, and water are all materials.

mathematics
NOUN **Mathematics** is the study of numbers, quantities, and shapes.

math
NOUN **Math** is an abbreviation of **mathematics**.

matter matters, mattering, mattered
VERB **1** If something **matters** to you, you care about it and feel it is important.
NOUN **2** A **matter** is something that you have to deal with or think about. *This is a matter for the police.*

mattress mattresses
NOUN A **mattress** is a large flat cushion which is put on a bed to make it comfortable to lie on.

may
VERB If someone says you **may** do something, you are allowed to do it.

May
NOUN **May** is the fifth month of the year. It has 31 days.

maybe
ADVERB You say **maybe** when something is possible, but you are not sure about it. *Maybe we could go tomorrow.*

mayor mayors
NOUN The **mayor** of a town or city is the man or woman who has been chosen to be its leader.

maze mazes
NOUN A **maze** is a system of paths which is made like a puzzle so that it is difficult to find your way through it.

meadow meadows
NOUN A **meadow** is a field of grass and wild flowers.

meal meals
NOUN A **meal** is food that people eat, usually at set times during the day.

mean means, meaning, meant; meaner, meanest
VERB **1** If you ask what something **means**, you want it explained to you.
VERB **2** If you **mean** what you say, you are serious about it.
VERB **3** If something **means** a lot to you, it is important to you.
VERB **4** If you **mean** to do something, you intend to do it. *I meant to phone you, but I didn't have time.*
ADJECTIVE **5** Someone who is **mean** is unkind or not nice.

meaning meanings
NOUN The **meaning** of a word or sentence is the thing or idea that it is explaining. *Do you know the meaning of the proverb "Look before you leap"?*

meanwhile
ADVERB **Meanwhile** means while something else is happening.

measles

NOUN **Measles** is an illness caught especially by children. It gives you a fever and red spots on your skin.

measure **measures, measuring, measured**

VERB **1** If you **measure** something, you find out how large or heavy it is.
NOUN **2** A **measure** is a unit in which something such as size, or speed, is expressed. *Yards are a measure of distance.*
See *Measures* on page 270.

measurement **measurements**

NOUN A **measurement** is a result that you get by measuring something.

meat **meats**

NOUN **Meat** is the flesh of animals that is cooked and eaten.

mechanical

ADJECTIVE A **mechanical** object has moving parts and is used to do a physical task.

medal **medals**

NOUN A **medal** is a small metal disc or cross given as an award for bravery or as a prize for a sport.

medical

ADJECTIVE **Medical** means to do with medicine or the care of people's health.

medicine **medicines**

NOUN **Medicine** is a tablet or liquid given to people who are ill to make them better.

medium

ADJECTIVE **Medium** means somewhere in the middle of two extremes. *He's of medium height – neither tall nor short.*

meet **meets, meeting, met**

VERB If you **meet** someone, you go to the same place at the same time as they do.

meeting **meetings**

NOUN A **meeting** is when a group of people meet to talk about particular things.

melon **melons**

NOUN A **melon** is a large fruit that is sweet and juicy inside. It has a thick, hard, green or yellow skin.
See *Fruit* on page 257.

melt **melts, melting, melted**

VERB When something like ice **melts**, it changes from a solid into a liquid because it has become warmer.

member **members**

NOUN A **member** of a group is one of the people, animals, or things belonging to that group.
membership NOUN

memorize **memorizes, memorizing, memorized**

VERB If you **memorize** something, you learn it so that you can repeat it exactly using only your memory.

memory **memories**

NOUN **1** Your **memory** is what allows you to remember things.
NOUN **2** A **memory** is something you remember from the past.

men

NOUN **Men** is the plural of **man**.

mend **mends, mending, mended**

VERB If you **mend** something that is broken or does not work, you repair it so that it can be used again.

mental

ADJECTIVE **Mental** means to do with your mind or brain. For example, mental math is working out the answers to calculations in your head.

mention mentions, mentioning, mentioned

VERB If you **mention** something, you talk about it briefly.

menu menus

NOUN **1** A **menu** is a list of food that you can order in a restaurant.

NOUN **2** A **menu** on a computer is a list of choices.

mercury

NOUN **Mercury** is a silver-colored metal. Liquid mercury is used in thermometers.

mercy

NOUN If you show **mercy** to someone, you do not hurt or punish them.

mermaid mermaids

NOUN In stories, a **mermaid** is a woman with a fish's tail.

merry merrier, merriest

ADJECTIVE **Merry** means happy and cheerful.

mess messes

NOUN If you say something is a **mess**, you mean it is very untidy.

messy ADJECTIVE

message messages

NOUN A **message** is words that you send or leave when you cannot speak directly to someone.

messenger messengers

NOUN A **messenger** is a person who takes a message to someone.

met

VERB **Met** is the past tense of **meet**.

metal metals

NOUN A **metal** is a hard, strong material that melts when it is heated, such as iron, gold, or steel. Metals are used to make things like jewelry, tools, cars, and machines.

meter meters

NOUN **1** A **meter** is an instrument for measuring something, such as the amount of gas that you have used.

NOUN **2** A **meter** (m) is a measure of length. It is equal to 39.37 inches.

NOUN **3** In poetry, **meter** is the rhythmic arrangement of words and syllables.

method methods

NOUN A **method** is a particular way of doing something.

metric

ADJECTIVE **Metric** relates to the system of measurement that uses meters, kilograms, and liters.

metronome metronomes

NOUN A **metronome** is device that produces a regular beat that helps musicians keep time as they play.

mice

NOUN **Mice** is the plural of **mouse**.

micro-

PREFIX **Micro-** means small. See *Prefixes* on page 264.

microchip microchips

NOUN A **microchip** is a small piece of silicon on which electronic circuits for a computer are printed.

microphone microphones

NOUN A **microphone** is a piece of equipment that is used to make sounds louder, or to record them.

microscope microscopes

NOUN A **microscope** is a piece of equipment which makes small objects appear much larger.

microscopic ADJECTIVE

a
b
c
d
e
f
g
h
i
j
k
l
Mm
n
o
p
q
r
s
t
u
v
w
x
y
z

microwave **microwaves**

NOUN A **microwave** is a type of oven which cooks food very quickly.

mid-

PREFIX Mid- is used to form words that refer to the middle part of a place or period of time, for example "midday." See *Prefixes* on page 264.

midday

NOUN **Midday** is 12 o'clock (noon) in the middle of the day.

middle **middles**

NOUN **1** The **middle** of something is the part farthest from the edges.
ADJECTIVE **2** The **middle** one in a series or a row is the one that has an equal number of people or things on each side of it.

midnight

NOUN **Midnight** is 12 o'clock at night.

might

VERB **1** If you say something **might** happen, you are not sure if it will.
VERB **2** If you say something **might** be true, you are not sure about it.

migrate **migrates, migrating, migrated**

VERB When birds, fish, or animals **migrate**, they move to another place at a particular time of year so that they can find food.

mild **milder, mildest**

ADJECTIVE **1** Something that is **mild** is gentle and does no harm. *You need to use a mild shampoo.*
ADJECTIVE **2** **Mild** weather in the winter is warmer than usual.

mile **miles**

NOUN A **mile** is a unit of distance equal to 5,280 feet.

military

ADJECTIVE **Military** has to do with the armed forces of a country.

milk

NOUN **Milk** is the white liquid that female mammals make in their bodies to feed their young. People drink milk from cows and use it to make butter, cheese, and yogurt.

mill **mills**

NOUN **1** A **mill** is a building in which grain is crushed to make flour. The photo shows a water mill. The water makes the mill wheel turn.

NOUN **2** A **mill** is also a factory used for making things such as cotton or paper.

millennium **millennia** or **millenniums**

NOUN A **millennium** is a period of 1000 years.

milliliter **milliliters**

NOUN A **milliliter** is a measure of volume and capacity. There are 1000 milliliters in a liter.

millimeter **millimeters**

NOUN A **millimeter** (mm) is a measure of length. There are 1000 millimeters in a meter. There are 10 millimeters in a centimeter.

million **millions**

NOUN A **million** is the number 1,000,000.

millionaire **millionaires**

NOUN A **millionaire** is a person who has more than a million dollars.

mince

NOUN **Mince** means to cut or chop into very small pieces.

mincemeat

NOUN **Mincemeat** is a sticky mixture of dried fruit and other sweet things.

mind minds, minding, minded

NOUN **1** Your **mind** is your ability to think, together with your memory, and all the thoughts you have.

NOUN **2** If you **change your mind**, you change a decision you have made.

VERB **3** If you **mind** about something, it worries you or makes you angry.

mine mines

PRONOUN **1** **Mine** refers to something belonging to the person who is speaking or writing. *That book is* **mine**.

NOUN **2** A **mine** is a place under the ground where people dig out things like diamonds, coal, or other minerals.

NOUN **3** A **mine** can be a bomb hidden in the ground or under water, which explodes when people or things touch it.

mineral minerals

NOUN **Minerals** are substances such as tin, salt, or coal that are formed naturally in rocks and in the earth.

mini-

PREFIX **Mini-** is used to form nouns that refer to something smaller or less important than similar things, for example a minibus.

See *Prefixes* on page 264.

minibus minibuses

NOUN A **minibus** is a van with seats in the back that is used as a small bus.

minister ministers

NOUN **1** A **minister** is an important member of the government of a country.

NOUN **2** A **minister** is also a person in charge of a church.

minor

ADJECTIVE Something that is **minor** is not very important or serious. *She had a* **minor** *accident.*

mint mints

NOUN **1** **Mint** is a small plant. Its leaves have a strong taste and smell, and are used in cooking.

NOUN **2** A **mint** is a kind of candy.

NOUN **3** A **mint** is also a place where coins are made.

minus

PREPOSITION **1** You use **minus** to show that one number is being subtracted from another. For example, ten minus six equals four (written $10 - 6 = 4$).

ADJECTIVE **2** Minus is used when talking about temperatures below 0° Fahrenheit. *The temperature is* **minus** *two degrees.*

minute minutes

(*said* **min**-nit) NOUN **1** A **minute** is a unit of time equal to 60 seconds.

(*said* my-**nyoot**) ADJECTIVE **2** Something **minute** is extremely small.

miracle miracles

NOUN **1** A **miracle** is a wonderful event, believed to have been caused by God.

NOUN **2** A **miracle** can also be any very surprising event. *By some* **miracle** *he got to school early.*

mirror mirrors

NOUN A **mirror** is a piece of glass that reflects light. When you look in a mirror you can see yourself.

mis-

PREFIX **Mis-** is added to some words to form other words, often ones that refer to things being done wrongly, for example "misprint" or "misunderstand." See *Prefixes* on page 264.

misbehave misbehaves, misbehaving, misbehaved

VERB If a child **misbehaves**, they are naughty or behave badly.

a b c d e f g h i j k l **Mm** n o p q r s t u v w x y z

mischief

NOUN **Mischief** is silly things that some children do to annoy other people.

mischievous

ADJECTIVE **1** A **mischievous** person likes to have fun by embarrassing people or playing tricks.

ADJECTIVE **2** A **mischievous** child is often naughty, but does not do any real harm.

miserable

ADJECTIVE Someone who is **miserable** is unhappy.

miserably ADVERB

misery

NOUN **Misery** is great unhappiness.

misfortune **misfortunes**

NOUN **Misfortune** is bad luck.

mislay **mislays, mislaying, mislaid**

VERB If you **mislay** something, you forget where you have put it.

mislead **misleads, misleading, misled**

VERB To **mislead** someone is to give them an idea that is not true.

misprint **misprints**

NOUN A **misprint** is a mistake in something that has been printed, for example "cow" instead of "cot."

miss **misses, missing, missed**

VERB **1** If you are aiming at something and **miss**, you fail to hit it.

VERB **2** If you **miss** a bus or train, you are too late to get on it.

VERB **3** If you **miss** somebody, you are lonely without them.

Miss

NOUN **Miss** is used before the name of a girl or an unmarried woman.

missile **missiles**

NOUN A **missile** is a weapon that goes through the air and explodes when it reaches its target.

missing

ADJECTIVE If something is **missing**, it is not in its usual place and you cannot find it.

misspell **misspells, misspelling, misspelled**

VERB If you **misspell** a word, you spell it wrongly.

mist **mists**

NOUN A **mist** is a large number of tiny drops of water in the air. When there is a mist, you cannot see very far.

misty ADJECTIVE

mistake **mistakes**

NOUN A **mistake** is something that is done wrong.

misunderstand **misunderstands, misunderstanding, misunderstood**

VERB If you **misunderstand** someone, you do not understand them properly.

mix **mixes, mixing, mixed**

VERB If you **mix** things, you stir them or put them together. *The children made paste by* **mixing** *flour and water.*

mixture **mixtures**

NOUN A **mixture** is several different things mixed up.

moan **moans, moaning, moaned**

VERB If you **moan**, you make a low, sad sound because you are in pain or trouble.

moat **moats**

NOUN A **moat** is a wide water-filled ditch around a building such as a castle.

mobile **mobiles**

ADJECTIVE **1** If you are **mobile**, you are able to travel or move to another place.

NOUN **2** A **mobile** is a decoration that you hang up so that it moves around when a breeze blows.

mobile phone **mobile phones**

NOUN A **mobile phone** is a telephone you can carry around.

model **models**

NOUN **1** A **model** is a small copy of something. It shows what it looks like or how it works.

NOUN **2** A **model** is also someone who shows clothes to people by wearing them.

modern

ADJECTIVE **Modern** has to do with new ideas and equipment. *We live in a* **modern** *house.*

modest

ADJECTIVE People who are **modest** do not boast about themselves.

moist **moister, moistest**

ADJECTIVE Something that is **moist** is slightly wet.

moisten VERB

moisture

NOUN **Moisture** is tiny drops of water in the air or on a surface.

mole **moles**

NOUN **1** A **mole** is a small, burrowing animal with tiny eyes and dark silky fur.

NOUN **2** A **mole** is also a small dark lump on someone's skin.

moment **moments**

NOUN **1** A **moment** is a very short time.

NOUN **2** A **moment** is also a point in time when something happens. *At that* **moment**, *the teacher came into the room.*

Monday **Mondays**

NOUN **Monday** is the day between Sunday and Tuesday.

money

NOUN **Money** is the coins or bills you use to buy something.

mongrel **mongrels**

NOUN A **mongrel** is a dog with parents of different breeds.

monitor **monitors**

NOUN A **monitor** is the part of a computer that contains the screen.

monkey **monkeys**

NOUN A **monkey** is an animal that lives in hot countries. It has a long tail and climbs trees.

monster **monsters**

NOUN A **monster** is an imaginary creature that is large and terrifying.

month **months**

NOUN A **month** is a measure of time. There are 12 months in a year.

mood **moods**

NOUN Your **mood** is the way you are feeling about things at a particular time, such as how cheerful or angry you are.

moon **moons**

NOUN The **moon** is a satellite that moves around the Earth. It shines in the sky at night. You can only see it because the moon's surface reflects sunlight.

moonlight

NOUN **Moonlight** is the light that comes from the moon at night.

moor **moors**

NOUN A **moor** is an open area of land covered mainly with grass and heather.

moose

NOUN A **moose** is a large North American deer. Moose have very flat, branch-shaped horns called antlers.

mop **mops**

NOUN A **mop** is a tool for washing floors. It has a long handle with a sponge or pieces of string fixed to the end.

more

ADJECTIVE OR ADVERB **More** means a greater number or amount of something. It is the comparative of "many" or "much." *Jill thinks football is **more** fun than math. He has **more** chips than I.*

morning **mornings**

NOUN **Morning** is the part of the day before noon.

mosque **mosques**

NOUN A **mosque** is a building where Muslims worship.

mosquito **mosquitoes** or **mosquitos**

NOUN A **mosquito** is a small flying insect that lives in damp places. The female bites people and other animals to suck their blood.
See Insects on page 259.

moss **mosses**

NOUN **Moss** is a small green plant without roots. It grows in flat clumps on trees, rocks, and damp ground.

most

ADJECTIVE, ADVERB, OR NOUN **Most** means the greatest number or amount of something. It is the superlative of "many" or "much." ***Most** children like candy. I saw the **most** fantastic movie. The **most** I can give you is three pieces.*

moth **moths**

NOUN A **moth** is an insect like a butterfly that usually flies at night.

mother **mothers**

NOUN A **mother** is a woman who has a child or children of her own.

motion **motions**

NOUN A **motion** is a movement.

motive **motives**

NOUN A **motive** is a reason for doing something. *There was no **motive** for the attack.*

motor **motors**

NOUN A **motor** is part of a vehicle or machine. The motor uses fuel to make the vehicle or machine work.

motorcycle **motorcycles**

NOUN A **motorcycle** is a two-wheeled vehicle that is driven by an engine.

motorist **motorists**

NOUN A **motorist** is someone who travels by car.

motto **mottoes** or **mottos**

NOUN A **motto** is a short sentence that is meant to guide behavior or state what someone believes or stands for.

mound **mounds**

NOUN 1 A **mound** is a hill or a pile, as in a **mound** of garbage.
NOUN 2 A **mound** is also a slightly raised area for the pitcher in the center of a baseball diamond.

mount **mounts, mounting, mounted**

VERB If you **mount** a horse, you climb on its back.

mountain **mountains**

NOUN A **mountain** is a very high piece of land with steep sides.

a b c d e f g h i j k l **Mm** n o p q r s t u v w x y z

mouse mice

NOUN **1** A **mouse** is a small rodent with a long tail.

NOUN **2** A **mouse** is also a small object that you use to move the cursor on a computer screen.

mousse

NOUN **Mousse** is a fluffy, cold dessert.

mouth mouths

NOUN **1** Your **mouth** is your lips, or the space behind them, where your tongue and teeth are.

NOUN **2** The **mouth** of a cave or hole is the entrance to it.

NOUN **3** The **mouth** of a river is the place where it flows into the sea.

move moves, moving, moved

VERB **1** To **move** means to go to a different place or position.

VERB **2** To **move** something means to change its place or position.

movement NOUN

mow mows, mowing, mowed

VERB If a person **mows** an area of grass, they cut it with a lawnmower.

Mr. (*said* **miss**-ter)

Mr. is used before a man's name.

Mrs. (*said* **miss**-iz)

Mrs. is used before the name of a married woman.

Ms. (*said* **miz**)

Ms. can be used before a woman's name. Some women choose to be called Ms. because it says nothing about whether they are married.

much

ADVERB **1** You use **much** to show that something is true to a great extent. *I feel much better now.*

ADVERB **2** If something does not happen **much**, it does not happen very often.

ADJECTIVE **3** You use **much** to ask questions or give information about the size or amount of something. *How much money do you need?*

mud

NOUN **Mud** is wet sticky earth.

muddy ADJECTIVE

muddle muddles

NOUN If things such as papers are in a **muddle**, they are all mixed up.

muffled

ADJECTIVE A **muffled** sound is quiet or difficult to hear.

mug mugs

NOUN A **mug** is a large deep cup, usually with straight sides and a handle.

multiple multiples

NOUN The **multiples** of a number are other numbers that it will divide into exactly. For example, 6, 9, and 12 are multiples of 3.

multiplication

NOUN **Multiplication** is when you multiply one number by another. The sign you use for multiplication is ×.

multiply multiplies, multiplying, multiplied

VERB **1** When something **multiplies**, it increases greatly in number. *Fleas multiply very fast.*

VERB **2** When you **multiply** a number, you make it bigger by a number of times. For example, two multiplied by three (two plus two plus two) equals six. $2 \times 3 = 6$ or $2 + 2 + 2 = 6$

a
b
c
d
e
f
g
h
i
j
k
l
Mm
n
o
p
q
r
s
t
u
v
w
x
y
z

multiracial

ADJECTIVE **Multiracial** means involving people of different races.

mumble **mumbles, mumbling, mumbled**

VERB If you **mumble**, you speak very quietly and not clearly.

mumps

NOUN **Mumps** is an illness that causes your neck to swell.

munch **munches, munching, munched**

VERB If you **munch** something, you chew it steadily and thoroughly.

murder **murders**

NOUN **Murder** is the deliberate killing of a person.

murmur **murmurs, murmuring, murmured**

VERB If you **murmur**, you say something very softly.

muscle **muscles**

NOUN **Muscles** are the parts inside your body that you use when you move.

museum **museums**

NOUN A **museum** is a building where many interesting or valuable objects are kept and displayed.

mushroom **mushrooms**

NOUN A **mushroom** is a small fungus with a short thick stem and a round top. You can eat some kinds of mushrooms, but others are poisonous.

music

NOUN **1 Music** is a pattern of sounds made by people singing or playing instruments.

NOUN **2 Music** is also the written symbols that stand for musical sounds.

musical

ADJECTIVE **Musical** means relating to playing or studying music. *He wants to learn to play a **musical** instrument.*

musician **musicians**

NOUN A **musician** is a person who plays a musical instrument well.

Muslim **Muslims**

NOUN A **Muslim** is a person who follows the religion of Islam.

must

VERB If something **must** happen, it is important or necessary that it happens. *You **must** be home by 5 p.m.*

mustard

NOUN **Mustard** is a hot, spicy, yellow paste made from mustard seeds.

my

ADJECTIVE **My** refers to something belonging or relating to the person speaking or writing. *I held **my** breath.*

myself

PRONOUN **Myself** is used when the person speaking does something and no one else does it. *I hung the picture **myself**.*

mysterious

ADJECTIVE Something that is **mysterious** is strange and puzzling.

mystery **mysteries**

NOUN **1** A **mystery** is something strange that cannot be explained.

NOUN **2** A **mystery** is also a story in which strange things happen.

myth **myths**

NOUN A **myth** is a story which was made up long ago to explain natural events and religious beliefs.

Nn

nail nails

NOUN **1** A **nail** is a small piece of metal with a sharp point at one end, which you hammer into objects to hold them together.

NOUN **2** Your **nails** are the thin hard areas at the ends of your fingers and toes.

naked

ADJECTIVE Someone who is **naked** is not wearing any clothes.

name names

NOUN A **name** is what someone or something is called.

nanny nannies

NOUN A **nanny** is someone trained to look after young children in the children's home.

narrative narratives

NOUN A **narrative** is a story or an account of events.

narrator narrators

NOUN A **narrator** is a person who tells a story or explains what is happening.

narrow narrower, narrowest

ADJECTIVE Something **narrow** is a short distance from one side to the other. *The stream was narrow enough to jump across.*

nasty nastier, nastiest

ADJECTIVE **1** Something that is **nasty** is very unpleasant.

ADJECTIVE **2** Someone who is **nasty** is very unkind.

nastily ADVERB

nation nations

NOUN A **nation** is a country with its own laws.

national

ADJECTIVE Something that is **national** has to do with the whole of a country. *USA Today is a national newspaper.*

native

ADJECTIVE **1** Your **native** country is the country where you were born.

ADJECTIVE **2** Your **native** language is the language that you first learned to speak.

ADJECTIVE **3** Animals or plants that are **native** to a place live there naturally. They have not been brought there by people.

natural

ADJECTIVE **1** **Natural** means existing or happening in nature. For example, an earthquake is a natural disaster.

ADJECTIVE **2** Something that is **natural** is normal and to be expected.

nature

NOUN **1** **Nature** is animals, plants, and all the other things in the world not made by people.

NOUN **2** The **nature** of a person or thing is their basic character.

naughty naughtier, naughtiest

ADJECTIVE A child who is **naughty** behaves badly.

navigate navigates, navigating, navigated

VERB When someone **navigates**, they work out the direction in which a ship, plane, or car should go, using maps and sometimes instruments.

a b c d e f g h i j k l m **Nn** o p q r s t u v w x y z

navy navies

NOUN **1** A **navy** is the part of a country's armed forces that fights at sea.
ADJECTIVE **2** Something that is **navy** is a very dark blue.
See *Colors* on page 271.

near nearer, nearest

ADJECTIVE **1** Something that is **near** is not far away. *Where is the nearest garage?*
ADVERB **2** If you are **near** something or somewhere, you are not far away from it. *We must be getting nearer.*

nearly

ADVERB **Nearly** means almost but not quite. *I nearly caught him, but he ran off.*

neat neater, neatest

ADJECTIVE Something that is **neat** is very tidy and clean.

necessary

ADJECTIVE Something that is **necessary** is needed or must be done.
necessarily ADVERB

neck necks

NOUN Your **neck** is the part of your body that joins your head to the rest of your body.

necklace necklaces

NOUN A **necklace** is a piece of jewelry that you wear around your neck.

need needs, needing, needed

VERB **1** If you **need** something, you must have it in order to live and be healthy.
VERB **2** Sometimes you **need** something to help you do a particular job. *Now I need a paintbrush.*
VERB **3** If you **need** to do something, you have to do it.

needle needles

NOUN **1** A **needle** is a small thin piece of metal used for sewing. It has a hole in one end and a sharp point at the other. You put thread through the hole.
NOUN **2** A **needle** is also a thin metal tube with a sharp point, that people like doctors use to give injections.
NOUN **3** **Needles** are long, thin pieces of metal or plastic used for knitting.
NOUN **4** The thin leaves on pine trees are called **needles**.

negative negatives

ADJECTIVE **1** A **negative** sentence is one that has the word "no" or "not" in it.
ADJECTIVE **2** A **negative** number is less than zero.
NOUN **3** A **negative** is a film from a camera. You can get your photographs printed from negatives.

neglect neglects, neglecting, neglected

NOUN If you **neglect** something, you do not look after it.

neighbor neighbors

NOUN Your **neighbor** is someone who lives near you.

neighborhood neighborhoods

NOUN A **neighborhood** is a district where people live. *This is a friendly neighborhood.*

nephew nephews

NOUN Someone's **nephew** is a son of their sister or brother. See **niece**.

nerve nerves

NOUN **1** Your **nerves** are the long thin threads in your body that carry messages between your brain and the other parts of your body.
NOUN **2** **Nerve** is courage. *I wanted to go on the ride, but I didn't have the nerve.*

nervous

ADJECTIVE **1** If you are **nervous**, you are worried about doing something.
ADJECTIVE **2** A **nervous** person is easily frightened.

nest nests

NOUN A **nest** is a place that a bird or other animal makes for its babies.

net nets

NOUN **1 Net** is material made from threads woven together with small spaces in between.

NOUN **2** The **net** is the same as the Internet.

ADJECTIVE **3** A **net** amount is what's left after everything necessary has been taken away.

ADJECTIVE **4** The **net** weight of something is its weight without its packaging.

netherworld

NOUN The **netherworld** is the world of the dead.

netizen netizens

NOUN A **netizen** is an active participant in the on-line community of the Internet.

nettle nettles

NOUN A **nettle** is a wild plant covered with little hairs that sting.

never

ADVERB **Never** means at no time in the past or future. *You must **never** cross the road without looking carefully.*

new newer, newest

ADJECTIVE **1** Something that is **new** has just been made or bought. *They have built some **new** houses close to us.*

ADJECTIVE **2** New can mean different. *My dad starts a **new** job today.*

news

NOUN **News** is information about something that has just happened.

newspaper newspapers

NOUN A **newspaper** is sheets of paper that are printed and sold regularly. Newspapers contain news and articles.

newt newts

NOUN A **newt** is a small animal that looks like a lizard. It lives near water. *See Amphibians on page 259.*

next

ADJECTIVE **1** The **next** period or thing is the one that comes immediately after this one. *The **next** program will follow after the break.*

ADJECTIVE **2** The **next** place is the one nearest to you. *She's in the **next** room.*

nib nibs

NOUN A **nib** is a small pointed piece of metal at the end of a pen. Ink comes out of the nib as you write.

nibble nibbles, nibbling, nibbled

VERB If you **nibble** something, you eat it slowly by taking small bites out of it.

nice nicer, nicest

ADJECTIVE **1** You say something is **nice** when you like it. *This cake is **nice**.*

ADJECTIVE **2** If you say the weather is **nice**, it is warm and pleasant.

ADJECTIVE **3** If you are **nice** to people, you are friendly and kind.

nickname nicknames

NOUN A **nickname** is a name that is given to a person by friends or family. *The baby's name is Sam, but his **nickname** is Dribbler.*

niece nieces

NOUN Someone's **niece** is a daughter of their sister or brother. See **nephew**.

night nights

NOUN The **night** is the time between evening and morning when it is dark.

nightfall

NOUN **Nightfall** is the time of day when it starts to get dark.

nightingale **nightingales**

NOUN A **nightingale** is a small brown European bird. Nightingales sing after dark as well as during the day.

nightmare **nightmares**

NOUN A **nightmare** is a frightening dream.

no

1 You say **no** when you do not want something or do not agree. *"More tea?"* *"**No**, thank you."*

ADJECTIVE **2** You can use **no** to mean not any. *I had **no** help at all.*

ADVERB **3** You can use **no** to mean not. *Competition entries must be in **no** later than Friday.*

nobody

PRONOUN **Nobody** means not a single person.

nocturnal

ADJECTIVE An animal that is **nocturnal** is active mostly at night.

nod **nods, nodding, nodded**

VERB If you **nod**, you move your head quickly down and up to answer yes to a question, or to show that you agree.

noise **noises**

NOUN **1** A **noise** is a sound that someone or something makes.

NOUN **2** Noise is loud or unpleasant sounds.

noisy ADJECTIVE

non-

PREFIX Putting **non-** in front of a word makes it mean the opposite. *This is a **non**-smoking area.*

See *Prefixes* on page 264.

none

PRONOUN **None** means not any, or not one. ***None** of us wanted to go.*

nonfiction

NOUN **Nonfiction** is writing that is based on fact. For example, dictionaries are nonfiction. See **fiction**.

nonsense

NOUN **Nonsense** is words that do not make sense.

noon

NOUN **Noon** is 12 o'clock in the middle of the day.

no one

PRONOUN **No one** means not a single person.

normal

ADJECTIVE Something that is **normal** is what you would expect.

north

NOUN **North** is one of the four main points of the compass. If you face the point where the sun rises, north is on your left. See **compass point**.

northern ADJECTIVE

northeast

NOUN **Northeast** is halfway between north and east.

northwest

NOUN **Northwest** is halfway between north and west.

nose **noses**

NOUN Your **nose** is the part of your face that sticks out above your mouth. It is used for smelling and breathing.

nostril **nostrils**

NOUN Your **nostrils** are the two openings at the end of your nose. You breathe through your nostrils.

note notes

NOUN **1** A **note** is a short written message.

NOUN **2** You take **notes** to help you remember what has been said.

NOUN **3** A **note** is also a single sound in music.

NOUN **4** A bank **note** is a printed piece of paper that is used as money.

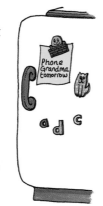

nothing

PRONOUN **Nothing** means not anything.

notice notices, noticing, noticed

VERB **1** If you **notice** something, you pay attention to it. *She **noticed** that it was raining.*

NOUN **2** A **notice** is a sign that tells people something. *The **notice** said, "Cameras are not allowed in the museum."*

notorious

ADJECTIVE A **notorious** person is known for having done something bad.

noun nouns

NOUN In grammar, a **noun** is a word which names a person, a thing or an idea. "James," "newt," and "success" are all nouns.

See *Noun on page 262.*

nourishment

NOUN **Nourishment** is the food that you need in order to grow and stay healthy.

nourishing ADJECTIVE

novel novels

NOUN A **novel** is a long written story that has been made up by the author. Novels are fiction.

November

NOUN **November** is the 11th month of the year. It has 30 days.

now

ADVERB **Now** means at the present time.

nowhere

ADVERB **Nowhere** means not anywhere.

nude

ADJECTIVE Someone who is **nude** is not wearing any clothes.

nudge nudges, nudging, nudged

VERB If you **nudge** somebody, you push them gently, usually with your elbow.

nuisance nuisances

NOUN If you say that someone or something is a **nuisance**, you mean they annoy you.

numb

ADJECTIVE If something is **numb**, it does not feel anything. *My foot is so cold it is **numb**.*

number numbers

NOUN A **number** is a word or sign that tells you how many of something there are.

See *Number bank on page 272.*

numeral numerals

NOUN A written symbol, like 8, is called a **numeral**.

numerous

ADJECTIVE If there are **numerous** things or people, there are a lot of them.

nurse nurses

NOUN A **nurse** is a person whose job is to care for people who are ill or injured.

nursery nurseries

NOUN **1** A **nursery** is a place where young children can be looked after during the day.

NOUN **2** A **nursery** can also be a place where plants are grown and sold.

nut nuts

NOUN **1** A **nut** is the hard fruit of certain trees, such as walnuts and chestnuts.

NOUN **2** A **nut** is also a small piece of metal with a hole in it. It screws onto a bolt to fasten things together.

nylon

NOUN **Nylon** is a strong artificial material.

Oo

oak oaks
NOUN An **oak** is a large tree with nuts called acorns. The wood of oak trees is often used to make furniture.

oar oars
NOUN An **oar** is a wooden pole with a wide flat end, used for rowing a boat.

oasis oases
NOUN An **oasis** is a place in a desert where water and plants are found.

oats
PLURAL NOUN **Oats** are the grains of a cereal. They are used especially for making porridge or for feeding animals.

obedient
ADJECTIVE If you are **obedient**, you do what you are told to do.

obey obeys, obeying, obeyed
VERB If you **obey** someone, you do as they say.

object objects
NOUN **1** An **object** is anything that you can touch or see, and that is not alive.
NOUN **2** In grammar, the **object** of a verb or preposition is the word or phrase which describes the person or thing affected. In the sentence "She fed the cat," "cat" is the object.

oblong oblongs
NOUN An **oblong** is a four-sided shape with two parallel short sides and two parallel long sides. See **rectangle**.
See *Colors and flat shapes* on page 271.

observe observes, observing, observed
VERB If you **observe** something or somebody, you watch them carefully.

obstinate
ADJECTIVE Someone who is **obstinate** is determined to do what they want and will not change their mind.

obvious
ADJECTIVE Something that is **obvious** is easy to see or understand.

occasion occasions
NOUN An **occasion** is an important event or celebration.

occasional
ADJECTIVE **Occasional** means happening sometimes, but not regularly or often.
occasionally ADVERB

occupant occupants
NOUN The **occupant** of a place is the person who lives or works there.

occupy occupies, occupying, occupied
VERB **1** To **occupy** a place means to live, stay, or work in it.
VERB **2** If something **occupies** you, you are busy doing it or thinking about it.
ADJECTIVE **3** If something like a chair is **occupied**, someone is using it.

occur occurs, occurring, occurred
VERB **1** When something **occurs**, it happens.
VERB **2** If something **occurs** to you, you suddenly think of it or realize it.

ocean oceans
NOUN An **ocean** is one of the five large seas on the Earth's surface.

o'clock
ADVERB You say **o'clock** after numbers when you say a time that is exactly on the hour.

octagon octagons
NOUN An **octagon** is a flat shape with eight straight sides.
octagonal ADJECTIVE
See *Colors and flat shapes* on page 271.

a b c d e f g h i j k l m n **Oo** p q r s t u v w x y z

Pp

pace paces
NOUN **1** The **pace** of something is the speed at which it happens.
NOUN **2** A **pace** is a step that you take when you walk.

pack packs, packing, packed
VERB **1** When you **pack**, you put your clothes in a case or bag.
NOUN **2** A **pack** is a set of playing cards.
NOUN **3** A **pack** of wolves or other animals is a group that hunts together. See *Collective nouns* on page 262.

package packages
NOUN A **package** is a small parcel.

packaging
NOUN **Packaging** is the container that something is sold or sent in.

packet packets
NOUN A **packet** is a thin cardboard box or paper container.

pad pads
NOUN **1** A **pad** is a number of pieces of paper fixed together on one side.
NOUN **2** An animal's **pads** are the soft parts under its paws.

paddle paddles, paddling, paddled
VERB **1** If you **paddle** in the sea, you stand or walk in the shallow water.
VERB **2** If you **paddle** a small boat such as a canoe, you use a special type of oar called a paddle to move the boat along.

padlock padlocks
NOUN A **padlock** is a special kind of lock. You can use it to lock gates and bicycles.

page pages
NOUN A **page** is one side of a piece of paper in a book or newspaper.

pagoda pagodas
NOUN A **pagoda** is a tall building which is used as a temple. Pagodas can be seen in China, Japan, and southeast Asia.

paid
VERB **Paid** is the past tense of **pay**.

pail pails
NOUN A **pail** is a bucket.

pain pains
NOUN A **pain** is an unpleasant feeling that you have in part of your body if you have been hurt or are ill.

painful
ADJECTIVE If you say that something is **painful**, you mean it is hurting you.
painfully ADVERB

paint paints, painting, painted
NOUN **1** **Paint** is a colored liquid that you put onto a surface to make it look fresh.
VERB **2** When you **paint** a picture, you use paint to make a picture on paper or canvas.

painting paintings
NOUN A **painting** is a picture that has been painted.

pair pairs
NOUN **1** A **pair** is a set of two things that go together. *I need a new **pair** of shoes.*
NOUN **2** Some objects, such as pants and scissors, have two main parts which are the same size and shape. This sort of object is also called a **pair**.

palace palaces
NOUN A **palace** is a large, important house, especially one which is the home of a king, queen, or president.

pale paler, palest
ADJECTIVE Something that is **pale** is light in color, and not strong or bright.

a
b
c
d
e
f
g
h
i
j
k
l
m
n
o
Pp
q
r
s
t
u
v
w
x
y
z

palm **palms**

NOUN **1** The **palm** of your hand is the inside surface of it. Your fingers are not part of your palm.

NOUN **2** A **palm** is a tree which grows in hot countries. It has long pointed leaves that grow out of the top of a tall trunk.

pan **pans**

NOUN A **pan** is a container with a long handle that is used for cooking.

pancake **pancakes**

NOUN A **pancake** is a thin flat cake made of flour, eggs, and milk, which is fried.

panda **pandas**

NOUN A **panda** is an animal like a black and white bear that lives in the bamboo forests of China.

pane **panes**

NOUN A **pane** is a sheet of glass in a window or door.

panic **panics, panicking, panicked**

VERB If you **panic**, you suddenly get so worried you cannot act sensibly.

pant **pants, panting, panted**

VERB If you **pant**, you breathe quickly with your mouth open. You usually pant when you have been running fast.

panther **panthers**

NOUN **Panther** is another name for a black leopard.

pantomime **pantomimes**

NOUN A **pantomime** is a play or scene acted out with gestures instead of words.

pants

PLURAL NOUN **Pants** are a piece of clothing wth two legs that covers the lower part of the body.

paper **papers**

NOUN **1** **Paper** is the material that you write on or wrap things in.

NOUN **2** A newspaper is also called a **paper**.

parable **parables**

NOUN A **parable** is a short story which aims to teach you something about the way you should behave.

parachute **parachutes**

NOUN A **parachute** is a large piece of thin cloth. It has strings fixed to it so that a person attached to it can float down to the ground from an aircraft.

parade **parades**

NOUN A **parade** is a lot of people marching in the road on a special day.

paraffin

NOUN **Paraffin** is a white, waxy substance used to make candles or seal jars.

paragraph **paragraphs**

NOUN A **paragraph** is a section of a piece of writing. Paragraphs begin on a new line.

parallel

ADJECTIVE Two lines, or other things that are **parallel**, are the same distance apart all the way along. *The road along the coast is **parallel** with the sea.*

paralyzed

ADJECTIVE Someone who is **paralyzed** cannot move or feel some or all of their body.

parcel **parcels**

NOUN A **parcel** is one or more objects wrapped in paper. This is usually done so that it can be sent by mail.

parent **parents**

NOUN Your **parents** are your mother and father.

park **parks, parking, parked**

NOUN **1** A **park** is an area of land with grass and trees, usually in a town. People go there to walk or play.

VERB **2** When someone **parks** a vehicle, they put it somewhere until they need it again.

parliament **parliaments**

NOUN The **parliament** of a country is the people who make the country's laws.

parrot **parrots**

NOUN A **parrot** is a brightly colored bird with a curved beak.

parsnip **parsnips**

NOUN A **parsnip** is a long, pointed, cream-colored root vegetable. See *Vegetables* on page 256.

part **parts**

NOUN **1** A **part** of something is one of the pieces that it is made from. *We need a new part for the washing machine.*

NOUN **2** A **part** is also a particular bit of something, such as an area or a body. *This part of the park is for young children only.*

NOUN **3** If you have a **part** in a play, you are one of the people in it.

participle **participles**

NOUN In grammar, a **participle** is a form of a verb. English has two participles – the past participle and the present participle. In the sentence, "He has gone" the word "gone" is a past participle; in the sentence, "She is winning" the word "winning" is a present participle.

particular

ADJECTIVE When you talk about a **particular** person or thing, you mean just that person or thing and not others of the same kind.

partly

ADVERB **Partly** means not completely. *The table was **partly** covered with a cloth.*

partner **partners**

NOUN Your **partner** is the person you are doing something with, for example when dancing or playing games.

party **parties**

NOUN A **party** is a group of people having fun together.

pass **passes, passing, passed**

VERB **1** If you **pass** someone, you go past them without stopping.

VERB **2** If you **pass** something to someone, you hand it to them.

VERB **3** If you **pass** a test or an exam, you are successful in it.

passage **passages**

NOUN **1** A **passage** is a long, narrow space with walls on both sides.

NOUN **2** A **passage** is also a section in a piece of writing. *There's a wonderful **passage** in the book that describes their arrival at the castle.*

passenger **passengers**

NOUN A **passenger** is a person who travels in a vehicle, but is not the driver.

passive

NOUN In grammar, the **passive voice** is the form of the verb in which the person or thing to which an action is being done is the subject of the sentence. For example, the sentence, "The ball was hit by the boy" is in the passive voice. See **voice**.

passport **passports**

NOUN A **passport** is a book with your name and photograph in it, that you need when you leave your own country.

a
b
c
d
e
f
g
h
i
j
k
l
m
n
o
Pp
q
r
s
t
u
v
w
x
y
z

password

password **passwords**

NOUN A **password** is a secret word or phrase that you must say to be allowed into a particular place.

past

NOUN **1** The **past** is the period of time before the present.

ADVERB **2** If you go **past** something, you move toward it and continue until you are on the other side.

PREPOSITION **3** You use **past** when you are telling the time. *It's ten **past** three.*

NOUN **4** In grammar, the **past tense** of a verb is the form used to show that something happened in the past.

pasta

NOUN **Pasta** is a type of food made from flour, eggs, and water, which is formed into different shapes. Spaghetti, macaroni, and noodles are types of pasta.

paste **pastes**

NOUN **Paste** is a thick wet mixture that is easy to spread.

pastime **pastimes**

NOUN A **pastime** is something you like to do in your free time.

pastry

NOUN **Pastry** is a food made of flour, fat, and water, rolled flat, and used for making pies.

pasture **pastures**

NOUN **Pasture** is land that is used for farm animals to graze on.

pat **pats, patting, patted**

VERB If you **pat** something, you hit it gently, usually with your open hand.

patch **patches**

NOUN A **patch** is a piece of material you put over a hole in something to mend it.

path **paths**

NOUN A **path** is a strip of ground that people walk on.

patience

NOUN **Patience** is being able to wait calmly for something, or to do something difficult without giving up.

patient **patients**

ADJECTIVE **1** If you are **patient**, you are able to wait calmly for something, or to do something difficult without giving up.

NOUN **2** A **patient** is someone who is being treated by a doctor.

patrol **patrols, patrolling, patrolled**

VERB When people like the police **patrol** a particular area, they go around it to make sure there is no trouble or danger.

pattern **patterns**

NOUN A **pattern** is a regular way something is organized. For example, lines and shapes can make patterns.

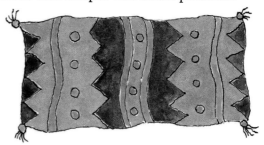

pause **pauses, pausing, paused**

VERB If you **pause** while you are doing something, you stop for a moment.

pavement **pavements**

NOUN **Pavement** is a hard material, such as concrete or asphalt, that covers roads and sidewalks.

paw **paws**

NOUN A **paw** is the foot of some animals. Paws have claws at the front and soft pads underneath.

pay **pays, paying, paid**

VERB When a person **pays** someone, they give them money in exchange for work or for things that they have bought.
payment NOUN

PC **PCs**

NOUN A **PC** is a personal computer.

PE

NOUN **PE** is an abbreviation of **physical education**.

pea **peas**

NOUN **Peas** are round green seeds which are eaten as a vegetable. They grow inside a covering called a pod.
See *Vegetables* on page 256.

peace

NOUN **1 Peace** is a feeling of quiet and calm.

NOUN **2** When a country has **peace** or is **at peace**, it is not fighting a war.

peaceful

ADJECTIVE A **peaceful** place is quiet and calm.

peach **peaches**

NOUN A **peach** is a round juicy fruit with a large pit in the middle. It has sweet yellow flesh and a yellow and red skin.
See *Fruit* on page 257.

peacock **peacocks**

NOUN A **peacock** is a large male bird with bright blue and green feathers, and long tail feathers which it spreads in a fan. The female is called a peahen.

peak **peaks**

NOUN **1** The **peak** of a mountain is the pointed top of it.

NOUN **2** The **peak** of a cap is the part that sticks out at the front.

peanut **peanuts**

NOUN **Peanuts** are small hard seeds which grow under the ground. You can buy roasted and salted peanuts to eat.

pear **pears**

NOUN A **pear** is a sweet, juicy fruit which grows on trees. It is narrow near its stalk, and wider and rounded at the bottom. See *Fruit* on page 257.

pearl **pearls**

NOUN A **pearl** is a hard, round object which grows inside the shell of an oyster. It is creamy-white in color. Pearls are used to make valuable jewelry.

pebble **pebbles**

NOUN A **pebble** is a small, smooth stone found on seashores and river beds.

peck **pecks, pecking, pecked**

VERB When a bird **pecks**, it bites at something with its beak.

peculiar

ADJECTIVE Something that is **peculiar** is strange or unusual.

pedal **pedals**

NOUN The **pedals** on a bicycle are the two parts that you push with your feet to make it move.

pedestrian **pedestrians**

NOUN A **pedestrian** is a person who is walking.

peek **peeks, peeking, peeked**

VERB If you **peek** at something, you have a quick look at it.

peel **peels, peeling, peeled**

VERB If you **peel** fruit or vegetables, you remove the skin.

peep **peeps, peeping, peeped**

VERB If you **peep** at something, you look at it very quickly, and usually secretly.

peg **pegs**

NOUN **1** A **peg** is a thin piece of metal or plastic that is used to hang things on.

NOUN **2** A **peg** is also used to hold things down.

a
b
c
d
e
f
g
h
i
j
k
l
m
n
o
Pp
q
r
s
t
u
v
w
x
y
z

pelican pelicans

NOUN A **pelican** is a water bird. Its large beak has a soft lower part like a pouch.

pen pens

NOUN A **pen** is a long thin tool that you use to write in ink.

penalty

NOUN A **penalty** is a punishment.

pencil pencils

NOUN A **pencil** is a long thin piece of wood with a dark material called graphite in the middle. It is used for writing or drawing.

pendulum pendulums

NOUN A **pendulum** is a large weight which hangs from a clock. It swings from side to side to keep the clock going at the right speed.

penguin penguins

NOUN A **penguin** is a large black and white bird found in the Antarctic. Penguins cannot fly. They use their wings for swimming in the water.

peninsula peninsula

NOUN A **peninsula** is a piece of land that juts out into the water.

penknife penknives

NOUN A **penknife** is a small knife with blades that fold back into the handle.

penny pennies

NOUN A **penny** is the coin that is the smallest unit of money in the United States and Canada. One hundred pennies equal one dollar.

pentagon pentagons

NOUN A **pentagon** is a flat shape that has five straight sides.
pentagonal ADJECTIVE
See *Colors and flat shapes* on page 271.

people

PLURAL NOUN **People** are men, women, and children.

pepper peppers

NOUN **1 Pepper** is a hot-tasting powder which is used to flavor food.
NOUN **2** A **pepper** is a red, green, or yellow vegetable. It can be cooked or eaten raw in salads.

percent

PHRASE You use **percent** to talk about amounts as a proportion of 100. For example, ten percent (10%) means 10 out of every 100.

perch perches

NOUN A **perch** is a short piece of wood for a bird to stand on.

percussion

ADJECTIVE **Percussion** instruments are instruments that you play by hitting them. Drums and cymbals are percussion instruments.

perfect

ADJECTIVE **1** Something that is **perfect** is done so well it could not be done better.
ADJECTIVE **2** If you say something is **perfect**, you mean it is wonderful.
perfectly ADVERB

perform performs, performing, performed

VERB If someone **performs**, they do something to entertain an audience.

performance performances

NOUN A **performance** is something done in front of people, like acting or dancing.

perfume perfumes

NOUN **1** A **perfume** is a pleasant smell.

NOUN **2** Perfume is a liquid that you put on your body so that you smell nice.

perhaps

ADVERB **1** If you say **perhaps** something will happen, you mean it might happen, but you are not sure.

ADVERB **2** You can also say **perhaps** when you are suggesting something. *He's late – perhaps he missed the train.*

perimeter perimeters

NOUN The **perimeter** of a shape is the distance all around it.

period periods

NOUN A **period** is a particular length of time. *Mrs. Smith will be away for a period of six months.*

periscope periscopes

NOUN A **periscope** is a tube with mirrors. When you look in one end, you can see what would otherwise be out of sight.

permanent

ADJECTIVE Something that is **permanent** lasts forever, or for a very long time.

permission

NOUN If you have **permission** to do something, you are allowed to do it.

permit permits, permitting, permitted

VERB If someone **permits** you to do something, they allow you to do it.

persist persists, persisting, persisted

VERB If you **persist**, you go on doing something even when it is difficult, or other people have told you to stop.

person people

NOUN A **person** is a man, woman, or child.

personal

ADJECTIVE **Personal** matters relate to your feelings, relationships, and health, which you may not want to talk about with other people.

persuade persuades, persuading, persuaded

VERB If someone **persuades** you to do something, you agree because they gave you a good reason.

persuasion NOUN

persuasive

ADJECTIVE **1** Someone who is **persuasive** is good at persuading others to believe or do a particular thing.

ADJECTIVE **2** Persuasive text aims to persuade the reader of something.

pest pests

NOUN A **pest** is an insect, rat, or other small animal that causes damage.

pester pesters, pestering, pestered

VERB If you **pester** someone, you keep bothering them.

pet pets

NOUN A **pet** is a tame animal that you keep and look after in your home.

petal petals

NOUN A **petal** is part of a flower. Petals may have bright colors or scents to attract insects.

pew

NOUN A **pew** is a long wooden bench with a high back that people sit on in church.

phantom phantoms

NOUN A **phantom** is a ghost.

a
b
c
d
e
f
g
h
i
j
k
l
m
n
o
Pp
q
r
s
t
u
v
w
x
y
z

phone

phone **phones**
NOUN **Phone** is an abbreviation of **telephone**.

photo **photos**
NOUN **Photo** is an abbreviation of **photograph**.

photocopier **photocopiers**
NOUN A **photocopier** is a machine that makes copies of documents.

photocopy **photocopies**
NOUN A **photocopy** is a copy of a document produced by a photocopier.

photograph **photographs**
NOUN A **photograph** is a picture that is made using a camera.

phrase **phrases**
NOUN A **phrase** is a short group of words used together.

physical
ADJECTIVE **1** **Physical** means to do with things that can be touched or seen.
ADJECTIVE **2** **Physical** also means to do with a person's body, rather than their mind.
physically ADVERB

piano **pianos**
NOUN A **piano** is a large musical instrument with black and white keys that you press with your fingers.

pick **picks, picking, picked**
VERB **1** To **pick** means to choose. *We need to **pick** three more people for our team.*
VERB **2** When you **pick** flowers or fruit, you take them off the plant.
VERB **3** If you **pick** something **up**, you lift it up from where it is.

pickle **pickles**
NOUN **Pickles** are vegetables, such as cucumbers, that have been kept in vinegar or salt water.

picnic **picnics**
NOUN A **picnic** is a meal that you take with you and eat out of doors.

pictograph **pictograghs**
NOUN **1** A **pictograph** is a picture or symbol used instead of a word or words.
NOUN **2** A **pictograph** is also a graph that uses pictures to show information.

picture **pictures**
NOUN A **picture** is a drawing, painting, or photograph.

pie **pies**
NOUN A **pie** is fruit, vegetables, meat, or fish baked in pastry.

piece **pieces**
NOUN A **piece** is a part of something.

pier **piers**
NOUN A **pier** is a long platform which sticks out over the sea. Piers can be used as a docking place for boats.

pierce **pierces, piercing, pierced**
VERB If a sharp object **pierces** something, it goes through it and makes a hole in it.

pig **pigs**
NOUN A **pig** is a farm animal kept for its meat. It has pinkish skin and short legs.

pigeon **pigeons**
NOUN A **pigeon** is a large bird with gray feathers, often seen in towns.

piglet **piglets**
NOUN A **piglet** is a young pig.
See *Young animals* on page 260.

pile **piles**
NOUN A **pile** is a lot of things, such as books, which have been put one on top of the other.

pill **pills**
NOUN A **pill** is medicine made into a small round object that you swallow.

pillar **pillars**
NOUN A **pillar** is a tall post made of something such as stone or brick. It usually helps to hold up a building.

pillbox **pillboxes**
NOUN A **pillbox** is a box for pills.

pillow **pillows**
NOUN A **pillow** is a bag filled with soft material to rest your head on in bed.

pilot **pilots**
NOUN A **pilot** is a person who is trained to fly an aircraft.

pimple **pimples**
NOUN A **pimple** is a small red spot, especially on your face.

pin **pins**
NOUN A **pin** is a small thin piece of metal with a point at one end. Pins can be pushed through things such as pieces of paper or cloth, to hold them together.

pincers
PLURAL NOUN **1** The **pincers** of a crab or lobster are its front claws.
PLURAL NOUN **2 Pincers** are also a tool used for gripping and pulling things.

pinch **pinches, pinching, pinched**
VERB If someone **pinches** you, they squeeze part of you quickly between their thumb and first finger.

pine **pines**
NOUN A **pine** is a tall evergreen tree with sharp, thin leaves called needles.

pineapple **pineapples**
NOUN A **pineapple** is a large oval fruit with yellow flesh and a thick, lumpy skin. Pineapples grow in hot countries.

pink **pinker, pinkest**
ADJECTIVE Something that is **pink** has a color between white and red.
See *Colors* on page 271.

pint **pints**
NOUN A **pint** is a measure for liquids. A pint is equal to just over half a liter.

pipe **pipes**
NOUN A **pipe** is a long, hollow tube, usually made of metal or plastic. Pipes are used to carry liquid or gas.

pirate **pirates**
NOUN In the past, a **pirate** was a robber who stole from ships.

pistol **pistols**
NOUN A **pistol** is a small gun.

pit **pits**
NOUN **1** A **pit** is a large hole that has been dug in the ground.
NOUN **2** A **pit** is also a large, hard seed in the middle of some fruits.

pitch **pitches, pitching, pitched**
VERB **1 Pitch** means to throw or toss something, such as a baseball.
NOUN **2** The **pitch** of a sound is how high or low it is.
VERB **3** When you **pitch** a tent, you put it up so that you can use it.

pity
NOUN **1** If you feel **pity** for someone, you feel sorry for them.
NOUN **2** If you say something is a **pity**, you mean it is disappointing. *What a pity Mark isn't coming.*

pizza

pizza pizzas

NOUN A **pizza** is a flat, round piece of dough covered with cheese, tomato, and other food.

place places

NOUN **1** A **place** is any building or area.
NOUN **2** A **place** is also the position where something belongs. *Please put the tools back in their right place.*

place value

NOUN In math, the **place value** of a digit tells you what the digit is worth in hundreds, tens, or ones.

plague plagues

NOUN A **plague** is a disease that spreads quickly and kills many people. *The bubonic plague killed thousands of people in Europe in the 1300s.*

plaice

NOUN A **plaice** is a flat sea fish.

plain plainer, plainest; plains

ADJECTIVE **1** A **plain** object has no pattern on it. *She wore a plain skirt.*
ADJECTIVE **2** If something is **plain**, it is clear and easy to see.
NOUN **3** A **plain** is a large, flat area of land with very few trees on it.

plait plaits, plaiting, plaited

VERB **1** If you **plait** three lengths of hair or rope together, you twist them over each other in turn.
NOUN **2** A **plait** is a length of hair that has been braided.

plan plans, planning, planned

NOUN **1** If you have a **plan**, you have thought of a way of doing something.
NOUN **2** A **plan** is a drawing that shows what something looks like from above.
VERB **3** If you **plan** what you are going to do, you decide exactly how to do it.

plane planes

NOUN **1** A **plane** is a flying vehicle. It has wings and one or more engines. **Plane** is an abbreviation of **airplane**.
NOUN **2** A **plane** is also a tool used for smoothing wood.

planet planets

NOUN A **planet** is a large round object in space that moves around a star. Earth is one of the nine planets that go around the sun.

plank planks

NOUN A **plank** is a long, flat piece of wood.

plant plants, planting, planted

NOUN **1** A **plant** is any living thing that is not an animal. Plants can make their own food.
VERB **2** When you **plant** things, such as seeds, flowers, or trees, you put them in the ground so that they will grow.

plaster plasters

NOUN **Plaster** is a smooth paste that dries and forms a hard layer. It is used to cover walls and ceilings inside buildings.

plastic

NOUN **1** **Plastic** is a light artificial material that does not break easily. It is used to make all sorts of things, such as buckets, bowls, and plates.
ADJECTIVE **2** Something that is **plastic** is made of plastic.

plastic surgery plastic surgeries

NOUN **Plastic surgery** is an operation on skin to repair damage or to improve someone's appearance.

plate plates

NOUN A **plate** is a flat dish for food.

platform **platforms**

NOUN **1** A **platform** is the area in a station where you wait for the train.

NOUN **2** A **platform** is also a raised area for people to stand on so that they can be seen more easily.

play **plays, playing, played**

VERB **1** When you **play**, you spend time doing things you enjoy.

VERB **2** When one person or team **plays** another, they take part in a game and each side tries to win.

VERB **3** If you **play** a musical instrument, you make musical sounds with it.

NOUN **4** A **play** is a story which is acted on the stage, or on radio or television.

player NOUN

playground **playgrounds**

NOUN A **playground** is a piece of land for children to play on.

playmate **playmates**

NOUN A **playmate** is a child who plays with another child.

playtime

NOUN **Playtime** is a break in the school day when you can play.

pleasant

ADJECTIVE If something is **pleasant**, you enjoy it or like it.

please **pleases, pleasing, pleased**

VERB If you **please** someone, you make them feel happy.

pleasure

NOUN **Pleasure** is a feeling of happiness or enjoyment.

pleat **pleats**

NOUN A **pleat** is a permanent fold in fabric.

pleated ADJECTIVE

plenty

NOUN If there is **plenty** of something, there is more than enough of it.

pliers

PLURAL NOUN **Pliers** are a tool used for pulling out small things like nails, or for bending or cutting wire.

plot **plots, plotting, plotted**

NOUN **1** A **plot** is a secret plan.

NOUN **2** The **plot** of a film, novel, or play is the story and the way it develops.

NOUN **3** A **plot** of land is a small piece that has been marked out for a special purpose, such as building houses or growing vegetables.

VERB **4** If people **plot** something, they plan secretly to do it.

plow **plows**

NOUN A **plow** is a farming tool that is pulled across a field to turn the soil over.

pluck **plucks, plucking, plucked**

VERB **1** When someone **plucks** a musical instrument, such as a guitar, they pull the strings and let them go quickly.

VERB **2** When you **pluck** a feather, flower, or fruit, you pull it from where it is growing.

plug **plugs, plugging, plugged**

NOUN **1** A **plug** is a small object that joins pieces of equipment to the electricity supply.

VERB **2** If someone **plugs** a hole, they block it with something.

plum **plums**

NOUN A **plum** is a small fruit with a thin, dark red or yellow skin and juicy flesh. It has a large pit in the middle.

See *Fruit* on page 257.

a
b
c
d
e
f
g
h
i
j
k
l
m
n
o
Pp
q
r
s
t
u
v
w
x
y
z

a
b
c
d
e
f
g
h
i
j
k
l
m
n
o
Pp
q
r
s
t
u
v
w
x
y
z

plumber plumbers
NOUN A **plumber** is a person who fits and repairs water pipes.

plump plumper, plumpest
ADJECTIVE Someone or something that is **plump** is somewhat fat.

plunge plunges, plunging, plunged
VERB If someone **plunges** into the water, they dive or throw themselves into it.

plural plurals
NOUN **Plural** means more than one. The **plural** of "boy" is "boys." The **plural** of "box" is "boxes." See **singular**.

plus
PREPOSITION **1** You use **plus** (+) to show that one number is being added to another. Two **plus** two equals four.
PREPOSITION **2** You can use **plus** when you mention an additional item. You get a television **plus** a free radio.

p.m.
ADVERB **p.m.** is the time between 12 noon and 12 midnight. See **a.m.**

poach poaches, poaching, poached
VERB If you **poach** an egg, you remove its shell and cook the egg gently in boiling water.

pocket pockets
NOUN A **pocket** is a small bag that is sewn into clothing.

pod pods
NOUN A **pod** is a seed cover. Peas and beans grow inside pods. See **pea**.

poem poems
NOUN A **poem** is a piece of writing in short lines, which sometimes rhyme. The lines usually have a particular rhythm.

poet poets
NOUN A **poet** is a person who writes poems.

poetry
NOUN **Poetry** is writing in which the lines have a rhythm and sometimes rhyme.

point points, pointing, pointed
NOUN **1** The **point** of something, such as a pin, is the sharp end of it.
NOUN **2** A **point** is a position or time. I'll call you at some **point** during the day.
NOUN **3** The **point** of doing something is the reason for doing it. The **point** of playing is to have fun.
NOUN **4** In a game or sport, a **point** is part of the score.
NOUN **5** The decimal **point** in a number is the dot separating the whole number from the fraction.
VERB **6** If you **point** at something, you show where it is by using your finger.
VERB **7** If something **points** in a particular direction, it faces that way.

pointed
ADJECTIVE Something that is **pointed** has a point at one end.

poison poisons
NOUN **Poison** is something that harms or kills people or animals if it gets into their body.
poisonous ADJECTIVE

poke pokes, poking, poked
VERB If you **poke** something, you push it hard with your finger.

polar bear polar bears
NOUN A **polar bear** is a large, white bear that lives near the North Pole.

pole poles
NOUN **1** A **pole** is a long, round post, used especially for holding things up.
NOUN **2** A **pole** is also one of the two points on the Earth that are the farthest from the equator. They are known as the North Pole and the South Pole.

preserve **preserves, preserving, preserved**
VERB **1** If you **preserve** something, you do something to keep it the way it is.
VERB **2** To **preserve** food means to stop it from going bad.

president **presidents**
NOUN The **president** of a country or an organization is the head of it.

press **presses, pressing, pressed**
VERB **1** If you **press** something against something else, you hold it there firmly.
*He **pressed** the phone against his ear.*
NOUN **2** Newspapers, and the journalists who work for them, are called the **press**.

pressure
NOUN **Pressure** is the force of one thing pressing or pushing on another.

pretend **pretends, pretending, pretended**
VERB If you **pretend**, you act as though something is true although it is not.
*Let's **pretend** to be working.*

pretty **prettier, prettiest**
ADJECTIVE Someone who is **pretty** is nice to look at.

prevent **prevents, preventing, prevented**
VERB If you **prevent** someone from doing something, you stop them from doing it.

prey
NOUN The **prey** of an animal is the creatures that it hunts for food.
bird of prey PHRASE A **bird of prey** is a bird, such as an eagle or a hawk, that kills and eats smaller birds and animals.

price **prices**
NOUN The **price** of something is the amount of money that you must pay to buy it.

prick **pricks, pricking, pricked**
VERB To **prick** something means to make a tiny hole in it with something sharp.

prickle **prickles**
NOUN **Prickles** are small, sharp points or thorns on plants.

pride
NOUN **1** **Pride** is the good feeling you have when you have done something well.
NOUN **2** A **pride** of lions is a group of lions that live together.
See *Collective nouns* on page 262.

prime minister **prime ministers**
NOUN The **prime minister** of a country is the leader of that country's government.

prince **princes**
NOUN A **prince** is the son of a king or queen.

princess **princesses**
NOUN A **princess** is the daughter of a king or queen, or the wife of a prince.

print **prints, printing, printed**
VERB **1** When someone **prints** something, such as a poster or a newspaper, they use a machine to make lots of copies of it.
VERB **2** If you **print** words, you write in letters that are not joined together.

printer **printers**
NOUN **1** A **printer** is a machine that is linked to a computer to print information on paper.
NOUN **2** A **printer** is also a person who prints things, like books and magazines.

print-out **print-outs**
NOUN A **print-out** is a printed copy of information from a computer.

prism **prisms**
NOUN **1** A **prism** is an object made of clear glass with many flat sides. It separates light passing through it into the colors of the rainbow.
NOUN **2** A **prism** is also any three-dimensional shape that has the same size and shape of face at each end.

prison

prison **prisons**
> NOUN A **prison** is a building where people are kept when they have broken the law.

prisoner **prisoners**
> NOUN **1** A **prisoner** is someone who is kept in prison as a punishment.
> NOUN **2** A **prisoner** is also someone who has been captured by an enemy.

private
> ADJECTIVE If something is **private**, it is for one person or group only. *All the rooms have a private bath.*
> in private PHRASE If you do something **in private**, you do it without other people being there.

prize **prizes**
> NOUN A **prize** is something that is given to someone as a reward.

probable
> ADJECTIVE Something that is **probable** is likely to be true, or likely to happen.
> probably ADVERB

problem **problems**
> NOUN **1** A **problem** is something that is difficult.
> NOUN **2** A **problem** is also something, like a puzzle, that you have to work out.

process **processes**
> NOUN A **process** is a series of actions for doing or making something.

procession **processions**
> NOUN A **procession** is a line of people walking or riding through the streets on a special occasion.

prod **prods, prodding, prodded**
> VERB If you **prod** something, you push it with your finger.

produce **produces, producing, produced**
> VERB **1** To **produce** something means to make it.
> VERB **2** If you **produce** an object from somewhere, such as a pocket, you bring it out so that it can be seen.
> VERB **3** Someone who **produces** a play, film or television program, gets it ready to show to the public.

product **products**
> NOUN **1** A **product** is something that is made to be sold.
> NOUN **2** In math, the **product** of two numbers is the answer you get when you multiply them together. For example, the product of four and two is eight.

profit **profits**
> NOUN A **profit** is the money you gain when you sell something for more than it cost you to make or buy.

program **programs**
> NOUN **1** A **program** is a set of instructions that a computer uses in order to do particular things.
> NOUN **2** A radio or television **program** is the thing that is being broadcast.
> NOUN **3** A **program** is a plan of things that will take place.

progress **progresses, progressing, progressed**
> NOUN **1** Progress is moving forward or getting better at something. *I'm making progress with my spelling.*
> VERB **2** If you **progress**, you get better at something.

project **projects**
> NOUN A **project** is work that you do to learn about something and then write about it.

promise **promises, promising, promised**
> VERB If you **promise** to do something, you mean you really will do it.

prong **prongs**

NOUN The **prongs** of a fork are the long pointed parts.

pronoun **pronouns**

NOUN **1** In grammar, a **pronoun** is a word that is used to replace a noun.

NOUN **2 Personal pronouns** replace the subject or object of a sentence. In the sentence "She caught a fish," "she" is a personal pronoun.

NOUN **3 Possessive pronouns** replace the subject or object when you want to show who owns it. In the sentence "This book is mine," "mine" is a possessive pronoun.

See Pronoun on page 263.

pronounce **pronounces, pronouncing, pronounced**

VERB To **pronounce** a word means to say it in a particular way.

pronunciation

NOUN **Pronunciation** is the way a word is usually said.

proof

NOUN **Proof** of something is the facts that show that it is true or that it exists.

prop **props, propping, propped**

VERB If you **prop** an object somewhere, you support it against something.

propeller **propellers**

NOUN A **propeller** is the blades that turn to drive an aircraft or ship.

proper

ADJECTIVE **1 Proper** means right. *Put those things back in the **proper** place.*

ADJECTIVE **2** You can also use **proper** to mean real. *You need a **proper** screwdriver for that job.*

properly

ADVERB If something is done **properly**, it is done correctly.

proper noun **proper nouns**

NOUN A **proper noun** is the name of a particular person or place. It starts with a capital letter. "Ben" and "London" are both proper nouns.

See Noun on page 262.

property **properties**

NOUN **1** Someone's **property** is the things that belong to them.

NOUN **2** A **property** is a building and the land belonging to it.

prophet **prophets**

NOUN A **prophet** is a person who predicts what will happen in the future.

proportion **proportions**

NOUN The **proportion** of one amount to another is its size in comparison with the other amount. *There was a large **proportion** of boys in the class.*

prose

NOUN **Prose** is written language that is not poetry or a play.

protect **protects, protecting, protected**

VERB To **protect** someone or something is to prevent them from being harmed.

protection NOUN

protein **proteins**

NOUN **Protein** is a substance found in meat, eggs, and milk that is needed by bodies for growth.

protest **protests**

NOUN A **protest** is something you say or do to show that you disagree with something.

proud **prouder, proudest**

ADJECTIVE If you feel **proud**, you feel glad about something you have done, or about something that belongs to you. *She was **proud** of her new bike.*

prove **proves, proving, proved**
VERB When you **prove** something, you show that it is definitely true.

proverb **proverbs**
NOUN A **proverb** is a short sentence that people say which gives advice about life. For example, the proverb "Look before you leap," means that you should think carefully before you do something.

provide **provides, providing, provided**
VERB If you **provide** something for someone, you give it to them so that they have it when they need it.

prune **prunes, pruning, pruned**
VERB 1 When someone **prunes** a tree, they cut off some of the branches so that it will grow better.
NOUN 2 A **prune** is a dried plum.

psalm **psalms**
NOUN A **psalm** is a poem or prayer from the Bible.

pub **pubs**
NOUN A **pub** is a building where adults go to drink and talk with their friends.

public
ADJECTIVE Something that is **public** can be used by anyone. For example, anyone can pay to travel on public transportation, such as trains and buses.

publish **publishes, publishing, published**
VERB When a company **publishes** a book, newspaper, or magazine, they print copies of it and sell them.
publisher NOUN

pudding **puddings**
NOUN A **pudding** is a sweet food which is usually eaten after the main part of a meal.

puddle **puddles**
NOUN A **puddle** is a small, shallow pool of liquid.

pull **pulls, pulling, pulled**
VERB 1 When you **pull** something, you hold it firmly and move it toward you.

VERB 2 When you **pull** a curtain, you move it across a window.
VERB 3 When a vehicle **pulls away**, **pulls out**, or **pulls in**, it moves in that direction.

pulley **pulleys**
NOUN A **pulley** is for lifting heavy weights. The weight is attached to a rope or a chain, which passes over a wheel.

pullover **pullovers**
NOUN A **pullover** is a shirt or sweater you can pull over your head.

pulse
NOUN Your **pulse** is the regular beating of blood through your body. You can feel your pulse in your neck or wrist.

pump **pumps, pumping, pumped**
NOUN 1 A **pump** is a machine that is used to force gas or liquid to move the way it is wanted.
VERB 2 To **pump** is to force gas or liquid somewhere using a pump. *I must pump up these balloons.*

pumpkin **pumpkins**
NOUN A **pumpkin** is a very large, orange-colored vegetable with a thick skin. It is soft inside, with a lot of seeds.

pun **puns**
NOUN A **pun** is a joke using a word which has two different meanings. For example, the sentence "My dog's a champion boxer," has a pun on the word "boxer."

punch **punches, punching, punched**
VERB If you **punch** someone, you hit them hard with your fist.

punctual
ADJECTIVE Someone who is **punctual** arrives somewhere or does something at exactly the right time.

punctuation

NOUN **Punctuation** is the marks such as periods and commas that you use in writing.

punctuate VERB

See *Punctuation* on page 264.

puncture **punctures**

NOUN A **puncture** is a small hole made by a sharp object.

punish **punishes, punishing, punished**

VERB To **punish** someone means to make them suffer because they have done something wrong.

punishment NOUN

pupil **pupils**

NOUN **1** The **pupils** at a school are the children who go there.

NOUN **2** Your **pupils** are the small, round black circles in the center of your eyes.

puppet **puppets**

NOUN A **puppet** is a kind of doll that you can move. Some puppets have strings which you can pull. Others are made so that you can put your hand inside.

puppy **puppies**

NOUN A **puppy** is a young dog.

See *Young animals* on page 260.

purchase **purchases, purchasing, purchased**

VERB When you **purchase** something, you buy it.

pure **purer, purest**

ADJECTIVE Something that is **pure** is not mixed with anything else.

purple

ADJECTIVE Something that is **purple** is of a reddish-blue color.

See *Colors* on page 271.

purpose **purposes**

NOUN A **purpose** is the reason for doing something.

on purpose PHRASE If you do something **on purpose**, you mean to do it. It does not happen by accident.

purr **purrs, purring, purred**

VERB When a cat **purrs**, it keeps making a low sound that shows it is happy.

purse **purses**

NOUN A **purse** is a small bag that people keep their money in.

push **pushes, pushing, pushed**

VERB When you **push** something, you press it hard.

pushup **pushups**

NOUN A **pushup** is an exercise in which you raise your body off the floor from a lying position by pushing up with your arms.

put **puts, putting, put**

VERB **1** When you **put** something somewhere, you move it there.

VERB **2** If you **put** something **off**, you delay doing it.

VERB **3** If you **put** a light **out**, you make it stop shining.

puzzle **puzzles, puzzling, puzzled**

VERB **1** If something **puzzles** you, you do not understand it.

NOUN **2** A **puzzle** is a game or question that needs a lot of thought to solve it.

pylons **pylons**

NOUN A **pylon** is a tall, metal tower that supports electrical cables.

pyramid **pyramids**

NOUN **1** A **pyramid** is a solid shape with a flat base and flat triangular faces that meet at the top in a point.

See *Solid shapes* on page 271.

PLURAL NOUN **2** The **pyramids** are ancient stone structures built over the bodies of Egyptian kings and queens.

a
b
c
d
e
f
g
h
i
j
k
l
m
n
o
Pp
q
r
s
t
u
v
w
x
y
z

a
b
c
d
e
f
g
h
i
j
k
l
m
n
o
p
Qq
r
s
t
u
v
w
x
y
z

Qq

quack **quacks, quacking, quacked**
VERB When a duck **quacks**, it makes a loud, harsh sound.

quadrilateral **quadrilaterals**
NOUN A **quadrilateral** is a flat shape with four straight sides.
See *Colors and flat shapes* on page 271.

quaint **quainter, quaintest**
ADJECTIVE Something that is **quaint** is unusual and rather pretty.

qualify **qualifies, qualifying, qualified**
VERB **1** When someone **qualifies**, they pass the examination they need to do a particular job.
VERB **2** You **qualify** if you get enough points in a competition to go on to the next stage.

quality **qualities**
NOUN The **quality** of something is how good or bad it is, compared with other things of the same kind.

quantity **quantities**
NOUN A **quantity** is an amount you can measure or count. *We shall need a huge quantity of food for the weekend.*

quarrel **quarrels**
NOUN A **quarrel** is an angry argument.

quarry **quarries**
NOUN A **quarry** is a deep hole that has been dug in a piece of land. Quarries are dug to provide materials, such as stone, for building and other work.

quarter **quarters**
NOUN A **quarter** is one of four equal parts of something.
See *Fractions* on page 272.

quay **quays**
(*said* **kee**)
NOUN A **quay** is a place where boats are tied up to be loaded or unloaded.

queen **queens**
NOUN **1** A **queen** is a woman who rules a country. Queens are not chosen by the people. They are born into a royal family.
NOUN **2** The wife of a king is also called a **queen**.
NOUN **3** In the insect world, a **queen** is a large female bee, ant, or wasp which can lay eggs.

query **queries, querying, queried**
NOUN **1** A **query** is a question.
VERB **2** If you **query** something, you ask about it because you think it might not be right.

question **questions**
NOUN A **question** is words you say or write when you want to ask something.

question mark **question marks**
NOUN A **question mark** is the punctuation mark (**?**) which you use in writing at the end of a question.
See *Punctuation* on page 264.

questionnaire **questionnaires**
NOUN A **questionnaire** is a list of questions which asks for information for a survey.

queue **queues**
NOUN A **queue** is a line of people or vehicles waiting for something.

quiche **quiches**
NOUN A **quiche** is a sort of tart with a filling of eggs, and cheese or other food.

quick **quicker, quickest**

ADJECTIVE **1** Someone or something that is **quick** moves very fast.

ADJECTIVE **2** Something that is **quick** lasts only a short time. *I'll have a **quick** look at it.*

quickly

ADVERB Things that happen **quickly**, happen very fast.

quiet **quieter, quietest**

ADJECTIVE **1** Someone or something that is **quiet** makes only a little noise or no noise at all.

ADJECTIVE **2** Quiet also means peaceful. *Let's have a **quiet** evening at home.*

quilt **quilts**

NOUN A **quilt** is a soft cover for a bed.

quit **quits, quitting, quit**

VERB **1** If you **quit** something, you stop doing it. *Quit teasing me!*

VERB **2** If you **quit**, you leave. *My dad has just **quit** his job.*

VERB **3** If you **quit** a file on a computer, you close it.

quite

ADVERB **1** Quite means rather. *I think he's **quite** nice.*

ADVERB **2** Quite can also mean completely. *The work is now **quite** finished.*

quiver **quivers, quivering, quivered**

VERB **1** If something **quivers**, it trembles.

NOUN **2** A **quiver** is a container for carrying arrows.

quiz **quizzes**

NOUN A **quiz** is a game or test. Someone tries to find out how much you know by asking you questions.

quotation **quotations**

NOUN A **quotation** is an extract from a book or speech that you use in your own work.

quotation marks

PLURAL NOUN **Quotation marks** are punctuation marks (" ") or (' ') used in writing to show where speech begins and ends.

quote **quotes, quoting, quoted**

VERB **1** If you **quote** something that someone has written or said, you repeat their exact words.

NOUN **2** A **quote** is a piece out of a book or speech.

quotient **quotients**

NOUN In math, a **quotient** is a whole number you get when you divide one number into another. For example, if you divide eight by two, the quotient is four.

a
b
c
d
e
f
g
h
i
j
k
l
m
n
o
p
Qq
r
s
t
u
v
w
x
y
z

Rr

rabbit **rabbits**

NOUN A **rabbit** is a small furry animal with long ears.

race **races, racing, raced**

NOUN **1** A **race** is a competition to see who is the fastest.

NOUN **2** A **race** is also a large group of people who look alike in some way. For example, different races have different skin color, or differently shaped eyes.

VERB **3** If you **race** someone, you try to beat them in a race.

rack **racks**

NOUN A **rack** is a frame that is used for holding things or for hanging things on.

racket **rackets**

NOUN **1** A **racket** is a bat with a frame and strings across and down it. It is used in tennis and similar games.

NOUN **2** If someone makes a **racket**, they make a loud, unpleasant noise.

radar

NOUN **Radar** is a way of showing the position and speed of ships and aircraft when they cannot be seen. Radio signals give the information on a screen.

radiator **radiators**

NOUN **1** A **radiator** is a hollow metal object that can be filled with liquid in order to heat a room.

NOUN **2** In a car, the **radiator** holds the water that is used to cool the engine.

radio **radios**

NOUN A **radio** is a piece of equipment which receives sounds through the air. You can use a radio to listen to programs that are broadcast.

radish **radishes**

NOUN A **radish** is a small salad vegetable with a red skin and white flesh. *See Vegetables on page 256.*

radius **radii**

NOUN The **radius** of a circle is the length of a straight line drawn from its center to any point on its edge.

raffle **raffles**

NOUN A **raffle** is a way of raising money. You buy a numbered ticket and win a prize if your number is chosen.

raft **rafts**

NOUN A **raft** is a floating platform. Rafts are often made of large pieces of wood fixed together.

rag **rags**

NOUN **1** A **rag** is a piece of old cloth that you can use to clean or wipe things.

NOUN **2** **Rags** are old, torn clothes.

rage

NOUN **Rage** is great anger. *Dad's face showed his rage.*

ragged

ADJECTIVE Clothes that are **ragged** are old and torn.

raid **raids**

NOUN A **raid** is a sudden attack against an enemy.

rail **rails**

NOUN **1** A **rail** is a horizontal bar that is firmly fixed to posts. Rails are used as fences, or for people to lean on.

NOUN **2** **Rails** are the heavy metal bars that trains run on.

railing **railings**

NOUN A **railing** is a kind of fence made from metal bars.

railway **railways**
NOUN A **railway** is a route along which trains travel on metal rails.

rain **rains, raining, rained**
NOUN **1 Rain** is water that falls from the clouds in small drops.
VERB **2** When it is **raining**, rain is falling.

rainbow **rainbows**
NOUN A **rainbow** is an arch of different colors that sometimes appears in the sky when the sun shines through rain.

rainforest **rainforests**
NOUN A **rainforest** is a dense forest in a tropical area where there is a lot of rain.

raise **raises, raising, raised**
VERB **1** If you **raise** something, you move it so that it is higher.
VERB **2** If you **raise** your voice, you speak more loudly.
VERB **3** To **raise** money for a cause means to get people to give money toward it.

raisin **raisins**
NOUN A **raisin** is a dried grape.

rake **rakes**
NOUN A **rake** is a garden tool with a row of metal teeth fixed to a long handle.

ram **rams, ramming, rammed**
VERB **1** If one vehicle **rams** another, it crashes into it.
NOUN **2** A **ram** is an adult male sheep.

Ramadan
NOUN **Ramadan** is the ninth month of the Muslim year, when Muslims eat and drink nothing from sunrise to sunset.

ramp **ramps**
NOUN A **ramp** is a sloping surface between two places at different levels.

ran
VERB **Ran** is the past tense of **run**.

ranch **ranches**
NOUN In the United States, a **ranch** is a large farm for raising cattle, sheep, or horses.

rang
VERB **Rang** is the past tense of **ring**.

range **ranges**
NOUN **1** The **range** of something is the area or distance over which it can be used.
NOUN **2** A **range** is a row of hills or mountains.

rank **ranks**
NOUN A **rank** is a position that a person holds in an organization. The higher the rank, the more important they are.

rap **raps, rapping, rapped**
VERB **1** If you **rap** something, you hit it with a series of quick blows.
NOUN **2 Rap** is a style of poetry spoken to music with a strong beat.

rapid
ADJECTIVE Something that is **rapid** is very quick.

rare **rarer, rarest**
ADJECTIVE Something that is **rare** is not often seen, or does not happen very often.

rash **rashes**
NOUN A **rash** is a lot of spots that appear on your skin in certain illnesses.

raspberry **raspberries**
NOUN A **raspberry** is a small red fruit which is soft and juicy, with a lot of small seeds.
See *Fruit* on page 257.

rat **rats**
NOUN A **rat** is a rodent with a long tail.

a
b
c
d
e
f
g
h
i
j
k
l
m
n
o
p
q
Rr
s
t
u
v
w
x
y
z

rather

ADVERB **1 Rather** means quite. *I'm rather angry about that.*

ADVERB **2** You can say **rather** if there is something else you want to do. *I don't want to go out. I'd rather watch television.*

rattle **rattles, rattling, rattled**

VERB **1** When something **rattles**, it makes short, rapid, knocking sounds. *Can you stop that window rattling?*

NOUN **2** A baby's **rattle** is a toy that makes a noise when it is shaken.

raw

ADJECTIVE Food that is **raw** is not cooked.

ray **rays**

NOUN A **ray** is a line of light.

razor **razors**

NOUN A **razor** is a tool that people use for shaving.

re-

PREFIX **Re-** is added to words to show that something is done again. For example, to "reread" means to read again. *See Prefixes on page 264.*

reach **reaches, reaching, reached**

VERB **1** When you **reach** a place, you arrive there.

VERB **2** If you **reach** somewhere, you stretch out your hand. *He reached across the table for the salt.*

react **reacts, reacting, reacted**

VERB When you **react** to something, you behave in a particular way because of it. *He reacted badly to the news.*

reaction NOUN

read **reads, reading, read**

VERB **1** When you **read**, you look at words and understand what they mean.

VERB **2** When you **read aloud**, you say the words that are written.

reading **readings**

NOUN **Reading** is the activity of reading books or other written material.

ready

ADJECTIVE If someone or something is **ready**, they are properly prepared for doing something.

real

ADJECTIVE **1** Something that is **real** is true. It is not imaginary. *I've seen a real princess.*

ADJECTIVE **2** You also say **real** when you mean the thing itself and not a copy. *I've got a lovely toy pony. But Jenny's got a real one.*

realize **realizes, realizing, realized**

VERB If you **realize** something, you work it out or notice it. *I've just realized you must be Tara's sister.*

really

ADVERB You can use **really** to make something you are saying stronger. *I really don't like that boy.*

rear

NOUN The **rear** of something is the part that is at the back of it.

rearrange **rearranges, rearranging, rearranged**

VERB To **rearrange** something means to organize or arrange it in a different way.

reason **reasons**

NOUN The **reason** for something is why it happens. *I'm sorry I'm late, but there is a good reason.*

reasonable

ADJECTIVE **1** People who are **reasonable** behave in a fair and sensible way.

ADJECTIVE **2** A price that is **reasonable** seems fair and not too high.

reasonably ADVERB

rebel **rebels, rebelling, rebelled**
VERB To **rebel** means to fight against authority.
rebellious ADJECTIVE

receive **receives, receiving, received**
VERB When you **receive** something, you get it after it has been given or sent to you.

recent
ADJECTIVE Something that is **recent** happened only a short time ago.
recently ADVERB

recipe **recipes**
NOUN A **recipe** is a list of ingredients and instructions for cooking something.

recite **recites, reciting, recited**
VERB When you **recite** something like a poem, you say it aloud from memory.

reckon **reckons, reckoning, reckoned**
VERB If you **reckon** that something is true, you think it is true.

recognize **recognizes, recognizing, recognized**
VERB If you **recognize** someone, you realize that you know who they are.

recommend **recommends, recommending, recommended**
VERB If you **recommend** something to someone, you tell them it is good.

record **records, recording, recorded**
NOUN 1 If you keep a **record** of something, you keep a written account, or store information in a computer.
NOUN 2 A **record** is also the best that has been done so far.
VERB 3 If someone **records** information, they write it down, put it onto tape or film, or into a computer.
VERB 4 To **record** sound means to put it on tape or compact disc.

recorder **recorders**
NOUN A **recorder** is a small musical instrument which you play by blowing into one end and putting your fingers over the holes.

recover **recovers, recovering, recovered**
VERB When you **recover** from something such as an illness, you become well again.

recreation
NOUN **Recreation** is all the things that you like doing in your spare time.
recreational ADJECTIVE

rectangle **rectangles**
NOUN A **rectangle** is a flat shape with four straight sides and four right angles.
rectangular ADJECTIVE
See *Colors and flat shapes* on page 271.

recycle **recycles, recycling, recycled**
VERB To **recycle** used products means to process them so they can be used again.

red **redder, reddest**
ADJECTIVE Something that is **red** is the color of a ripe tomato.
See *Colors* on page 271.

redraft **redrafts, redrafting, redrafted**
VERB If you **redraft** a piece of text, you make another draft.

reduce **reduces, reducing, reduced**
VERB To **reduce** something means to make it smaller in size or amount.

reed

reed **reeds**

NOUN A **reed** is a plant with a tall, hollow stem. Reeds grow in or near water.

reef **reefs**

NOUN A **reef** is a long line of rocks that is just below the surface of the sea.

reel **reels**

NOUN A **reel** is a round object that you wrap thread, wire, or film around.

refer **refers, referring, referred**

VERB If you **refer** to someone or something, you mention them.

referee **referees**

NOUN A **referee** is a person whose job is to make sure that the players in a game follow the rules properly.

reference book **reference books**

NOUN A **reference book** is a book that gives you information in a way that is easy to find. Dictionaries and encyclopedias are reference books.

refill **refills, refilling, refilled**

NOUN **1** A **refill** is a full container that replaces an empty one. *Have you got a refill for this pen?*

VERB **2** If you **refill** something, you fill it again after it has been emptied.

reflect **reflects, reflecting, reflected**

VERB **1** When a surface **reflects** rays of something, like light or heat, the rays bounce back from the surface.

VERB **2** When a mirror **reflects** a person or thing, it shows what they look like.

reflection **reflections**

NOUN A **reflection** is what you see when you look in a mirror or shiny surface.

refreshing

ADJECTIVE Something that is **refreshing** makes you feel energetic or cool again after you have been tired or hot.

refreshments

PLURAL NOUN **Refreshments** are drinks and snacks.

refrigerator **refrigerators**

NOUN A **refrigerator** is a large, cooled container in which you store food to keep it fresh.

refuse **refuses, refusing, refused**

(*said* rif-**yooz**) VERB **1** If you **refuse** to do something, you say you will not do it.

(*said* ref-**yoos**) NOUN **2 Refuse** is rubbish or waste.

region **regions**

NOUN A **region** is a large area of land.

register **registers, registering, registered**

NOUN **1** A **register** is an official list or record of things.

VERB **2** When something is **registered**, it is recorded on an official list. *The car was registered in my mother's name.*

regret **regrets, regretting, regretted**

VERB If you **regret** something, you wish it had not happened.

regular

ADJECTIVE **1** Something that is **regular** does not change its pattern, for example, a regular heartbeat.

ADJECTIVE **2** A **regular** polygon has all its angles and sides equal.

rehearsal **rehearsals**

NOUN A **rehearsal** is a practice of a play, dance, or piece of music, to prepare for a public performance.

reign **reigns, reigning, reigned**

VERB **1** When a king or queen **reigns**, they rule a country.

NOUN **2** The **reign** of a king or queen is the period during which they reign.

rim rims

NOUN **1** The **rim** of a container, such as a cup, is the edge around the top.

NOUN **2** The **rim** of a round object, such as a wheel, is the outside edge of it.

rind rinds

NOUN The **rind** of a fruit, such as an orange or a lemon, is its thick, outer skin.

ring rings, ringing, rang, rung

NOUN **1** A **ring** is an ornament that people wear on a finger.

NOUN **2** Anything in the shape of a circle can be called a **ring**.

NOUN **3** A **ring** is the area in which a boxing or wrestling match takes place.

VERB **4** When a bell **rings**, it makes a loud clear sound.

rinse rinses, rinsing, rinsed

VERB When you **rinse** something, you wash it in clean water with no soap.

rip rips, ripping, ripped

VERB If someone **rips** something, they tear it violently.

ripe riper, ripest

ADJECTIVE When fruit or grain is **ripe**, it is ready to be eaten or harvested.

ripple ripples

NOUN A **ripple** is a little wave on the surface of water.

rise rises, rising, rose, risen

VERB **1** If something **rises**, it moves upward.

VERB **2** When the sun or the moon **rises**, it appears above the horizon.

risk risks

NOUN A **risk** is a danger that something bad might happen.

take a risk PHRASE If someone **takes a risk**, they do something knowing that it could be dangerous.

risky ADJECTIVE

rival rivals

NOUN Your **rival** is someone who is trying to win the same things you are.

river rivers

NOUN A **river** is a large amount of fresh water flowing toward the sea.

road roads

NOUN A **road** is a wide path with a smooth surface, specially treated so that people and vehicles can travel on it easily.

roam roams, roaming, roamed

VERB If you **roam**, you wander around without any particular purpose.

roar roars, roaring, roared

VERB If something **roars**, it makes a very loud noise, like a lion. *The car **roared** off down the road.*

roast roasts, roasting, roasted

VERB When someone **roasts** meat or other food, they cook it in an oven or over a fire.

rob robs, robbing, robbed

VERB If someone **robs** you, they steal something from you.

robber NOUN   **robbery** NOUN

robin robins

NOUN A **robin** is a small brown bird with a red neck and chest.

robot robots

NOUN A **robot** is a machine which is programmed to move and perform tasks automatically.

rock rocks, rocking, rocked

NOUN **1** Rock is the very hard material that is in the earth. Cliffs and mountains are made of rock.

NOUN **2** A **rock** is a large piece of stone.

VERB **3** When something **rocks**, it moves slowly backward and forward, or from side to side.

NOUN **4** Rock or **rock music** is music with a very strong beat.

rocky ADJECTIVE

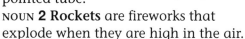

a
b
c
d
e
f
g
h
i
j
k
l
m
n
o
p
q
Rr
s
t
u
v
w
x
y
z

rocket rockets

NOUN **1** A **rocket** is a space vehicle, usually shaped like a long, pointed tube.

NOUN **2 Rockets** are fireworks that explode when they are high in the air.

rod rods

NOUN A **rod** is a long, thin pole or bar, usually made of wood or metal. *His uncle gave him a new fishing rod.*

rode

VERB **Rode** is the past tense of **ride**.

rodent rodents

NOUN A **rodent** is a small mammal with sharp front teeth for gnawing. Rats, mice, squirrels, and hamsters are rodents.

roll rolls, rolling, rolled

VERB **1** When something **rolls**, or when you roll it, it moves along a surface, turning over and over.

NOUN **2** A **roll** of something, like paper, is a long piece of it that has been rolled into a tube.

NOUN **3** A **roll** is a small loaf of bread for one person.

Rollerblade Rollerblades

NOUN; TRADEMARK **Rollerblades** are roller skates which have the wheels set in one straight line on the bottom of the boot.

roller skate roller skates

NOUN **Roller skates** are shoes with four small wheels underneath.

roof roofs

NOUN **1** The **roof** of a building or car is the covering on top of it.

NOUN **2** The **roof** of your mouth, or of a cave, is the highest part.

room rooms

NOUN **1** A **room** is a section in a building, divided from other rooms by walls.

NOUN **2** If there is plenty of **room**, there is a lot of space.

root roots

NOUN **1** A **root** is the part of a plant that grows underground.

NOUN **2** The **root** of a hair, tooth, or nail is the part that you cannot see because it is covered with skin.

root word root words

NOUN A **root word** is a word to which prefixes and suffixes can be added to make other words. In the word "clearly," the root word is "clear."

rope ropes

NOUN **Rope** is thick, strong string.

rose roses

NOUN **1** A **rose** is a flower. Most roses grow on thorny stems.

VERB **2 Rose** is also the past tense of **rise**.

rot rots, rotting, rotted

VERB **1** When vegetables and other foods **rot**, they go bad.

VERB **2** When wood **rots**, it becomes soft and can easily be pulled to pieces.

rotate rotates, rotating, rotated

VERB When something **rotates**, it turns with a circular movement.

rotten

ADJECTIVE Something that is **rotten** has gone bad or soft so that it cannot be used.

rough rougher, roughest

ADJECTIVE **1** If something is **rough**, the surface is uneven and not smooth.

ADJECTIVE **2** If someone is being **rough**, they are not being gentle.

ADJECTIVE **3** A **rough** estimate is not meant to be exact.

ADJECTIVE **4** A **rough** draft is an early version of something you are writing.

roughly

ADVERB **1** If you say **roughly**, you mean approximately. *There are **roughly** twice as many boys as girls in this club.*

ADVERB **2** If someone speaks **roughly** to you, they sound angry and aggressive.

round   rounder, roundest

ADJECTIVE **1** Something **round** is shaped like a ball or a circle.

NOUN **2** Rounds is the regular route or course of action followed by a mail carrier, doctor or guard.

round up or **round down** PHRASE If you **round a number**, you raise it up or lower it down to the nearest 10, 100, or 1000. *If you **round** 34 to the nearest ten, it would be 30. 675 **rounded up** to the nearest hundred is 700.*

roundabout

ADJECTIVE A **roundabout** route is an indirect way of getting from one place to another.

round trip   round trips

NOUN A **round trip** means to travel to a place and back again.

roundup   roundups

NOUN A **roundup** is the gathering together of cattle for branding or shipping to market.

rouse

VERB **1** When you **rouse** someone, you wake them up.

VERB **2** His speech **roused** the crowd, making them excited and interested.

route   routes

NOUN A **route** is a way from one place to another. *David took his usual **route** to school.*

routine   routines

ADJECTIVE **1** Routine things happen regularly.

NOUN **2** Your **routine** is the usual way that you do things.

row   rows, rowing, rowed

NOUN **1** A **row** of people or things is several of them arranged in a line.

VERB **2** When you **row** a boat, you use oars to make it move through the water.

royal

ADJECTIVE **1** Someone who is **royal** belongs to the family of a king or queen.

ADJECTIVE **2** Something that is **royal** is connected with a royal family.

rub   rubs, rubbing, rubbed

VERB When you **rub** something, you wipe it hard.

rubber   rubbers

NOUN **1** Rubber is a strong stretchy material that is made from the sap of a tree. It is used to make things like tires.

NOUN **2** Rubbers are low boots that protect shoes from water.

rubbish

NOUN **1** Rubbish is waste material, such as used paper or empty cans.

NOUN **2** If you say something is **rubbish**, you think it is of very poor quality.

ruby   rubies

NOUN A **ruby** is a dark red jewel.

rudder   rudders

NOUN A **rudder** is a piece of wood or metal on the back of a boat or plane which is moved to make the boat or plane turn.

a b c d e f g h i j k l m n o p q **Rr** s t u v w x y z

rude

rude **ruder, rudest**

ADJECTIVE If someone is **rude**, they behave badly and are not polite. *It's **rude** to stare at people.*

rug **rugs**

NOUN A **rug** is a piece of thick material, like a small carpet.

rugby

NOUN **Rugby** is a game played with an oval ball. Two teams try to score points by carrying the ball across a line, or by kicking the ball over a bar.

ruin **ruins, ruining, ruined**

VERB **1** To **ruin** something means to spoil it completely. *Mark and Joe **ruined** my party by fighting.*

NOUN **2** The **ruins** of a building are the parts of it that are left after it has fallen down or been badly damaged.

rule **rules, ruling, ruled**

VERB **1** To **rule** a country means to be in charge of the way the country works.

NOUN **2** **Rules** tell you what you are allowed to do and what you are not allowed to do. They are used in games, and in places such as schools.

ruler **rulers**

NOUN **1** A **ruler** is a person who rules a country.

NOUN **2** A **ruler** is also a long, flat piece of wood or plastic with straight edges, used for measuring or drawing straight lines.

rumor **rumors**

NOUN A **rumor** is a story or piece of information which a lot of people are talking about, but which may not be true.

run **runs, running, ran, run**

VERB **1** When you **run**, you move quickly, leaving the ground during each stride.

VERB **2** When liquid **runs**, it flows. *Don't leave the hot water **running**.*

VERB **3** Someone who **runs** something, like a school or country, is in charge of it.

VERB **4** When a vehicle, such as a train or bus **runs** somewhere, it travels at set times. *The bus **runs** every 20 minutes.*

VERB **5** If you **run** out of something, you have no more of it left.

rung **rungs**

NOUN **1** A **rung** is a wooden or metal step on a ladder.

VERB **2** **Rung** is the past participle of **ring**.

running

NOUN **1** **Running** is the activity of running, especially as a sport.

ADJECTIVE **2** **Running** water is flowing rather than standing still.

runway **runways**

NOUN A **runway** is a long, narrow strip of ground at an airport which planes use when they take off or land.

rush **rushes, rushing, rushed**

VERB If you **rush** somewhere, you go there quickly.

rust **rusts, rusting, rusted**

NOUN **1** **Rust** is a reddish-brown substance that forms on iron or steel, which has been in contact with water.

VERB **2** When something **rusts**, rust forms on it.

rusty ADJECTIVE

rustle **rustles, rustling, rustled**

VERB When something **rustles**, it makes soft sounds as it moves. *Dry leaves **rustled** underfoot.*

rut **ruts**

NOUN A **rut** is a deep groove in the ground made by the wheels of a vehicle.

Ss

sack **sacks**

NOUN A **sack** is a large, strong bag made of cloth or plastic.

sad **sadder, saddest**

ADJECTIVE If you are **sad**, you are unhappy because something has happened that you do not like.

saddle **saddles**

NOUN A **saddle** is a seat for a rider on a horse or bicycle.

safari **safaris**

NOUN A **safari** is a journey to see wild animals.

safari park **safari parks**

NOUN A **safari park** is a large protected area of land where wild animals live and move around freely.

safe **safer, safest; safes**

ADJECTIVE 1 If you are **safe**, you are not in any danger.

ADJECTIVE 2 If something is in a **safe** place, it cannot be lost or stolen.

NOUN 3 A **safe** is a strong, metal box with special locks. People keep money or valuable things in a safe.

safety NOUN

said

VERB **Said** is the past tense of **say**.

sail **sails, sailing, sailed**

NOUN 1 A **sail** is a large piece of material attached to a boat. The wind blows against the sail and pushes the boat along.

NOUN 2 A **sail** is also one of the flat pieces of wood on the top of a windmill.

VERB 3 To **sail** a boat means to make it move across water using its sails.

sailor **sailors**

NOUN A **sailor** is a person who works on a ship as a member of the crew.

salad **salads**

NOUN A **salad** is a mixture of raw vegetables, for example lettuce, cucumber, and tomatoes.

sale **sales**

NOUN 1 The **sale** of anything is the selling of it for money.

NOUN 2 A **sale** is a time when a shop sells things at less than their usual price.

saliva

NOUN **Saliva** is the liquid in your mouth that helps you eat food.

salmon

NOUN A **salmon** is a large, silvery fish. Salmon live in the sea, but they swim up rivers to lay their eggs.

salt

NOUN **Salt** is a white powder or crystal with a bitter taste. Salt is found in the earth and in sea water. It is used to flavor or preserve food.

salute **salutes, saluting, saluted**

NOUN 1 A **salute** is a sign of respect used especially in the armed forces.

VERB 2 If you **salute** someone, you assume a prescribed position.

same

ADJECTIVE 1 If two things are the **same**, they are exactly like each other in some way. *Look! Your dress is the **same** as mine.*

ADJECTIVE 2 **Same** means one shared thing and not two different ones. *Amy and I are in the **same** class.*

sample **samples**

NOUN A **sample** of something is a small quantity of it that you can try.

a
b
c
d
e
f
g
h
i
j
k
l
m
n
o
p
q
r
Ss
t
u
v
w
x
y
z

sand

NOUN **Sand** is tiny grains of rock, shells, and other material. Most deserts and beaches are made of sand.

sandal **sandals**

NOUN **Sandals** are light shoes for warm weather. The soles are held on by straps which go over your foot.

sandbox **sandboxes**

NOUN A **sandbox** is a shallow box in the ground with sand in it, where small children can play.

sandwich **sandwiches**

NOUN A **sandwich** is two slices of bread with a layer of food in between.

sang

VERB **Sang** is the past tense of **sing**.

sank

VERB **Sank** is the past tense of **sink**.

sap

NOUN **Sap** is the liquid that carries food through plants and trees.

sardine **sardines**

NOUN A **sardine** is a small sea fish.

sari **saris**

NOUN A **sari** is a piece of clothing worn especially by Asian women.

sat

VERB **Sat** is the past tense of **sit**.

satchel **satchels**

NOUN A **satchel** is a leather or cloth bag with a long strap.

satellite **satellites**

NOUN **1** A **satellite** is a natural object in space that moves around a larger object. The moon is a satellite of the Earth.

NOUN **2** A **satellite** is also an object sent into space to send signals back to Earth.

satellite dish **satellite dishes**

NOUN A **satellite dish** is a receiver for signals from an artificial satellite.

satellite television

NOUN **Satellite television** is where the programs are sent from an artificial satellite. They can be received using a satellite dish.

satisfactory

ADJECTIVE Something that is **satisfactory** is good enough for its purpose.

satisfy **satisfies, satisfying, satisfied**

VERB To **satisfy** someone means to give them enough of something to make them pleased or contented.

Saturday **Saturdays**

NOUN **Saturday** is the day between Friday and Sunday.

sauce **sauces**

NOUN A **sauce** is a thick liquid served with other food to add to the taste.

saucepan **saucepans**

NOUN A **saucepan** is a deep, metal cooking pot, usually with a long handle. Most saucepans have lids.

saucer **saucers**

NOUN A **saucer** is a small plate on which you place a cup.

sausage **sausages**

NOUN A **sausage** is a finely minced meat mixture put into a skin.

savage

ADJECTIVE A **savage** animal is wild and fierce.

save **saves, saving, saved**

VERB **1** If you **save** someone or something, you help them to escape from harm or danger. *He fell in the river and his father dived in to save him.*

VERB **2** If you **save** money, you gradually collect it by not spending it all.

savings

PLURAL NOUN Your **savings** are the money you have saved.

saw **saws, sawing, sawed, sawn**

VERB **1 Saw** is the past tense of **see**.

NOUN **2** A **saw** is a tool for cutting wood and other materials. It has a blade with sharp teeth along one edge.

VERB **3** If you **saw** something, you cut it with a saw.

sawdust

NOUN **Sawdust** is the dust and small bits of wood made when wood is sawn.

say **says, saying, said**

VERB When you **say** something, you speak words.

scald **scalds, scalding, scalded**

VERB If you **scald** yourself, you burn yourself with very hot liquid or steam.

scale **scales**

NOUN **1** The **scale** of a map is a key that shows how its size relates to the place in the real world.

NOUN **2** The **scales** of a fish or reptile are the small pieces of hard skin covering its body.

scales

PLURAL NOUN **Scales** are a piece of equipment you use for weighing things.

scamper **scampers, scampering, scampered**

VERB When people or small animals **scamper**, they move quickly and lightly.

scan **scans, scanning, scanned**

VERB **1** If you **scan** a piece of writing, you look through it quickly.

VERB **2** If a machine **scans** something, it examines it using a beam of light, X-rays, or sound waves.

scar **scars**

NOUN A **scar** is a mark that is left on the skin after a wound has healed.

scarce **scarcer, scarcest**

ADJECTIVE Something that is **scarce** is not often found.

scare **scares, scaring, scared**

VERB Someone or something that **scares** you makes you feel frightened.

scarecrow **scarecrows**

NOUN A **scarecrow** is an object in the shape of a person, put in a field of crops to frighten birds away.

scared

ADJECTIVE If you are **scared**, you are frightened.

scarf **scarves**

NOUN A **scarf** is a piece of cloth that you wear around your neck to keep you warm.

scarlet

ADJECTIVE Something **scarlet** is a bright red color.

scatter **scatters, scattering, scattered**

VERB **1** If you **scatter** things, you throw or drop a lot of them all over an area.

VERB **2** If people **scatter**, they suddenly move away in different directions.

scene **scenes**

NOUN **1** The **scene** of an event is the place where it happened. *The police went to the scene of the crime.*

NOUN **2** A **scene** is part of a play or film in which things happen in one place.

scenery **sceneries**

NOUN **1 Scenery** is what you can see when you are out in the country.

NOUN **2 Scenery** is also all the cloths and boards that are used as a background for the stage in a theater.

scent

scent **scents**
NOUN A **scent** is a pleasant smell.

scheme **schemes, scheming, schemed**
NOUN **1** A **scheme** is a plan for doing something.
VERB **2** When people **scheme**, they make secret plans.

school **schools**
NOUN **1** A **school** is a place for teaching and learning.
NOUN **2** You can refer to a large group of dolphins or fish as a **school**.
See *Collective nouns* on page 262.

science
NOUN **Science** is the study of plants and animals, materials, and things like electricity, forces, light, and sound.

science fiction
NOUN **Science fiction** is stories about events happening in the future or in other parts of the universe.

scientist **scientists**
NOUN A **scientist** is a person who finds out why things happen by doing tests and by careful study.

scissors
PLURAL NOUN **Scissors** are a cutting tool with two sharp blades.

scoop **scoops, scooping, scooped**
VERB **1** If you **scoop** something up, you pick it up using a spoon or the palm of your hand.
NOUN **2** A **scoop** is an object like a large spoon which is used for picking up food, such as ice cream.

score **scores, scoring, scored**
VERB **1** If someone **scores**, they get a goal or other point in a game.
NOUN **2** The **score** in a game is the number of points made by each team or player.

scowl **scowls, scowling, scowled**
VERB If you **scowl**, you look very cross.

scramble **scrambles, scrambling, scrambled**
VERB If you **scramble** over rough or difficult ground, you move over it quickly, using your hands to help you.

scrap **scraps**
NOUN A **scrap** of something is a small piece of it. *I need a **scrap** of paper.*

scrapbook **scrapbooks**
NOUN A **scrapbook** is a book in which you stick things such as pictures or newspaper articles.

scrape **scrapes, scraping, scraped**
VERB If you **scrape** something, you take off its surface by pulling a rough or sharp object over it.

scratch **scratches, scratching, scratched**
VERB **1** If you **scratch** your skin, you rub your fingernails against it.
VERB **2** If you **scratch** something, you damage it by making small cuts on it. *I fell into the hedge and **scratched** my bike.*
NOUN **3** A **scratch** is a small cut.

scream **screams, screaming, screamed**
VERB If you **scream**, you shout or cry in a loud high-pitched voice.

screech **screeches, screeching, screeched**
VERB To **screech** means to make an unpleasant high-pitched noise. *The car wheels **screeched**.*

screen **screens**
NOUN A **screen** is a flat surface on which pictures or words are shown, for example a television or computer screen.

screw **screws, screwing, screwed**

NOUN **1** A **screw** is a small, sharp piece of metal used for holding things together.

VERB **2** If you **screw** things together, you fasten them together using screws.

VERB **3** If you **screw** something onto something else, you fasten it there by twisting it around and around. *He screwed the top back onto the bottle of water.*

screwdriver **screwdrivers**

NOUN A **screwdriver** is a tool used for turning screws.

scribble **scribbles, scribbling, scribbled**

VERB If you **scribble**, you write quickly and roughly.

script **scripts**

NOUN The **script** of a play or film is the written version of it.

scrub **scrubs, scrubbing, scrubbed**

VERB If you **scrub** something, you rub it hard with a stiff brush and water.

sculptor **sculptors**

NOUN A **sculptor** is someone who makes sculptures.

sculpture **sculptures**

NOUN **1** A **sculpture** is a statue or model made by shaping stone, clay, or other materials.

NOUN **2** **Sculpture** is the art of making sculptures.

sea **seas**

NOUN The **sea** is the salty water that covers about three-quarters of the earth.

seagull **seagulls**

NOUN **Seagulls** are common, white, gray, and black birds that live near the sea.

seahorse **seahorses**

NOUN A **seahorse** is a small fish which swims upright, with a head that looks like a horse's head.

seal **seals, sealing, sealed**

NOUN **1** A **seal** is a large mammal with flippers that lives partly on land and partly in the sea.

VERB **2** If you **seal** an envelope, you stick down the flap.

seam **seams**

NOUN A **seam** is the line where two pieces of material are sewn together.

search **searches, searching, searched**

VERB If you **search** for something, you try to find it by looking carefully.

seasick

ADJECTIVE If you are **seasick** you feel nauseous and dizzy because of the tossing movement of a boat or ship.

season **seasons**

NOUN A **season** is one of the four parts of a year: spring, summer, autumn, and winter.

seat **seats**

NOUN A **seat** is a place where you can sit, for example, a chair or a stool.

seat belt **seat belts**

NOUN A **seat belt** is a strap that you fasten across your body for safety when traveling in a car, truck, or aircraft.

seaweed

NOUN **Seaweed** is a plant that grows in the sea.

a
b
c
d
e
f
g
h
i
j
k
l
m
n
o
p
q
r
Ss
t
u
v
w
x
y
z

second seconds

ADJECTIVE **1** The **second** item in a series is the one counted as number two.

NOUN **2** A **second** is a short period of time. There are 60 seconds in a minute.

second person

NOUN In grammar, the **second person** is the person who is addressed in speech or writing. It is expressed as "you."

secret secrets

NOUN A **secret** is something that only a few people know and that they are not to tell other people.

section sections

NOUN A **section** of something is one of the separate parts it is divided into.

secure

ADJECTIVE **1** If you feel **secure**, you feel safe and confident.

ADJECTIVE **2** If something is **secure**, it is fixed firmly in position.

security NOUN

see sees, seeing, saw, seen

VERB **1** If you **see** something, you are looking at it or you notice it.

VERB **2** To **see** something also means to understand it. *I see what you mean.*

VERB **3** If you **see** someone, you visit them or meet them. *I went to see the doctor.*

seed seeds

NOUN The **seeds** of a plant are the small, hard parts from which new plants grow.

seek seeks, seeking, sought

VERB If you **seek** someone or something, you try to find them.

seem seems, seeming, seemed

VERB **1** If you say that someone **seems**, for example, to be happy or sad, you mean that is the way they look. *Tim seems to be a bit upset today.*

VERB **2** If something **seems** a certain way, that is the way it feels to you. *I only waited for ten minutes, but it seemed like hours.*

seen

VERB **Seen** is the past participle of **see**.

seesaw seesaws

NOUN A **seesaw** is a long plank balanced on a support in the middle. A child sits on each end.

segment segments

NOUN A **segment** of something is a small part of it.

seize seizes, seizing, seized

VERB If you **seize** something, you grab it firmly.

select selects, selecting, selected

VERB When you **select** someone or something, you choose them.

selfish

ADJECTIVE People who are **selfish** only think about themselves. They do not care about other people.

sell sells, selling, sold

VERB When someone **sells** something, they give it in exchange for money.

semester semesters

NOUN A **semester** is one of two terms that make up a school year.

semi-

PREFIX Putting **semi-** in front of a word makes it mean half or partly. For example, a "semicircle" is half of a circle.

See *Prefixes* on page 264.

semicircle semicircles

NOUN A **semicircle** is half of a circle.

See *Colors and flat shapes* on page 271.

semicolon **semicolons**

NOUN A **semicolon** is the punctuation mark (;) which is used in writing to separate different parts of a sentence or list, or to show a pause.
See Punctuation on page 264.

semifinal **semifinals**

NOUN The **semifinals** are the two matches in a competition played to decide who plays in the final.

send **sends, sending, sent**

VERB **1** When you **send** something to someone, you arrange for it to be delivered to them.
VERB **2** If someone **sends** someone somewhere, they tell them to go there. *She was sent home because she was ill.*
VERB **3** If someone **sends** for you, you get a message to go and see them.

senior

ADJECTIVE **Senior** means either older or more experienced.

sensation **sensations**

NOUN A **sensation** is a physical feeling.

sense **senses**

NOUN **1** Your **senses** are your power to see, hear, smell, touch, and taste.
NOUN **2** **Sense** is knowing the right thing to do. *You should have had more sense.*
NOUN **3** If something makes **sense**, you can understand it.

sensible

ADJECTIVE People who are **sensible** know what is the right thing to do.
sensibly ADVERB

sensitive

ADJECTIVE **1** If someone or something is **sensitive**, they are easily hurt. *He is very sensitive about his big ears.*
ADJECTIVE **2** If you are **sensitive** to other people's feelings, you understand them.

sent

VERB **Sent** is the past tense of **send**.

sentence **sentences**

NOUN A **sentence** is a group of words that mean something.

separate **separates, separating, separated**

ADJECTIVE **1** If two things are **separate**, they are not connected.
VERB **2** To **separate** people or things means to part them. *Separate the yolk from the white.*

September

NOUN **September** is the ninth month of the year. It has 30 days.

sequel **sequels**

NOUN A **sequel** to a book or movie is another book or movie which continues the story.

sequence **sequences**

NOUN A **sequence** of events is a number of them coming one after the other.

series

NOUN **1** A **series** is a number of things of the same kind that follow each other.
NOUN **2** A radio or television **series** is a set of programs about the same thing.

serious

ADJECTIVE **1** People who are **serious** are often quiet and do not laugh very much.
ADJECTIVE **2** Things that are **serious** are important and need careful thought.
ADJECTIVE **3** A **serious** problem or situation is very bad and worrying.

servant **servants**

NOUN A **servant** is someone paid to work in another person's house.

a
b
c
d
e
f
g
h
i
j
k
l
m
n
o
p
q
r
Ss
t
u
v
w
x
y
z

serve serves, serving, served
VERB **1** If you **serve** food or drink to people, you give it to them.
VERB **2** To **serve** customers in a store means to help them to buy what they want.

service services
NOUN A **service** is something useful that a person or company does for people.

sesame
NOUN A **sesame** is a small, oval seed, or the tropical plant from which the seed comes.

set sets, setting, set
NOUN **1** A **set** is a number of things of the same kind that belong together, for example a set of golf clubs or a set of tools.
VERB **2** When something such as jelly or concrete **sets**, it becomes firm or hard.
VERB **3** When the sun **sets**, it goes down behind the horizon.
VERB **4** When you **set** a clock or control, you adjust it to a particular position.

settee settees
NOUN A **settee** is a long, comfortable seat for two or more people.

setting settings
NOUN The **setting** of a story or play is where it takes place. *That old castle would make a great setting for a creepy story.*

settle settles, settling, settled
VERB **1** If you **settle**, you sit or make yourself comfortable.
VERB **2** If something such as dust or snow **settles**, it sinks slowly and becomes still.
VERB **3** If you **settle** something, you decide it.

several
ADJECTIVE **Several** people or things means a number of them. *He was gone for several hours.*

severe
ADJECTIVE **Severe** is used to describe something extremely bad or unpleasant. *She had a severe toothache.*

sew sews, sewing, sewed
VERB When someone **sews**, they join pieces of cloth together by using a needle and thread.

sewer sewers
NOUN A **sewer** is a large underground pipe that carries rainwater and waste away from houses and other buildings.

sex sexes
NOUN The two **sexes** are the two groups that people and other living things are divided into. One sex is male and the other is female. Only female animals can have babies.

shabby shabbier, shabbiest
ADJECTIVE Something that is **shabby** looks old and nearly worn out.

shade shades, shading, shaded
NOUN **1** Shade is the darkness in a place where the sun cannot reach. *She sat in the shade of an apple tree.*
NOUN **2** A **shade** is something that covers a light to stop it shining in your eyes.
VERB **3** If you **shade** something, you stop the sun from shining on it.
NOUN **4** Shade is how dark or light a color is. *I love this shade of blue.*

shadow shadows
NOUN A **shadow** is a dark shape. It is formed when something opaque blocks the light coming from a lamp or the sun.

shake shakes, shaking, shook, shaken
VERB **1** If you **shake** something, or it shakes, it moves quickly from side to side or up and down.
VERB **2** If your voice **shakes**, it trembles because you are nervous or angry.

shaky shakier, shakiest
ADJECTIVE If someone or something is **shaky**, they are weak and unsteady.
shakily ADVERB

shallow shallower, shallowest
ADJECTIVE Something that is **shallow**, such as a hole, a container, or water, measures only a short distance from top to bottom.

shame
NOUN **1** **Shame** is an unhappy feeling that people have when they have done something wrong or foolish.
NOUN **2** If you say something is a **shame**, you mean you are sorry about it. *It's a shame you can't come around.*

shampoo shampoos
NOUN **Shampoo** is a soapy liquid that you use for washing your hair.

shape shapes
NOUN **1** The **shape** of something is the form of its outline, for example whether it is round or square.
NOUN **2** A **shape** is something that has its outside edges joining in a particular way. Shapes can be flat (two-dimensional), like a circle or a triangle, or solid (three-dimensional), like a cube or sphere.
See *Colors and flat shapes* and *Solid shapes* on page 271.

share shares, sharing, shared
VERB **1** If you **share** something with another person, you both use it. *She shared a bedroom with her sister.*
VERB **2** If you **share** something among a group of people, you divide it so that everyone gets some.
NOUN **3** A **share** of something is a portion of it.

shark sharks
NOUN **Sharks** are large powerful fish with sharp teeth.

sharp sharper, sharpest
ADJECTIVE **1** A **sharp** object has a fine edge or point that is good for cutting or piercing things.
ADJECTIVE **2** A **sharp** person is quick to notice or understand things.
ADJECTIVE **3** A **sharp** pain is sudden and hurts a lot.

sharpen sharpens, sharpening, sharpened
VERB If you **sharpen** something, you make its edge or point sharper.

shatter shatters, shattering, shattered
VERB If something **shatters**, it breaks into a lot of small pieces.

shave shaves, shaving, shaved
VERB When a man **shaves**, he removes hair from his face with a razor.

shawl shawls
NOUN A **shawl** is a large piece of woolen cloth. Shawls are worn by women over their shoulders or head.

shear shears, shearing, sheared
VERB To **shear** a sheep means to cut the wool off it.

shears
PLURAL NOUN **Shears** are a tool like a large pair of scissors, used especially for cutting hedges.

shed sheds, shedding, shed
NOUN **1** A **shed** is a small building used for storing things.
VERB **2** When a tree **sheds** its leaves, they fall off.

a
b
c
d
e
f
g
h
i
j
k
l
m
n
o
p
q
r
Ss
t
u
v
w
x
y
z

sheep
NOUN A **sheep** is a farm animal with a thick, wool coat. Sheep are kept for meat or wool.

sheet sheets
NOUN 1 A **sheet** is a large piece of thin cloth which is put on a bed.
NOUN 2 A **sheet** of something, such as paper or glass, is a thin, flat piece.

shelf shelves
NOUN A **shelf** is something flat which is usually attached to a wall or inside a cupboard. It is for putting things on.

shell shells
NOUN 1 The **shell** of an egg or nut is the hard covering around it.

NOUN 2 The **shell** of an animal, such as a tortoise, is the hard covering on its back.

shelter shelters, sheltering, sheltered
NOUN 1 A **shelter** is a small building or covered place where people or animals can be safe from bad weather or danger.
VERB 2 If you **shelter** in a place, you stay there and are safe.

shepherd shepherds
NOUN A **shepherd** is a person who looks after sheep.

sheriff sheriffs
NOUN A **sheriff** is the chief person who enforces the law in a county.

sherry
NOUN A **sherry** is a strong, sweet wine.

shield shields, shielding, shielded
NOUN 1 A **shield** is a large piece of strong material, like metal or plastic, which soldiers or police officers carry to protect themselves.

VERB 2 To **shield** someone means to protect them from something.

shift shifts, shifting, shifted
VERB 1 If you **shift** something, you move it.
VERB 2 If something **shifts**, it moves.
NOUN 3 A **shift** is a set period during which people work in a factory or hospital. *My dad works the night **shift**.*

shimmer shimmers, shimmering, shimmered
VERB If something **shimmers**, it shines with a faint flickering light, for example as the moon does on water.

shin shins
NOUN Your **shin** is the front part of your leg, between your knee and your ankle.

shine shines, shining, shone
VERB 1 When something **shines**, it gives out a bright light.
VERB 2 If you make an object **shine**, you make it bright by polishing it.
shiny ADJECTIVE

ship ships
NOUN A **ship** is a large boat which carries passengers or cargo.

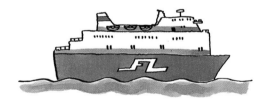

shirt shirts
NOUN A **shirt** is a light piece of clothing for the top part of your body, with a collar, sleeves, and buttons down the front.

shiver shivers, shivering, shivered
VERB When you **shiver**, your body shakes slightly, usually because you are cold or frightened.

shoal shoals
NOUN A **shoal** of fish is a large group of them swimming together.
See *Collective nouns* on page 262.

shock **shocks, shocking, shocked**
NOUN **1** If you have a **shock**, something happens suddenly which upsets you.
VERB **2** If you **shock** someone, you give them an unpleasant surprise.
shocking ADJECTIVE

shoe **shoes, shoeing, shod**
NOUN **1** **Shoes** are strong coverings for your feet.
VERB **2** To **shoe** a horse means to put horseshoes onto its hooves.

shoelace **shoelaces**
NOUN A **shoelace** is a long piece of material, like string, that is used to fasten a shoe.

shone
VERB **Shone** is the past tense of **shine**.

shook
VERB **Shook** is the past tense of **shake**.

shoot **shoots, shooting, shot**
NOUN **1** A **shoot** is a new part growing from a plant or tree.
VERB **2** To **shoot** means to fire a bullet from a gun, or an arrow from a bow.
VERB **3** If someone **shoots** in a game such as basketball, they try to score.
VERB **4** When a film is **shot**, it is filmed.

shop **shops, shopping, shopped**
NOUN **1** A **shop** is a place where things are sold.
VERB **2** When you **shop**, you go to the stores to buy things.

shopkeeper **shopkeepers**
NOUN A **shopkeeper** is a person who owns or looks after a small store.

shore **shores**
NOUN The **shore** of a sea or lake is the land along the edge of it.

short **shorter, shortest**
ADJECTIVE **1** Someone who is **short** is not as tall as most other people.
ADJECTIVE **2** Something that is **short** is not very long.
PHRASE **3** If one word is **short for** another, it is a quick way of saying it. *Phone is **short for** telephone.*

shorts
PLURAL NOUN **Shorts** are pants with short legs.

shot **shots**
VERB **1** **Shot** is the past tense of **shoot**.
NOUN **2** A **shot** is when a gun is fired.
NOUN **3** In basketball and tennis, a **shot** is the act of shooting or hitting the ball.

should
VERB **1** You use **should** to say that something ought to happen. *You **should** write a thank you letter.*
VERB **2** You also use **should** to say that you expect something to happen. *We **should** have heard by now.*

shoulder **shoulders**
NOUN Your **shoulders** are the parts of your body between your neck and the tops of your arms.

shout **shouts, shouting, shouted**
VERB If you **shout** something, you say it very loudly.

shove **shoves, shoving, shoved**
VERB If you **shove** someone or something, you push them roughly.

shovel **shovels, shoveling, shoveled**
NOUN **1** A **shovel** is a tool like a spade with a rounded blade.
VERB **2** If you **shovel** earth or snow, you move it with a shovel.

a
b
c
d
e
f
g
h
i
j
k
l
m
n
o
p
q
r
Ss
t
u
v
w
x
y
z

show

show **shows, showing, showed, shown**

VERB **1** If you **show** someone something, you let them see it. *Show me your passport.*

VERB **2** If you **show** someone how to do something, you do it yourself so that they can watch you.

VERB **3** If something **shows**, people can see it. *Do you think that mark will **show**?*

VERB **4** If you **show** your feelings, you let people see them.

NOUN **5** A **show** is something that you watch at the theater or on television.

shower **showers**

NOUN **1** A **shower** is a piece of equipment which sprays you with water so that you can wash yourself.

NOUN **2** A **shower** is also a short period of rain or snow.

shrank

VERB **Shrank** is the past tense of **shrink**.

shred **shreds, shredding, shredded**

NOUN **1** A **shred** of paper or material is a small narrow piece of it. *He tore the paper into **shreds**.*

VERB **2** If you **shred** something, you cut or tear it into small pieces.

shriek **shrieks, shrieking, shrieked**

VERB If you **shriek**, you give a sudden sharp scream.

shrill **shriller, shrillest**

ADJECTIVE A **shrill** sound is loud and high-pitched, like a whistle.

shrimp **shrimps**

NOUN A **shrimp** is a small, edible shellfish with a long tail and many legs.

shrink **shrinks, shrinking, shrank, shrunk**

VERB If something **shrinks**, it becomes smaller.

shrivel **shrivels, shriveling, shriveled**

VERB When something **shrivels**, it becomes dry and curled up.

shrug **shrugs, shrugging, shrugged**

VERB If you **shrug** your shoulders, you raise them slightly to show that you are not interested in something.

shrunk

VERB **Shrunk** is the past participle of **shrink**.

shudder **shudders, shuddering, shuddered**

VERB If you **shudder**, you tremble with fear or horror.

shuffle **shuffles, shuffling, shuffled**

VERB **1** If you **shuffle**, you walk without lifting your feet properly off the ground.

VERB **2** If you **shuffle** a pack of cards, you mix them up before you begin a game.

shut **shuts, shutting, shut**

VERB **1** If you **shut** something, such as a door, you move it so that it fills a gap.

VERB **2** When a shop **shuts** for the day, you can no longer go into it.

ADJECTIVE **3** If something is **shut**, it is closed.

shy **shier, shiest**

ADJECTIVE A **shy** person is nervous with people they do not know well.

sick **sicker, sickest**

ADJECTIVE If you are **sick**, you are ill.

side **sides**

NOUN **1** The **side** of something is to the left or right of it. *He parted his hair on the left **side**.*

NOUN **2** The **side** of something can be the edge of it. *A triangle has three **sides**.*

NOUN **3** The **sides** of a river are its banks.

NOUN **4** The **sides** of a piece of paper are its front and back.

NOUN **5** The two **sides** in a game are the teams playing against each other.

ADJECTIVE **6** A **side** road is a small road leading off a larger one.

sideways

ADVERB **Sideways** means moving or facing toward one side. *She had to squeeze **sideways** through the gap.*

sigh **sighs, sighing, sighed**
VERB When you **sigh**, you breathe out heavily. People usually sigh when they are tired, sad, or bored.

sight
NOUN **Sight** is being able to see.

sign **signs, signing, signed**
VERB **1** If you **sign** something, you write your name on it.
NOUN **2** A **sign** is a mark that means something, for example a plus sign (+).
NOUN **3** **Signs** can be words, pictures, or symbols that tell you something.

NOUN **4** You can make a **sign** with your body that means something to other people. For example, if you shake your head, it is a sign that you mean "No."

signal **signals, signaling, signaled**
NOUN **1** A **signal** is a message that is given by signs. A flashing light is a signal that a driver is turning left or right.
VERB **2** If you **signal** to someone, you do something to give them a message.

signature **signatures**
NOUN Your **signature** is the way you write your own name.

sign language
NOUN **Sign language** is a way of communicating using your hands. It is often used by deaf people.

Sikh **Sikhs**
NOUN A **Sikh** is a person who believes in Sikhism, an Indian religion which teaches that there is only one God.

silence
NOUN **Silence** is when there is no noise.

silent
ADJECTIVE **1** If someone or something is **silent**, they are not saying anything or making any noise.
ADJECTIVE **2** A **silent** letter is one that is written, but not pronounced, for example, the "g" in the word "gnat."
See *Silent letters* on page 261.

silhouette **silhouettes**
NOUN A **silhouette** is the outline of a dark shape against a light background.

silk **silks**
NOUN **Silk** is a fine, soft cloth. It is made from threads produced by a kind of caterpillar called a silkworm.
silky ADJECTIVE

silly **sillier, silliest**
ADJECTIVE If someone says you are **silly**, they mean you are behaving in a foolish or childish way.

silver
NOUN **Silver** is a grayish-white metal used for making jewelry.

similar
ADJECTIVE If things are **similar**, they are somewhat alike.

simile **similes**
NOUN A **simile** is an expression in which a person or thing is described as being similar to someone or something else. "She turned as red as a beet" is a simile.

simple **simpler, simplest**
ADJECTIVE Something that is **simple** is easy to do or understand.
simply ADVERB

simplify **simplifies, simplifying, simplified**
VERB To **simplify** something means to make it easier to do or understand.

since

PREPOSITION 1 Since means from a particular time until now. *I've been waiting **since** half past three.*
CONJUNCTION 2 Since also means because. *I had a drink, **since** I was feeling thirsty.*

sincere

ADJECTIVE If you are **sincere**, you say things that you really mean.
sincerely ADVERB

sing sings, singing, sang, sung

VERB 1 If you **sing** a song, you make music with your voice.
VERB 2 When birds **sing**, they make pleasant sounds.

single

ADJECTIVE 1 Single means one of something. *We can't park here. It's a **single** yellow line.*
ADJECTIVE 2 People who are **single** are not married.
ADJECTIVE 3 A **single** bed or bedroom is for one person.
NOUN 4 A **single** in baseball allows the runner to get to first base.

singular

NOUN Singular means one. *The **singular** of "girls" is "girl." The **singular** of "children" is "child."* See **plural**.

sink sinks, sinking, sank, sunk

NOUN 1 A **sink** is a large basin with faucet and a drain.
VERB 2 If something **sinks**, it moves slowly down until it disappears, especially below the surface of water.
VERB 3 To **sink** something sharp into an object means to make it go deeply into it. *The tiger **sank** its teeth into his leg.*

sip sips, sipping, sipped

VERB If you **sip** a drink, you drink it a little at a time.

sir

NOUN Sir is a polite way of addressing a man. *Please **sir**, can I leave early?*

siren sirens

NOUN A **siren** is something that makes a loud, wailing noise as a warning. Fire engines, police cars, and ambulances have sirens.

sister sisters

NOUN Your **sister** is a girl or woman who has the same parents as you.

sit sits, sitting, sat

VERB 1 When you **sit**, you put your bottom on something such as a chair or the floor.
VERB 2 When a bird **sits** on its eggs, it covers them with its body to hatch them.

site sites

NOUN A **site** is a piece of ground that is used for a particular purpose. *Let's stop at the next camp **site**.*

situation situations

NOUN A **situation** is the things that are happening to you. *You have put me in a difficult **situation**.*

size sizes

NOUN 1 The **size** of something is how big or small it is.
NOUN 2 Size is also one in a series of standard measurements for clothing, shoes, and so on.

sizzle sizzles, sizzling, sizzled

VERB If something **sizzles**, it makes a hissing sound. *The meat **sizzled** in the frying pan.*

skate skates

NOUN 1 Skates are ice skates or roller skates.
NOUN 2 A **skate** is an edible flat sea fish.

skateboard skateboards

NOUN A **skateboard** is a narrow board on wheels which you stand on and ride for fun.

skeleton **skeletons**

NOUN Your **skeleton** is all the bones in your body joined together. It supports your body and protects your organs.

sketch **sketches**

NOUN A **sketch** is a quick drawing.

ski **skis**

NOUN **Skis** are long pieces of wood, metal, or plastic that you fasten to special boots so that you can move easily on snow.

skid **skids, skidding, skidded**

VERB If a vehicle **skids**, it slides out of control, for example, because the road is wet or icy.

skill **skills**

NOUN **Skill** is the ability to do something well.

skillful ADJECTIVE

skim **skims, skimming, skimmed**

VERB 1 If you **skim** something from the surface of a liquid, you remove it.

VERB 2 If you **skim** a piece of writing, you read it to get a general idea of what it is about.

skin **skins**

NOUN 1 Your **skin** is the natural covering of your body.

NOUN 2 The **skin** of a fruit or vegetable is its outer covering.

skinny **skinnier, skinniest**

ADJECTIVE A **skinny** person is very thin.

skip **skips, skipping, skipped**

VERB 1 When you **skip**, you move along almost as though you were dancing, with little jumps.

VERB 2 If you **skip** with a rope, you swing the rope over your head and under your feet while jumping.

VERB 3 If you **skip** something, you leave it out. *I'm going to skip lunch.*

skirt **skirts**

NOUN A **skirt** is a piece of clothing worn by women and girls. It hangs from the waist.

skull **skulls**

NOUN Your **skull** is the bony part of your head. It protects your brain, which is inside it.

sky **skies**

NOUN The **sky** is the space around the earth which you can see when you stand outside and look upward.

skyscraper **skyscrapers**

NOUN A **skyscraper** is a very tall building.

slab **slabs**

NOUN A **slab** is a thick, flat piece of something, such as stone or concrete.

slack **slacker, slackest**

ADJECTIVE Something that is **slack** is loose, and not firmly stretched.

slam **slams, slamming, slammed**

VERB If you **slam** a door, you shut it hard so that it makes a loud noise.

slang

NOUN **Slang** is words that you use in everyday talk, but not when you are writing or being polite.

slant **slants, slanting, slanted**

VERB If something **slants**, it is not straight, but lies at an angle.

a
b
c
d
e
f
g
h
i
j
k
l
m
n
o
p
q
r
Ss
t
u
v
w
x
y
z

slap slaps, slapping, slapped

VERB If you **slap** someone, you hit them with the palm of your hand.

slate slates

NOUN **Slate** is a dark gray rock that can be split into thin layers. It is sometimes used for roofs.

sled sleds

NOUN A **sled** is a vehicle on runners used for traveling over snow.

sleek sleeker, sleekest

ADJECTIVE Hair or fur that is **sleek** is smooth and shiny.

sleep sleeps, sleeping, slept

VERB When you **sleep**, you close your eyes and your whole body rests.

sleepy ADJECTIVE

sleet

NOUN **Sleet** is a mixture of snow and rain.

sleeve sleeves

NOUN The **sleeves** of a coat or sweater are the parts that cover your arms.

sleigh sleighs

NOUN A **sleigh** is a sled pulled by animals.

slept

VERB **Slept** is the past tense of **sleep**.

slice slices, slicing, sliced

NOUN **1** A **slice** is a thin piece of food that has been cut from a larger piece.

VERB **2** If you **slice** food, you cut it into thin pieces.

slide slides, sliding, slid

VERB **1** When something **slides**, it moves smoothly over a surface.

NOUN **2** A **slide** is a piece of playground equipment for sliding down.

slight slighter, slightest

ADJECTIVE Something that is **slight** is small. *She has a slight cut.*

slightly ADVERB

slim slimmer, slimmest

ADJECTIVE Someone who is **slim** has a body that is thin, but not too thin.

slime

NOUN **Slime** is a thick, slippery substance which covers a surface and which looks unpleasant. *The pond was covered in green slime.*

slimy ADJECTIVE

sling slings, slinging, slung

NOUN **1** A **sling** is a piece of cloth which you hang from your neck to support a broken or injured arm.

VERB **2** If you **sling** something somewhere, you throw it carelessly.

slip slips, slipping, slipped

VERB **1** If you **slip**, you accidentally slide and lose your balance.

VERB **2** If you **slip** somewhere, you go there quickly and quietly. *She slipped out of the house.*

NOUN **3** A **slip** of paper is a small piece of paper.

slipper slippers

NOUN **Slippers** are soft, loose shoes that people wear in the house.

slippery

ADJECTIVE Something that is **slippery** is smooth, wet, or greasy. It is difficult to keep hold of or to walk on.

slit slits, slitting, slit

VERB **1** If you **slit** something, you make a long narrow cut in it. *He slit open the envelope.*

NOUN **2** A **slit** is a long narrow opening in something.

a b c d e f g h i j k l m n o p q r **Ss** t u v w x y z

slope slopes

NOUN A **slope** is a flat surface which has one end higher than the other.

slot slots

NOUN A **slot** is a narrow opening in something, usually for putting coins in.

slow slower, slowest

ADJECTIVE **1** Something that is **slow** moves along without much speed.
ADJECTIVE **2** If a watch or clock is **slow**, it shows a time that is earlier than the correct time.
slowly ADVERB

slug slugs

NOUN A **slug** is a small, slow-moving animal with a long, slimy body, like a snail, but without a shell.

sly slier, sliest

ADJECTIVE Someone who is **sly** is good at tricking people in a not very nice way.

smack smacks, smacking, smacked

VERB If a person **smacks** someone, they hit them with an open hand.

small smaller, smallest

ADJECTIVE Something that is **small** is not as large as other things of the same kind.

smart smarter, smartest

ADJECTIVE Someone who is **smart** is intelligent.

smash smashes, smashing, smashed

VERB **1** If something **smashes**, it falls and hits the ground. It makes a loud noise and breaks into lots of pieces. *The cup **smashed** when she dropped it.*
VERB **2** If someone or something **smashes** an object, they drop it or hit it so that it breaks into lots of pieces.

smell smells, smelling, smelled, or smelt

VERB **1** When you **smell** something, you notice it with your nose.
VERB **2** If something **smells** nice or nasty, people's noses tell them about it.
NOUN **3** Your sense of **smell** is your ability to smell things.

smile smiles, smiling, smiled

VERB When you **smile**, the corners of your mouth move upward and you look happy.

smoke smokes, smoking, smoked

NOUN **1** **Smoke** is a mixture of gas and small particles sent into the air when something burns.
VERB **2** If something is **smoking**, smoke is coming from it.

smooth smoother, smoothest

ADJECTIVE **1** Something which is **smooth** has no roughness, lumps, or holes in it.
ADJECTIVE **2** A **smooth** ride is one that is comfortable because there are no bumps.

smother smothers, smothering, smothered

VERB **1** If someone **smothers** a fire, they cover it with something in order to put it out.
VERB **2** If a lot of things **smother** something, they cover it all over. *The grass was **smothered** in daisies.*

smudge smudges, smudging, smudged

NOUN **1** A **smudge** is a dirty mark left on something.
VERB **2** If you **smudge** something, you make it dirty by touching it.

smug smugger, smuggest

ADJECTIVE Someone who is **smug** is too pleased with how good or clever they are.

smuggle smuggles, smuggling, smuggled

VERB To **smuggle** things or people into or out of a place means to take them there secretly, or against the law.

snack snacks

NOUN A **snack** is a small amount of food that you eat quickly. *I had an apple and some potato chips for a **snack**.*

a
b
c
d
e
f
g
h
i
j
k
l
m
n
o
p
q
r
Ss
t
u
v
w
x
y
z

snag snags

NOUN A **snag** is a small problem.

snail snails

NOUN A **snail** is a small, slow-moving animal with a shell on its back.

snake snakes

NOUN A **snake** is a long, thin reptile with scales on its skin and no legs. See *Reptiles* on page 259.

snap snaps, snapping, snapped

VERB **1** If something **snaps**, it breaks suddenly with a sharp, cracking noise.
VERB **2** If a dog **snaps** at you, it tries to bite you.
VERB **3** If someone **snaps** at you, they speak crossly.

snarl snarls, snarling, snarled

VERB When an animal **snarls**, it makes a fierce sound in its throat while showing its teeth.

snatch snatches, snatching, snatched

VERB If you **snatch** something, you take it quickly and suddenly.

sneak sneaks, sneaking, sneaked

VERB If you **sneak** somewhere, you go there very quietly, being careful that other people do not see or hear you.

sneer sneers, sneering, sneered

VERB If a person **sneers** at something, they show that they don't like it much.

sneeze sneezes, sneezing, sneezed

VERB When you **sneeze**, you blow out suddenly through your nose, making a loud noise.

sniff sniffs, sniffing, sniffed

VERB If you **sniff**, you breathe in through your nose hard enough to make a sound.

snooze snoozes, snoozing, snoozed

VERB If you **snooze**, you sleep lightly for a short time, especially during the day.

snore snores, snoring, snored

VERB When people **snore**, they breathe very noisily while they are sleeping.

snorkel snorkels

NOUN A **snorkel** is a tube that you breathe through when your face is just under the surface of the water.

snow snows, snowing, snowed

NOUN **1** Snow is flakes of ice crystals which fall from the sky in cold weather.
VERB **2** When it **snows**, snow falls from the sky.

snowball snowballs

NOUN A **snowball** is a ball of snow for throwing.

snowflake snowflakes

NOUN A **snowflake** is a soft piece of falling snow.

snowman snowmen

NOUN A **snowman** is a pile of snow that is made to look like a person.

snug snugger, snuggest

ADJECTIVE If you feel **snug**, you are warm and comfortable.

snuggle snuggles, snuggling, snuggled

VERB If you **snuggle** somewhere, you cuddle up to something or someone.

soak soaks, soaking, soaked

VERB **1** When liquid **soaks** something, it makes it very wet.
VERB **2** When something **soaks** up a liquid, the liquid is drawn up into it.

spill spills, spilling, spilled
VERB If you **spill** a liquid, you let it flow out of a container by mistake.

spin spins, spinning, spun
VERB **1** If something **spins**, it turns around and around quickly.
VERB **2** When someone **spins**, they make thread by twisting together pieces of fiber using a machine.
VERB **3** When spiders **spin**, they give out a sticky thread and make it into a web.

spinach
NOUN **Spinach** is a vegetable with large, green leaves.
See *Vegetables on page 256.*

spine spines
NOUN **1** Your **spine** is your backbone.
NOUN **2** Spines are long, sharp points on an animal's body or on a plant.

spiral spirals
NOUN A **spiral** is a continuous curve which winds around and around, with each curve above or outside the previous one.

spire spires
NOUN The **spire** of a church is the tall, cone-shaped structure on top.

spite spites, spiting, spited
VERB If you do something to **spite** someone, you do it deliberately to hurt or annoy them.
in spite of PHRASE When you say that you are doing something **in spite of** something else, you mean that you are not going to let it stop you. *In spite of the rain, I'm still going out.*

spiteful
ADJECTIVE A **spiteful** person does or says nasty things to people to hurt them.
spitefully ADVERB

splash splashes, splashing, splashed
VERB **1** If you **splash** around in water, you disturb the water in a noisy way.

VERB **2** If liquid **splashes** something, it scatters over it in a lot of small drops.
NOUN **3** A **splash** is the sound made when something hits or falls into water.

splendid
ADJECTIVE **Splendid** means extremely good.

splinter splinters, splintering, splintered
NOUN **1** A **splinter** is a thin, sharp piece of wood or glass which has broken off a larger piece.
VERB **2** If something **splinters**, it breaks into thin sharp pieces.

split splits, splitting, split
VERB **1** If something is **split**, it divides into two or more. *The village was **split** in two by the new road.*
VERB **2** If people **split** something between them, they share it.

spoil spoils, spoiling, spoiled
VERB **1** If you **spoil** something, you damage it, or make it less good than it was.
VERB **2** To **spoil** children means to give them everything they want, so that they become selfish.

spoke spokes
VERB **1** Spoke is the past tense of **speak**.
NOUN **2** The **spokes** of a wheel are the bars which connect the hub to the rim.

spoken
VERB **Spoken** is the past participle of **speak**.

sponge sponges
NOUN **1** A **sponge** is a soft thing with holes in it. It soaks up water and you use it for washing things.

NOUN **2** A **sponge** or **sponge cake** is a very light cake.

spoon

spoon spoons

NOUN A **spoon** is a utensil with a handle. It is used for eating, mixing, or serving food.

sport sports

NOUN **Sports** are games that you play which exercise your body.

spot spots, spotting, spotted

NOUN **1** **Spots** are small, round marks on a surface. Some fabrics have a pattern of spots.

NOUN **2** A **spot** can be a particular place. *This would be a nice* ***spot*** *for a picnic.*

NOUN **3** A **spot** can also be a small mark on a person's skin.

VERB **4** If you **spot** something, you notice it.

spotless

ADJECTIVE Something that is **spotless** is perfectly clean.

spout spouts

NOUN A **spout** is a tube with an end like a lip, for pouring liquid. *Teapots have a* ***spout***.

sprang

VERB **Sprang** is the past tense of **spring**.

sprawl sprawls, sprawling, sprawled

VERB If you **sprawl**, you sit or lie with your legs and arms spread out.

spray sprays, spraying, sprayed

NOUN **1** **Spray** is lots of small drops of liquid splashed or forced into the air.

VERB **2** To **spray** a liquid over something means to cover it with small drops of the liquid.

spread spreads, spreading, spread

VERB **1** If you **spread** something, you arrange it over a surface. *They* ***spread*** *their wet clothes out to dry.*

VERB **2** If you **spread** something, such as butter, you put a thin layer of it onto something.

VERB **3** If you **spread** parts of your body, such as your arms, you stretch them out until they are far apart.

spring springs, springing, sprang, sprung

NOUN **1** **Spring** is the season between winter and summer.

NOUN **2** A **spring** is a coil of wire which returns to its shape after being pressed or pulled.

NOUN **3** A **spring** is also a place where water comes up through the ground.

VERB **4** To **spring** means to jump. *The leopard* ***sprang*** *on its prey.*

springbok springboks

NOUN A **springbok** is a small South African antelope which moves in leaps.

sprinkle sprinkles, sprinkling, sprinkled

VERB If you **sprinkle** a liquid or powder over something, you scatter it over it.

sprint sprints, sprinting, sprinted

VERB To **sprint** means to run fast over a short distance.

sprout sprouts, sprouting, sprouted

VERB **1** When something **sprouts**, it starts to grow.

NOUN **2** **Sprouts** are small, round, green vegetables.

See *Vegetables* on page 256.

sprung

VERB **Sprung** is the past participle of **spring**.

spun

VERB **Spun** is the past tense of **spin**.

spurt spurts, spurting, spurted

VERB When a liquid or flame **spurts** out, it comes out quickly in a powerful stream. *Blood* ***spurted*** *from his arm.*

sudden

ADJECTIVE Something that is **sudden** happens quickly and unexpectedly.
suddenly ADVERB

suffer   **suffers, suffering, suffered**

VERB If someone is **suffering**, they feel pain or sadness.

suffix   **suffixes**

NOUN A **suffix** is a group of letters which is added to the end of a word to form a new word, for example "-able" or "-ful."
See *Suffixes* on page 265.

sugar

NOUN **Sugar** is a sweet substance used to sweeten food and drinks.

suggest   **suggests, suggesting, suggested**

VERB If you **suggest** something to someone, you give a plan or an idea for them to think about.
suggestion NOUN

suit   **suits, suiting, suited**

NOUN **1** A **suit** is a matching jacket and pants or skirt.
VERB **2** If something **suits** you, it is right for you.

suitable

ADJECTIVE Something that is **suitable** for a particular purpose is right for it. *Are these shoes **suitable** for running?*

suitcase   **suitcases**

NOUN A **suitcase** is a case that you carry clothes in when you are traveling.

sulk   **sulks, sulking, sulked**

VERB If you **sulk**, you are silent and bad-tempered for a while because you are annoyed about something.

sultana   **sultanas**

NOUN A **sultana** is a dried white grape.

sum   **sums**

NOUN **1** A **sum** is an amount of money.
NOUN **2** In math, the **sum** is the answer or total that you get when you add numbers. *The **sum** of 2 and 3 is 5.*

summarize   **summarizes, summarizing, summarized**

VERB To **summarize** something means to give a short account of its main points.

summary   **summaries**

NOUN If you give a **summary** of something, you give the main points.

summer   **summers**

NOUN **Summer** is the season between spring and autumn.

summit   **summits**

NOUN The **summit** of a mountain is its top.

sun   **suns**

NOUN The **sun** is the star that gives us heat and light.

sunburn

NOUN **Sunburn** is sore skin on someone's body when they have been in the sun for too long.

Sunday   **Sundays**

NOUN **Sunday** is the day between Saturday and Monday.

sundial   **sundials**

NOUN A **sundial** is an object that uses the sun to tell the time. It has a pointer that casts a shadow on a flat base marked with the hours.

sunflower

sunflower **sunflowers**
NOUN A **sunflower** is a tall plant with large yellow flowers.

sung
VERB **Sung** is the past participle of **sing**.

sunglasses
PLURAL NOUN **Sunglasses** are glasses with dark lenses that you wear to protect your eyes from the sun.

sunk
VERB **Sunk** is the past participle of **sink**.

sunlight
NOUN **Sunlight** is the bright light produced when the sun is shining.
sunlit ADJECTIVE

sunny **sunnier, sunniest**
ADJECTIVE When the weather is **sunny**, the sun is shining brightly.

sunrise **sunrises**
NOUN **Sunrise** is the time in the morning when the sun comes up.

sunset **sunsets**
NOUN **Sunset** is the time in the evening when the sun goes down.

sunshine
NOUN **Sunshine** is the bright light produced when the sun is shining.

super
ADJECTIVE **Super** means very nice or very good. *We've just seen a **super** movie.*

super-
PREFIX **Super-** is added to words to describe something that is larger or better, for example "supermarket."
See *Prefixes* on page 264.

superlative **superlatives**
NOUN In grammar, the **superlative** is the form of an adjective which has "the most" of that adjective. For example, "fattest" is the superlative of "fat."
See *Adjective* on page 263.

supermarket **supermarkets**
NOUN A **supermarket** is a large store which sells all kinds of food and things for the house.

supersonic
ADJECTIVE A **supersonic** aircraft can travel faster than the speed of sound.

superstitious
ADJECTIVE People who are **superstitious** believe in things like magic and powers that bring good or bad luck.

supper **suppers**
NOUN **Supper** is a meal or snack eaten in the evening.

supply **supplies, supplying, supplied**
VERB **1** If someone **supplies** you with something, they provide you with it.
NOUN **2** A **supply** of something is the amount of it which someone has. *The water **supply** is getting very low.*

support **supports, supporting, supported**
VERB **1** If you **support** someone, you want them to do well.
VERB **2** If something **supports** an object, it holds it up firmly.

suppose **supposes, supposing, supposed**
VERB **1** If you **suppose** that something is true, you think that it is likely to be true.
CONJUNCTION **2** You can use **suppose** or **supposing** when you are thinking about doing something. ***Supposing** we just left without saying anything, what do you think would happen?*
I suppose PHRASE You can say **I suppose** when you are not certain about something. *Yes, **I suppose** he could come.*

swallow

sure

ADJECTIVE **1** If you are **sure** something is true, you believe it is true.
ADJECTIVE **2** If something is **sure** to happen, it will definitely happen.
ADJECTIVE **3** If you are **sure** of yourself, you are very confident.
make sure PHRASE If you **make sure** of something, you check it. *Can you make sure we locked up properly?*

surf surfs, surfing, surfed

NOUN **1 Surf** is the white foam that forms on the top of waves when they break.
VERB **2** When you **surf**, you ride toward the shore on top of a large wave while standing on a special board.

VERB **3** When you **surf** the Internet, you go from web site to web site.

surface surfaces

NOUN The **surface** of something is the top or outside area of it.

surgeon surgeons

NOUN A **surgeon** is a doctor who performs operations.

surgery surgeries

NOUN **Surgery** is medical treatment in which part of the patient's body is cut open.

surname surnames

NOUN Your **surname** is the name you share with other members of your family. Typically, it is your last name.

surprise surprises

NOUN A **surprise** is something unexpected.

surrender surrenders, surrendering, surrendered

VERB If someone **surrenders**, they stop fighting and agree that they have lost.

surround surrounds, surrounding, surrounded

VERB If something **surrounds** something else, it is all around it.

surroundings

PLURAL NOUN Your **surroundings** are the area around you.

survey surveys

NOUN **1** A **survey** of something is a detailed examination of it, often in the form of a report.
VERB **2** A **survey** is also a set of questions to find out what people think about things.

survive survives, surviving, survived

VERB If someone **survives**, they continue to live after being close to death.

suspect suspects, suspecting, suspected

VERB If you **suspect** someone of doing something wrong, you think they have done it.

suspense

NOUN **Suspense** is excitement or worry caused by having to wait for something.

suspicious

ADJECTIVE **1** If you are **suspicious** of someone, you do not trust them.
ADJECTIVE **2** If something is **suspicious**, it makes you feel something is wrong.

swallow swallows, swallowing, swallowed

VERB **1** When you **swallow** food or drink, it goes down your throat.
NOUN **2** A **swallow** is a small bird with pointed wings and a long, forked tail.

217

swam

VERB **Swam** is the past tense of **swim**.

swamp swamps

NOUN A **swamp** is an area of extremely wet land.

swan swans

NOUN A **swan** is a large, white bird with a long neck that lives on rivers and lakes.

swap swaps, swapping, swapped

VERB If you **swap** something, you give it to someone and receive something else from them in exchange.

swarm swarms

NOUN A **swarm** is a large group of bees or other insects flying together.
See *Collective nouns* on page 262.

sway sways, swaying, swayed

VERB When people or things **sway**, they lean or swing slowly from side to side.

sweat

NOUN **Sweat** is the salty liquid which comes from your skin when you are hot.

sweater sweaters

NOUN A **sweater** is a knitted piece of clothing covering your upper body and arms.

sweatshirt sweatshirts

NOUN A **sweatshirt** is a piece of clothing made of thick cotton. It covers your upper body and arms.

sweep sweeps, sweeping, swept

VERB If you **sweep** a floor or a path, you clean it by pushing a broom over it.

sweet sweeter, sweetest; sweets

ADJECTIVE **1** Food or drink that is **sweet** has a taste of sugar.

PLURAL NOUN **2 Sweets** are things such as chocolates and candy.

ADJECTIVE **3** A **sweet** person is good-natured, gentle, and kind.

sweet corn

NOUN **Sweet corn** is a long stalk covered with juicy yellow seeds that can be eaten as a vegetable.
See *Vegetables* on page 256.

swell swells, swelling, swelled or swollen

VERB If something **swells**, it becomes larger and rounder than usual.

swept

VERB **Swept** is the past tense of **sweep**.

swerve swerves, swerving, swerved

VERB If something that is moving **swerves**, it suddenly changes direction.

swift swifter, swiftest

ADJECTIVE Something that is **swift** can move very quickly.

swim swims, swimming, swam, swum

VERB When you **swim**, you use your arms and legs to move through water.

swimming

NOUN **Swimming** is the activity of moving yourself through water.

swimming pool swimming pools

NOUN A **swimming pool** is a place made for people to swim in.

swimsuit swimsuits

NOUN A **swimsuit** is clothing worn for swimming; also called a bathing suit.

swine

NOUN **1** A **swine** is a pig or a hog.

NOUN **2** **Swine** also means a hateful, vicious, or greedy person.

swing swings, swinging, swung

VERB **1** If something **swings**, it keeps moving backward and forward, or from side to side, while it is hanging.

NOUN **2** A **swing** is a seat that hangs from a frame and moves backward and forward when you sit on it.

switch switches, switching, switched

NOUN **1** A **switch** is a small control for a piece of equipment such as a light or radio.

VERB **2** To **switch** is to change one thing for another. *I switched to another school when my family moved.*

swollen

ADJECTIVE Something that is **swollen** has swelled up.

swoop swoops, swooping, swooped

VERB When a bird **swoops**, it suddenly flies downward in a smooth curve.

sword swords

NOUN A **sword** is a weapon with a long blade and a short handle.

swum

VERB **Swum** is the past participle of **swim**.

swung

VERB **Swung** is the past tense of **swing**.

sycamore sycamores

NOUN A **sycamore** is a tree that has large five-pointed leaves.

syllable syllables

NOUN Each beat in a word is a **syllable**. For example, "cat" has one syllable, and "cattle" has two.

symbol symbols

NOUN A **symbol** is a sign or mark that stands for something else. For example, the symbol + stands for "plus."

symmetrical

ADJECTIVE If something is **symmetrical**, it has two halves that are exactly the same, except that one half is like a reflection of the other half.

symmetry

NOUN **1** **Symmetry** is when one half of something is exactly like a mirror image of the other half.

NOUN **2** The **line of symmetry** is the dividing line between two symmetrical halves.

sympathy

NOUN If you feel **sympathy** for someone who is unhappy, you are sorry for them.

synagogue synagogues

NOUN A **synagogue** is a building where Jewish people gather to worship.

synonym synonyms

NOUN **Synonyms** are words that have the same or similar meaning. The words "nice" and "pleasant" are synonyms. See *Synonyms* on page 266.

syrup

NOUN **Syrup** is a thick, sweet liquid made by boiling sugar with water.

system systems

NOUN **1** A **system** is a way of doing something. *I've got a new system for organizing my toys.*

NOUN **2** You can refer to a set of equipment as a **system**, for example, a central heating system.

a b c d e f g h i j k l m n o p q r **Ss** t u v w x y z

Tt

table tables
NOUN **1** A **table** is a piece of furniture with a flat top for putting things on.
NOUN **2** A **table** is also a set of facts or figures arranged in rows or columns.

tablet tablets
NOUN A **tablet** is a small, round pill made of powdered medicine.

table tennis
NOUN **Table tennis** is another name for ping pong. You use paddles to hit a small hollow ball over a low net across a table.

tackle tackles, tackling, tackled
VERB **1** If you **tackle** a difficult task, you deal with it in a determined way.
VERB **2** If you **tackle** someone in a game such as football, you try to get the ball away from them.

tactful
ADJECTIVE A **tactful** person is careful not to hurt someone else's feelings.
tactfully ADVERB

tadpole tadpoles
NOUN **Tadpoles** are small water animals that grow into frogs or toads. They have long tails and round, black heads.

tail tails
NOUN **1** A **tail** is the part of an animal, bird, or fish that grows out of the end of its body.
NOUN **2** The back part of a plane is called the **tail**.

take takes, taking, took, taken
VERB **1** If you **take** something, you put your hand around it and carry it. *Let me take your coat.*
VERB **2** If someone **takes** you somewhere, you go there with them.
VERB **3** If a person **takes** something that does not belong to them, they steal it.
VERB **4** If you **take away** one number or amount from another, you find out how much is left.

talcum powder
NOUN **Talcum powder**, or **talc**, is a soft powder which you put on your skin to help dry it and make it smell nice.

tale tales
NOUN A **tale** is a story.

talent talents
NOUN **Talent** is the natural ability a person has to do something well.

talk talks, talking, talked
VERB When you **talk**, you say things to someone.

talkative
ADJECTIVE Someone who is **talkative** talks a lot.

tall taller, tallest
ADJECTIVE **1** Someone who is **tall** stands higher than a lot of other people.
ADJECTIVE **2** You use **tall** to say how high somebody or something is. *My little brother is only three feet tall.*

tally tallies
NOUN A **tally** is a record of amounts which you add to as you go along.

tame tamer, tamest
ADJECTIVE A **tame** animal is not afraid of humans and will not hurt them.

tan

NOUN If someone has a **tan**, their skin has become darker than it usually is because they have been in the sun.

tangle **tangles, tangling, tangled**

NOUN **1** A **tangle** is a mass of things, such as hairs or fibers, that are knotted or coiled together and are hard to separate.
VERB **2** If something is **tangled**, it is twisted in knots.

tank **tanks**

NOUN **1** A **tank** is a large container for liquid or gas.
NOUN **2** A **tank** is also a vehicle for soldiers which moves on tracks. Tanks are covered with strong metal armor, and have guns or rockets.

tanker **tankers**

NOUN A **tanker** is a cargo ship that carries gas or liquid.

tap **taps, tapping, tapped**

NOUN **1** A **tap** is a handle which controls the flow of gas or liquid from a pipe.
VERB **2** If you **tap** something, you hit it lightly.

tape **tapes**

NOUN **1** Tape is a strip of sticky material which you use to stick things together.
NOUN **2** A **tape** is a long thin magnetic strip that you can record sounds or pictures on.

tape measure **tape measures**

NOUN A **tape measure** is a strip of plastic or metal that is marked in centimeters or inches. It is used to measure things.

tape recorder **tape recorders**

NOUN A **tape recorder** is a machine that records and plays sound on tape.

tar

NOUN **Tar** is a thick black substance that is used for making roads.

target **targets**

NOUN A **target** is something that people aim at and try to hit.

tart **tarts**

NOUN A **tart** is a piece of pastry filled with jam or fruit.

task **tasks**

NOUN A **task** is a piece of work which has to be done.

tassel **tassels**

NOUN A **tassel** is a tuft of loose threads tied by a knot and used for decoration.

taste **tastes, tasting, tasted**

NOUN **1** Your sense of **taste** is your ability to recognize the flavor of things in your mouth.
VERB **2** When you **taste** food, you take a little bit to see what it is like.

tasty **tastier, tastiest**

ADJECTIVE Something that is **tasty** has a pleasant flavor.

taught

VERB **Taught** is the past tense of **teach**.

tax **taxes**

NOUN **Tax** is money that people have to pay to the government.

taxi **taxis**

NOUN A **taxi** is a car that people pay to be driven somewhere in.

tea **teas**

NOUN **1** Tea is a drink made by pouring boiling water onto the dried leaves of the tea plant.
NOUN **2** Tea is also an afternoon meal.

tea bag **tea bags**

NOUN A **tea bag** is a small paper bag with tea leaves in it which is put in boiling water to make tea.

teach **teaches, teaching, taught**

VERB If someone **teaches** you something, they tell or show you how to do it.

teacher **teachers**

NOUN A **teacher** is a person whose job is to help people learn.

a
b
c
d
e
f
g
h
i
j
k
l
m
n
o
p
q
r
s
Tt
u
v
w
x
y
z

team **teams**
NOUN A **team** is a number of people working or playing together.

teapot **teapots**
NOUN A **teapot** is a container for making tea. It has a lid, a handle, and a spout.

tear **tears, tearing, tore, torn**
(*rhymes with* **fear**) NOUN **1** Tears are the drops of liquid that come out of your eyes when you cry.
(*rhymes with* **fair**) VERB **2** If you **tear** something, such as paper or fabric, you pull it apart.

tease **teases, teasing, teased**
VERB If someone **teases** you, they make fun of you.

teaspoon **teaspoons**
NOUN A **teaspoon** is a small spoon used for stirring drinks.

technology
NOUN **Technology** is the practical use of science in areas such as industry, farming, or medicine.

teddy bear **teddy bears**
NOUN A **teddy bear** is a child's soft toy which looks like a friendly bear.

teenager **teenagers**
NOUN A **teenager** is someone from 13 to 19 years of age.

teeth
NOUN **Teeth** is the plural of **tooth**.

telephone **telephones**
NOUN A **telephone**, or **phone**, is an instrument for talking to someone else who is in another place.

telescope **telescopes**
NOUN A **telescope** is an instrument for making objects that are far away look nearer and larger.

television **televisions**
NOUN A **television** is a machine that receives signals through the air or on cable and changes them into pictures and sounds.

tell **tells, telling, told**
VERB **1** If you **tell** someone something, you let them know about it.
VERB **2** If someone **tells** you to do something, they say you must do it.
VERB **3** If you **tell** the time, you find out what the time is by looking at a clock.

temper
NOUN **1** Someone's **temper** is how cheerful or how angry they are feeling.
NOUN **2** If you lose your **temper**, you become angry.

temperature **temperatures**
NOUN The **temperature** of something is how hot or cold it is.

temple **temples**
NOUN A **temple** is a building used for the worship of a god in various religions.

temporary
ADJECTIVE Something that is **temporary** only lasts for a short time.

tempt **tempts, tempting, tempted**
VERB If something **tempts** you, you want to do it, but you think it might be wrong.
tempting ADJECTIVE

tender
ADJECTIVE **1** Someone who is **tender** shows gentle and caring feelings.
ADJECTIVE **2** Meat or other food which is **tender** is very easy to cut or chew.

tennis
NOUN **Tennis** is a game for two or four players in which a ball is hit over a net.

tense **tenser, tensest; tenses**
ADJECTIVE **1** If you are **tense**, you are nervous and cannot relax.
NOUN **2** The **tense** of a verb is the form which shows whether you are talking about the past, present, or future.

tent **tents**
NOUN A **tent** is a shelter made of canvas or nylon, held up by poles and ropes.

tentacle **tentacles**
NOUN The **tentacles** of an animal, such as an octopus, are its long thin arms.

term **terms**
NOUN A **term** is one of the periods that each year is divided into at school.

terrace **terraces**
NOUN A **terrace** is a paved open area next to a house.

terrible
ADJECTIVE Something **terrible** is serious and unpleasant.
terribly ADVERB

terrify **terrifies, terrifying, terrified**
VERB If something **terrifies** you, it makes you feel extremely frightened.

territory **territories**
NOUN **1** The **territory** of a country is the land that it controls.
NOUN **2** An animal's **territory** is an area that it considers its own and defends when other animals try to enter it.

terror
NOUN **Terror** is great fear or panic.

test **tests, testing, tested**
VERB **1** If someone **tests** something, they try to find out whether it works properly.
NOUN **2** A **test** is something you have to do to show how much you know.

tetrahedron **tetrahedrons** or **tetrahedra**
NOUN A **tetrahedron** is a solid shape with four triangular faces.
See *Solid shapes* on page 271.

text **texts**
NOUN **Text** is any written material.

textbook **textbooks**
NOUN A **textbook** is a book about a particular subject for students to use.

than
PREPOSITION OR CONJUNCTION You use **than** to link two things that you are comparing. *She's older **than** me.*

thank **thanks, thanking, thanked**
VERB You **thank** people when you are grateful for something they have done.

that **those**
ADJECTIVE **1** You use **that** or **those** to describe something which is not the nearest one. *Give me **that** book, please.*
PRONOUN **2** You can use **that** or **those** to refer to people or things which have already been mentioned. *What about going by bus? Is **that** a good idea?*

thatched
ADJECTIVE A **thatched** roof is one made of straw or reeds.

thaw **thaws, thawing, thawed**
VERB When something that is frozen **thaws**, it melts.

theater **theaters**
NOUN A **theater** is a building where you go to see a play or movie.

their
ADJECTIVE **Their** refers to something belonging or relating to people or things that have already been mentioned. *Leave it to Sam and Joe. It's **their** problem.*

them
PRONOUN **Them** refers to people or things which have already been mentioned. *I don't want any sprouts. I don't like **them**.*

theme **themes**
NOUN A **theme** is the main idea in a piece of writing, painting, movie, or music.

themselves

PRONOUN If people do something **themselves**, no one else does it. *My parents had to educate **themselves**.*

then

ADVERB **Then** refers to a particular time in the past or future. *I left the room **then**.*

there

ADVERB **1 There** means in, at, or to that place. *He's sitting over **there**.*
PRONOUN **2 There** is used to say that something exists or does not exist. *Are **there** any more chips?*

therefore

ADVERB **Therefore** means as a result. *It was raining, **therefore** we stayed indoors.*

thermometer **thermometers**

NOUN A **thermometer** is an instrument that measures temperature.

thesaurus **thesauruses**

NOUN A **thesaurus** is a book in which words with similar meanings are grouped together.

these

ADJECTIVE OR PRONOUN **These** is the plural of **this**.

thick **thicker, thickest**

ADJECTIVE **1** An object that is **thick** has greater depth or width than other things of the same kind. *I'll have a **thick** slice, please.*
ADJECTIVE **2** Something that is **thick** is made up of a lot of things growing closely together. *She has long, **thick** hair.*
ADJECTIVE **3 Thick** liquids do not flow easily.

thief **thieves**

NOUN A **thief** is a person who steals something.

thigh **thighs**

NOUN Your **thighs** are the top parts of your legs above your knees.

thin **thinner, thinnest**

ADJECTIVE **1** Something that is **thin** is much narrower than it is long. *The witch's nose was long and **thin**.*
ADJECTIVE **2** A **thin** person weighs less than most people of the same height.
ADJECTIVE **3** Something such as paper or cloth that is **thin** has only a small distance between front and back.
ADJECTIVE **4 Thin** liquids are watery.

thing **things**

NOUN **1** A **thing** is an object, rather than an animal or human being.
PLURAL NOUN **2** Your **things** are your clothes or possessions.

think **thinks, thinking, thought**

VERB **1** When you **think**, you use your mind to consider ideas or problems.
VERB **2** If you say you **think** something is true, you mean you believe it is true, but you are not sure.

third person

NOUN In grammar, the **third person** refers to a person, thing, or group. It is expressed as "he," "she," "it," or "they."

thirsty

ADJECTIVE If you are **thirsty**, you feel that you need to drink something.
thirstily ADVERB

this **these**

ADJECTIVE **1 This** is used to refer to someone or something that is nearby. *Would you like to borrow **this** book?*
PRONOUN **2** You can use **this** to introduce someone. ***This** is Ranjit.*

thistle **thistles**

NOUN A **thistle** is a wild plant with prickly leaves and purple flowers.

thorn **thorns**

NOUN A **thorn** is one of the sharp points on the stem of a plant, such as a rose.

thorough

ADJECTIVE **1** Someone who is **thorough** is always careful in their work.
ADJECTIVE **2** A **thorough** action is one that is done carefully and completely. *The doctor gave him a **thorough** examination.*
thoroughly ADVERB

those

ADJECTIVE OR PRONOUN **Those** is the plural of **that**.

though

CONJUNCTION **1** You say **though** before something that makes another part of the sentence rather surprising. *She didn't take a coat, **though** it was raining.*
CONJUNCTION **2** You can use **though** to mean if. *It looks as **though** you were right.*

thought **thoughts**

VERB **1 Thought** is the past tense of **think**.
NOUN **2** A **thought** is an idea that you have in your mind.
NOUN **3 Thought** is the action of thinking carefully about something.

thoughtful

ADJECTIVE **1** If someone is **thoughtful**, they are thinking a lot.
ADJECTIVE **2** A **thoughtful** person remembers what other people want or need, and tries to be kind to them.
thoughtfully ADVERB

thoughtless

ADJECTIVE If you are **thoughtless**, you do not think about what other people feel.

thousand

NOUN A **thousand** is the number 1000.

thread **threads, threading, threaded**

NOUN **1** A **thread** is a long, fine piece of cotton, silk, nylon, or wool.
VERB **2** When you **thread** a needle, you put thread through the hole in the top.

threat **threats**

NOUN A **threat** is a warning that something unpleasant may happen.

threaten **threatens, threatening, threatened**

VERB If someone **threatens** you, they say that something unpleasant may happen if you do not do what they want.

three-dimensional

ADJECTIVE A **three-dimensional** or **3D** object or shape is not flat. It has height or depth, as well as length and width.
See *Solid shapes* on page 271.

threw

VERB **Threw** is the past tense of **throw**.

thrill **thrills**

NOUN A **thrill** is a sudden feeling of great excitement or pleasure.
thrilling ADJECTIVE

throat **throats**

NOUN **1** Your **throat** is the back of your mouth and the top part of the passages inside your neck.
NOUN **2** The front part of your neck is also called your **throat**.

throb **throbs, throbbing, throbbed**

VERB **1** If a part of your body **throbs**, you feel a series of strong beats or dull pains.
VERB **2** If something **throbs**, it vibrates and makes a loud rhythmic noise.

throne **thrones**

NOUN A **throne** is a special chair used by kings and queens on important occasions.

through

PREPOSITION **Through** means moving from one side of something to the other. *We found a path **through** the woods.*

a
b
c
d
e
f
g
h
i
j
k
l
m
n
o
p
q
r
s
Tt
u
v
w
x
y
z

throw

throw throws, throwing, threw, thrown
VERB If you **throw** an object that you are holding, you send it through the air.

thrush thrushes
NOUN A **thrush** is a songbird with a brown back and a pale spotted chest.

thrust thrusts, thrusting, thrust
VERB If you **thrust** something somewhere, you push or move it there quickly with a lot of force.

thud thuds
NOUN A **thud** is a dull sound, such as a heavy object makes when it falls onto a carpet.

thumb thumbs
NOUN Your **thumb** is the short, thick finger on the side of your hand.

thump thumps, thumping, thumped
VERB If you **thump** something, you hit it hard, usually with your fist. *He shouted and **thumped** the table.*

thunder
NOUN **Thunder** is the loud noise that you hear after a flash of lightning, in a storm.

thunderstorm thunderstorms
NOUN A **thunderstorm** is a storm with thunder, lightning, and heavy rain.

Thursday Thursdays
NOUN **Thursday** is the day between Wednesday and Friday.

tick ticks
NOUN A **tick** is an insect that attaches to your skin.

ticket tickets
NOUN A **ticket** is a small piece of card or paper that shows that you have paid for something, such as a train ride.

tickle tickles, tickling, tickled
VERB When you **tickle** someone, you move your fingers lightly over their body to make them laugh.

tide tides
NOUN The **tide** is the regular change in the level of the sea on the shore.

tidy tidier, tidiest; tidies, tidying, tidied
ADJECTIVE **1** Something that is **tidy** is neat and well arranged.
VERB **2** When you **tidy** a room, you put things away in their proper place.
tidily ADVERB

tie ties, tying, tied
NOUN **1** A **tie** is a long, narrow piece of cloth that is worn around the neck.
NOUN **2** A **tie** in a race or competition is when two people have the same result.
VERB **3** If you **tie** an object to something, you fasten it with something, such as string.

tiger tigers
NOUN A **tiger** is a large wild cat that lives in Asia. Its fur is usually orange with black stripes.

tight tighter, tightest
ADJECTIVE **1** Clothes that are **tight** fit too closely to your body.
ADJECTIVE **2** Something that is **tight** is firmly fastened and difficult to move.

tights
PLURAL NOUN **Tights** are a piece of clothing made of thin material that fit closely over your hips, legs, and feet.

tile tiles
NOUN A **tile** is a small, thin piece of something, such as slate or carpet, that is used to cover surfaces.

till tills
PREPOSITION OR CONJUNCTION **1** Till means the same as until. *Wait **till** morning... Wait **till** I get back.*
NOUN **2** A **till** is a drawer or box in a store or bank where money is kept.

a b c d e f g h i j k l m n o p q r s Tt u v w x y z

tilt **tilts, tilting, tilted**
VERB If you **tilt** something, you make it slope.

timber
NOUN **Timber** is wood used for building, and making furniture.

time
NOUN **1 Time** is what is measured in seconds, minutes, hours, days, and years. See *Time* on page 268.
NOUN **2** If it is **time** to do something, that thing ought to be done now.

times
NOUN **1 Times** is used after numbers to say how often something happens.
NOUN **2** In math, **times** is used to link numbers that are multiplied together. *Four **times** three is twelve.*

timetable **timetables**
NOUN A **timetable** is a list of the times when things happen, or when trains and buses go.

timid
ADJECTIVE A **timid** person is not brave.

tin **tins**
NOUN **1 Tin** is a soft silvery-white metal.
NOUN **2** A **tin** is a metal container with a lid, for storing food.

tingle **tingles, tingling, tingled**
VERB When part of your body **tingles**, you feel a slight prickling or stinging.

tinkle **tinkles, tinkling, tinkled**
VERB If something **tinkles**, it makes a sound like a small bell ringing.

tint
NOUN **1** A **tint** is a variety of color, often one with white added.
NOUN **2** A **tint** is also a pale, delicate color.

tiny **tinier, tiniest**
ADJECTIVE Something that is **tiny** is very small.

tip **tips, tipping, tipped**
VERB **1** If you **tip** an object, you move it so that it is no longer straight. *She **tipped** her chair back and almost fell over.*
NOUN **2** The **tip** of something long and narrow is the end of it.

tiptoe **tiptoes, tiptoeing, tiptoed**
VERB If you **tiptoe** somewhere, you walk there very quietly on your toes.

tired
ADJECTIVE If you are **tired**, you feel that you want to rest or sleep.

tissue **tissues**
NOUN A **tissue** is a piece of soft paper that you can use as a handkerchief.

title **titles**
NOUN **1** A **title** is the name of something, such as a book or movie.
NOUN **2** Someone's **title** is a name such as Mr., Mrs., or Sir that goes in front of their own name.

toad **toads**
NOUN A **toad** is an amphibian. It looks like a frog but it has a drier skin and lives mostly on land.
See *Amphibians* on page 259.

toadstool **toadstools**
NOUN A **toadstool** is a type of poisonous fungus.

toast
NOUN **Toast** is a slice of bread made brown and crisp by heating.

toboggan **toboggans**
NOUN A **toboggan** is a vehicle for traveling on snow. It has a flat seat, with two metal or wooden runners.

today

ADVERB **Today** is the day that is happening now.

toddler **toddlers**

NOUN A **toddler** is a small child who has only just learned to walk.

toe **toes**

NOUN Your **toes** are the five parts at the end of your foot which you can move.

toffee **toffees**

NOUN A **toffee** is a sticky, chewy candy made from butter and sugar.

together

ADVERB **1** If two people do something **together**, they both do it.

ADVERB **2** If two things happen **together**, they happen at the same time.

toilet **toilets**

NOUN **1** A **toilet** is a bowl connected to a drain and fitted with a seat. You use it to get rid of waste matter from your body.

NOUN **2** A **toilet** is also a small room containing a toilet.

told

VERB **Told** is the past tense of **tell**.

tomato **tomatoes**

NOUN A **tomato** is a soft, small, red fruit. It can be cooked or eaten raw in salads. See *Fruit on page 257.*

tomorrow

ADVERB **Tomorrow** is the day after today.

ton **tons**

NOUN A **ton** is a unit of weight equal to 2000 pounds.

tongue **tongues**

NOUN Your **tongue** is the soft, moving part inside your mouth. You use your tongue for tasting, eating, and speaking.

tongue twister **tongue twisters**

NOUN A **tongue twister** is a sentence or expression which is difficult to say properly. For example, "She sells seashells on the seashore" is a tongue twister.

tonight

ADVERB **Tonight** is the evening of today or the night that follows today.

tonsils

NOUN Your **tonsils** are the two flaps of soft tissue that lie one on each side of the throat.

too

ADVERB **1** **Too** means also, or as well. *I was there **too**.*

ADVERB **2** **Too** also means more than is needed. *I've had **too** much to eat.*

took

VERB **Took** is the past tense of **take**.

tool **tools**

NOUN A **tool** is anything that you use to help you do something, such as a hammer.

tooth **teeth**

NOUN **1** A **tooth** is one of the hard, white objects in your mouth. You use your teeth for biting and chewing food.

NOUN **2** The **teeth** of a comb, saw, or zipper are the parts that stick out in a row.

toothbrush **toothbrushes**

NOUN A **toothbrush** is a small brush that you use for cleaning your teeth.

toothpaste

NOUN **Toothpaste** is a substance which you use to clean your teeth.

top **tops**

NOUN **1** The **top** of something is its highest point, part, or surface.

NOUN **2** The **top** of a bottle, jar, or tube is its cap or lid.

topic **topics**

NOUN A **topic** is a particular subject that you write or talk about.

a b c d e f g h i j k l m n o p q r s **Tt** u v w x y z

torch **torches**

NOUN A **torch** is a flaming light that can be carried in the hand.

tore

VERB **Tore** is the past tense of **tear**.

torn

VERB **Torn** is the past participle of **tear**.

tornado **tornadoes** or **tornados**

NOUN A **tornado** is a very strong wind that moves around in a circle and can cause a lot of damage.

tortoise **tortoises**

NOUN A **tortoise** is a slow-moving reptile with a hard, thick shell.
See *Reptiles* on page 259.

toss **tosses, tossing, tossed**

VERB **1** If you **toss** something, you throw it lightly and carelessly.
VERB **2** If something **tosses**, it keeps moving from side to side. *An ocean liner tosses in rough seas.*

total **totals**

NOUN **1** A **total** is the number you get when you add several numbers together.
ADJECTIVE **2** Total means complete. *The party was a total success.*

touch **touches, touching, touched**

VERB **1** If you **touch** something, you feel it with your hand.
VERB **2** If two things are **touching**, there is no space between them.

tough **tougher, toughest**

ADJECTIVE Something that is **tough** is strong and difficult to cut, tear, or break.

tour **tours**

NOUN A **tour** is a journey to visit interesting places.

tourist **tourists**

NOUN A **tourist** is a person who visits places for pleasure and interest.

tournament **tournaments**

NOUN A **tournament** is a competition in which lots of matches are played, until just one person or team is left.

tow **tows, towing, towed**

VERB If a vehicle **tows** another vehicle, it pulls it along behind.

toward

PREPOSITION **1** If you move **toward** something, you go in that direction.
PREPOSITION **2** If you give money **toward** something, you help pay for it.

towel **towels**

NOUN A **towel** is a piece of soft thick cloth that you use to dry yourself with.

tower **towers**

NOUN A **tower** is a tall, narrow building or a tall part of a building.

town **towns**

NOUN A **town** is a place with a lot of streets and buildings where people live and work.

toy **toys**

NOUN A **toy** is something you play with, such as a doll or a model car.

trace **traces, tracing, traced**

VERB **1** If you **trace** something, such as a map, you copy it by covering it with a piece of thin paper and drawing over the lines underneath.
VERB **2** If you **trace** something, you find it after looking for it.

track **tracks**

NOUN **1** A **track** is a rough, narrow road or path.
NOUN **2** A **track** is also a special road or path that is used for racing.
NOUN **3** A railway **track** is a strip of ground with rails that trains travel on.

traction

NOUN **Traction** is the gripping power that keeps a moving body from slipping on a surface.

a
b
c
d
e
f
g
h
i
j
k
l
m
n
o
p
q
r
s
Tt
u
v
w
x
y
z

tractor

tractor tractors
NOUN A **tractor** is a vehicle with large rear wheels. Tractors are used on farms for pulling or lifting things.

trade trades
NOUN **Trade** is the buying and selling of goods or services. Trade can be between people, companies, or countries.

trademark trademarks
NOUN A **trademark** is a name or symbol that a manufacturer always uses on its products. It is usually protected by law so that nobody else can use it.

tradition traditions
NOUN A **tradition** is something that people have done or believed in for a long time.
traditional ADJECTIVE
traditionally ADVERB

traffic
NOUN **Traffic** is the movement of vehicles on the road, in the air, or on water.

traffic light traffic lights
NOUN **Traffic lights** are special signals to control the flow of traffic. They are usually placed where streets intersect. Red lights mean stop and green lights mean go.

traffic signal traffic signals
NOUN A **traffic signal** directs cars and trucks on the roads.

tragedy tragedies
NOUN **1** A **tragedy** is an event or situation that is very sad.
NOUN **2** A **tragedy** is also a serious play, that usually ends with the death of the main character.
tragic ADJECTIVE

trail trails, trailing, trailed
NOUN **1** A **trail** is a rough path across open country or through forests.
NOUN **2** A **trail** is also the scent, footprints, and other signs that people and animals leave behind them.
VERB **3** If you **trail** something or it **trails**, it drags along behind you.

trailer trailers
NOUN **1** A **trailer** is a vehicle pulled by a car, used for carrying things.
NOUN **2** A **trailer** can also be a series of short pieces from a movie or television program in order to advertise it.

train trains, training, trained
NOUN **1** A **train** is a number of railroad cars which are joined together and pulled by an engine along a railway.
VERB **2** If someone **trains** you to do a job, they teach you the skills you need.
VERB **3** If you **train** a dog, you teach it to behave properly.

trainer trainers
NOUN **1** A **trainer** is a person who coaches people in sports, such as boxing.
NOUN **2** **Trainers** also work with circus animals, show animals, or pets.

trait
NOUN A **trait** is a characteristic that makes one person or thing different from another.

trampoline trampolines
NOUN A **trampoline** is something that is used for jumping on. It is made of strong cloth held into a frame by springs.

transfer transfers, transferring, transferred
VERB If you **transfer** something, you move it to a different place or position.

a b c d e f g h i j k l m n o p q r s **Tt** u v w x y z

Uu

ugly **uglier, ugliest**
ADJECTIVE Someone or something that is **ugly** is not pleasant to look at.

umbrella **umbrellas**
NOUN An **umbrella** is a shelter from the rain. It consists of a folding frame covered in thin cloth, attached to a long stick.

un-
PREFIX **Un-** is added to the beginning of a word to make it mean the opposite, for example "happy" → "unhappy."
See *Prefixes* on page 264.

unable
ADJECTIVE If you are **unable** to do something, you cannot do it.

unaware
ADJECTIVE If you are **unaware** of something, you do not know about it.

unbearable
ADJECTIVE Something **unbearable** is so unpleasant, painful, or upsetting you feel you cannot stand it.

unbelievable
ADJECTIVE **1** Something **unbelievable** is extremely great or surprising. *She showed* **unbelievable** *courage.*
ADJECTIVE **2 Unbelievable** can also be used to describe something that is so unlikely you cannot believe it.

unbreakable
ADJECTIVE Something that is **unbreakable** cannot be broken.

uncertain
ADJECTIVE If you are **uncertain**, you are not sure what to do.

uncle **uncles**
NOUN Your **uncle** is the brother of one of your parents, or your aunt's husband.

uncomfortable
ADJECTIVE If you are **uncomfortable**, you do not feel at ease.

uncommon
ADJECTIVE Something **uncommon** does not often happen, or is not often seen.

unconscious
ADJECTIVE Someone who is **unconscious** is unable to see, hear, or feel anything that is going on. This is usually because they have fainted or have been badly injured.

under
PREPOSITION **1 Under** means below or beneath.

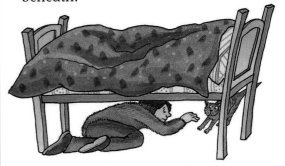

PREPOSITION **2 Under** can also mean less than. *Children* **under** *five can go in free.*

under-
PREFIX **1 Under-** is added to the beginning of a word to form a new word meaning under the thing mentioned, for example "ground" → "underground."
PREFIX **2 Under-** can also be used as a prefix to mean not enough. *The hungry rabbit was* **underfed**.
See *Prefixes* on page 264.

a
b
c
d
e
f
g
h
i
j
k
l
m
n
o
p
q
r
s
t
Uu
v
w
x
y
z

underground

underground

ADJECTIVE **1** Something **underground** is below the surface of the ground.

ADJECTIVE **2** An **underground** operation is a secret mission.

undergrowth

NOUN **Undergrowth** is bushes or plants growing together under the trees in a forest or jungle.

underline **underlines, underlining, underlined**

VERB If you **underline** a word or sentence, you draw a line under it.

underneath

PREPOSITION OR ADVERB **Underneath** means below or beneath. *They found the missing card **underneath** the table... They couldn't move the car because their cat was **underneath**.*

understand **understands, understanding, understood**

VERB If you **understand** something, you know what it means.

underwear

NOUN Your **underwear** is the clothing that you wear next to your skin under your other clothes.

undo **undoes, undoing, undid, undone**

VERB If you **undo** something that is tied up, you untie it.

undress **undresses, undressing, undressed**

VERB When you **undress**, you take off your clothes.

uneasy

ADJECTIVE If you are **uneasy**, you are worried that something is wrong.

unemployed

ADJECTIVE Someone who is **unemployed** does not have a job.

uneven

ADJECTIVE Something that is **uneven** does not have a flat, smooth surface.

unexpected

ADJECTIVE Something that is **unexpected** surprises you.

unexpectedly ADVERB

unfair

ADJECTIVE If you think that something is **unfair**, it does not seem right or reasonable to you.

unfairly ADVERB

unfortunate

ADJECTIVE **1** Someone who is **unfortunate** is unlucky.

ADJECTIVE **2** If you say something is **unfortunate**, you mean you wish it had not happened.

unfortunately ADVERB

unfriendly

ADJECTIVE Someone who is **unfriendly** is not kind to you.

ungrateful

ADJECTIVE If someone is **ungrateful**, they are not thankful for something that has been given to them or done for them.

unhappy **unhappier, unhappiest**

ADJECTIVE Someone who is **unhappy** is sad or miserable.

unhappily ADVERB

unhealthy **unhealthier, unhealthiest**

ADJECTIVE **1** Someone who is **unhealthy** is often ill.

ADJECTIVE **2** Something that is **unhealthy** is likely to cause illness.

unicorn **unicorns**

NOUN A **unicorn** is an imaginary animal like a white horse with a horn in the middle of its forehead.

uniform uniforms

NOUN A **uniform** is a special set of clothes that is worn by people to show that they belong to the same group.

unique

ADJECTIVE If something is **unique**, it is the only one of its kind.

unit units

NOUN **1** A **unit** is an amount that is used for measuring things. For example, a second is a unit of time.

NOUN **2** A *unit is a single person, thing, or group that is part of something larger, as in an apartment unit.*

unite unites, uniting, united

VERB If people **unite**, they work as a group.

united ADJECTIVE

universe

NOUN The **universe** is the whole of space including all the stars and planets.

university universities

NOUN A **university** is a place where people can carry on their education when they have left high school.

unkind

ADJECTIVE Someone who is **unkind** is rather cruel and unpleasant.

unleaded

ADJECTIVE **Unleaded** gasoline has a smaller amount of lead in it, in order to reduce the pollution from vehicles.

unless

CONJUNCTION You use **unless** to introduce a condition that is necessary for something else to happen. *I won't come **unless** you invite me.*

unlike

PREPOSITION If one thing is **unlike** another, the two things are different.

unlikely

ADJECTIVE If something is **unlikely**, it is probably not true or probably will not happen.

unload unloads, unloading, unloaded

VERB If people **unload** something, such as a truck, they take the load off it.

unlock unlocks, unlocking, unlocked

VERB If you **unlock** something, such as a door, you open it with a key.

unlucky

ADJECTIVE Someone who is **unlucky** has bad luck.

unluckily ADVERB

unnatural

ADJECTIVE Something **unnatural** is strange because it is not usual. *There was an **unnatural** stillness.*

unnaturally ADVERB

unnecessary

ADJECTIVE Something that is **unnecessary** is not needed.

unpack unpacks, unpacking, unpacked

VERB When you **unpack**, you take everything out of a suitcase, bag, or box.

unpleasant

ADJECTIVE Something that is **unpleasant** is rather nasty and not enjoyable.

unpopular

ADJECTIVE Someone or something that is **unpopular** is disliked by most people.

unsafe

ADJECTIVE If something like a building or a machine is **unsafe**, it is dangerous.

unselfish

ADJECTIVE People who are **unselfish** care more about other people than they do about themselves.

a b c d e f g h i j k l m n o p q r s t **Uu** v w x y z

untidy untidier, untidiest
ADJECTIVE **1** Someone who is **untidy** does not care whether things are neat and well arranged.
ADJECTIVE **2** An **untidy** place is not neat or well arranged.

untie unties, untying, untied
VERB If you **untie** something, you undo the knots in the string around it.

until
PREPOSITION OR CONJUNCTION **Until** means up to a certain time. *The shop was open until midnight... He waited until the dog was asleep.*

untrue
ADJECTIVE Something that is **untrue** is false and not based on facts.

unusual
ADJECTIVE Someone or something that is **unusual** is different from the ordinary.

up
PREPOSITION OR ADVERB **1** **Up** means toward or in a higher place. *She ran up the stairs... It was high up in the mountains.*
ADVERB **2** If an amount of something goes **up**, it increases. *The price of butter has gone up.*

uppercase
ADJECTIVE **Uppercase** letters are capital letters. See **lowercase**.

upright
ADJECTIVE If you are **upright**, you are standing up straight.

uproar uproars
NOUN An **uproar** is a lot of noise and shouting.

upset upsets, upsetting, upset
VERB **1** If someone **upsets** something, they turn it over by accident. *He upset a can of paint on the carpet.*
ADJECTIVE **2** If you are **upset**, you are unhappy or disappointed.

upside down
ADJECTIVE Something that is **upside down** has been turned so that the part that should be at the top is at the bottom.

upstairs
ADVERB **1** If you go **upstairs** in a building, you go up to a higher floor.
ADVERB **2** Someone or something that is **upstairs** is on a higher floor than you.

up-to-date
ADJECTIVE Something that is **up-to-date** is new or modern.

urgent
ADJECTIVE Something that is **urgent** needs to be done at once.

use uses, using, used
VERB If you **use** something, you do something with it that helps you.

used
VERB Something that **used** to be done was done in the past.
used to PHRASE If you are **used to** something, you are familiar with it and have often experienced it.

useful
ADJECTIVE If something is **useful**, it helps you in some way.

useless
ADJECTIVE If something is **useless**, you cannot use it.

usual
ADJECTIVE Something that is **usual** happens, or is done or used, most often.

usually
ADVERB If something **usually** happens, it happens most often.

wade wades, wading, waded
VERB To **wade** means to walk through fairly shallow water.

wafer wafers
NOUN A **wafer** is a thin, crisp cookie.

wag wags, wagging, wagged
VERB When a dog **wags** its tail, it waves it from side to side because it is happy.

wagon wagons
NOUN **1** A **wagon** is a strong cart for carrying heavy loads, usually pulled by a horse or tractor.

VERB **2** A **wagon** is also a child's toy vehicle with four wheels and a long handle for pulling.

wail wails, wailing, wailed
VERB If someone **wails**, they make a long crying noise.

waist waists
NOUN Your **waist** is the narrow middle part of your body, just below your chest.

wait waits, waiting, waited
VERB If you **wait**, you spend time before something happens.

wake wakes, waking, woke, woken
VERB When you **wake**, you stop sleeping.

walk walks, walking, walked
VERB When you **walk**, you move along by putting one foot in front of the other.

wall walls
NOUN **1** A **wall** is one of the vertical sides of a building or a room.

NOUN **2** A **wall** can also be used to divide or go around an area of land.

wallet wallets
NOUN A **wallet** is a small, flat case that fits in a pocket. It is used to hold things such as paper money and credit cards.

wallpaper wallpapers
NOUN **Wallpaper** is thick colored or patterned paper that is used for covering and decorating the walls of a room.

walnut walnuts
NOUN A **walnut** is a nut with a wrinkled shape and a light brown shell.

walrus walruses
NOUN A **walrus** is a mammal that lives in the sea and looks like a large seal. It has coarse whiskers and two long tusks.

wand wands
NOUN A **wand** is a long, thin rod that magicians wave when they are performing tricks and magic.

wander wanders, wandering, wandered
VERB If you **wander**, you walk around without going in any particular direction.

want wants, wanting, wanted
VERB If you **want** something, you wish for it or need it.

war wars
NOUN A **war** is a period of fighting between countries.

wardrobe wardrobes
NOUN A **wardrobe** is a tall closet where you can hang your clothes.

warehouse warehouses
NOUN A **warehouse** is a large building which is used to store things.

warm warmer, warmest
ADJECTIVE **1** Something that is **warm** has some heat, but not enough to be hot.

ADJECTIVE **2** Clothes and blankets that are **warm** are made of a material that stops you from feeling cold.

a
b
c
d
e
f
g
h
i
j
k
l
m
n
o
p
q
r
s
t
u
v

x
y
z

warmth

warmth

NOUN **Warmth** is a comfortable amount of heat.

warn warns, warning, warned

VERB If you **warn** someone, you tell them about a danger or problem that they might meet.

warning warnings

NOUN A **warning** is something that tells you about a possible problem or danger.

warren warrens

NOUN A **warren** is a group of holes in the ground which rabbits live in. The holes are connected by tunnels.

wary warier, wariest

ADJECTIVE If you are **wary** about something, you are careful because you are not sure about it. *The police officer told us to be wary of strangers.*

warily ADVERB

wash washes, washing, washed

VERB **1** If you **wash** something, you clean it with soap and water.
NOUN **2** Wash is clothes, towels, and bedding that need to be cleaned.

washable

ADJECTIVE Clothes or materials that are **washable** can be washed in water without being damaged.

washing machine washing machines

NOUN A **washing machine** is a machine for washing clothes in.

wasn't

CONTRACTION **Wasn't** is a short form of was not.

wasp wasps

NOUN A **wasp** is a flying insect that has a slender body. Female wasps can sting.

waste wastes, wasting, wasted

VERB **1** If you **waste** something, such as time or money, you use too much of it on something that is not important.
NOUN **2** Waste is material that is no longer wanted.

watch watches, watching, watched

NOUN **1** A **watch** is a small clock that you can wear on your wrist.
VERB **2** If you **watch** something, you look at it carefully to see what happens.

water waters, watering, watered

NOUN **1** Water is a clear liquid that all living things need in order to live.
VERB **2** If you **water** a plant or animal, you give it water to drink.

waterfall waterfalls

NOUN A **waterfall** is water that flows over the edge of a cliff to the ground below.

waterlogged

ADJECTIVE Land that is **waterlogged** is so wet the soil cannot absorb any more water.

waterproof

ADJECTIVE A material that is **waterproof** does not let water pass through it.

watertight

ADJECTIVE Something that is **watertight** is closed so tightly that it does not allow water to pass through.

wave **waves, waving, waved**
VERB **1** If you **wave**, you move your hand in the air, to say hello or goodbye.
VERB **2** If something **waves**, it moves gently up and down or from side to side. *The flags **waved** in the wind.*
NOUN **3** A **wave** is a raised line of water on the surface of the sea caused by wind or tides.
NOUN **4** A **wave** is also a gentle curving shape in someone's hair.

wax
NOUN **Wax** is a solid, slightly shiny substance, made of fat or oil. It is used to make candles and polish.

way **ways**
NOUN **1** A **way** of doing something is how it can be done.
NOUN **2** The **way** to a particular place is the direction you have to go to get there.

weak **weaker, weakest**
ADJECTIVE **1** People or animals that are **weak** do not have much strength or energy.
ADJECTIVE **2** If an object or part of an object is **weak**, it could break easily.
ADJECTIVE **3** Drinks, such as tea or coffee, that are **weak** do not have a strong taste.

wealthy **wealthier, wealthiest**
ADJECTIVE Someone who is **wealthy** has a lot of money.

weapon **weapons**
NOUN A **weapon** is an object, such as a gun or missile, which is used to hurt or kill people in a fight or war.

wear **wears, wearing, wore, worn**
VERB **1** When you **wear** things, such as clothes, you have them on your body.
VERB **2** When something **wears out**, it has been used so much that it cannot be used any more.

weary **wearier, weariest**
ADJECTIVE If you are **weary**, you are tired.
wearily ADVERB

weather
NOUN The **weather** is what it is like outside, for example raining, sunny, or windy.
See *Weather words* on page 269.

weave **weaves, weaving, wove, woven**
VERB When someone **weaves** cloth, they make it by crossing threads over and under each other, using a machine called a loom.

web **webs**
NOUN **1** A **web** is a fine net made by a spider to catch flies.
NOUN **2** The **web** is short for the World Wide Web, which is where information can be stored on the Internet.

webbed
ADJECTIVE **Webbed** feet have the toes connected by a piece of skin.

web site **web sites**
NOUN A **web site** is a group of pages on the Internet which contain information about a particular subject.

wedding **weddings**
NOUN A **wedding** is when a man and woman become husband and wife.

Wednesday **Wednesdays**
NOUN **Wednesday** is the day between Tuesday and Thursday.

weed **weeds**
NOUN A **weed** is any wild plant that grows where it is not wanted. Weeds grow strongly and stop other plants from growing properly.

week **weeks**
NOUN A **week** is a period of seven days.

a
b
c
d
e
f
g
h
i
j
k
l
m
n
o
p
q
r
s
t
u
v
Ww
x
y
z

weekend **weekends**

NOUN A **weekend** is Saturday and Sunday.

weep **weeps, weeping, wept**

VERB If someone **weeps**, they cry.

weigh **weighs, weighing, weighed**

VERB **1** If something **weighs** a particular amount, that is how heavy it is.

VERB **2** If you **weigh** something, you use scales to measure how heavy it is.

weight

NOUN The **weight** of something is its heaviness. Weight and mass are connected. Weight is usually measured in ounces and pounds. See **mass**.

weird **weirder, weirdest**

ADJECTIVE Something that is **weird** seems strange and peculiar.

welcome **welcomes, welcoming, welcomed**

VERB If you **welcome** someone, you speak to them in a friendly way when they arrive.

well **better, best; wells**

ADJECTIVE **1** If you are **well**, you are healthy.

ADVERB **2** If you do something **well**, you do it to a high standard.

NOUN **3** A **well** is a deep hole in the ground that has been dug to reach water or oil.

we'll **we'll**

CONTRACTION **We'll** is a short form of we will.

went

VERB **Went** is the past tense of **go**.

wept

VERB **Wept** is the past tense of **weep**.

west

NOUN The **west** is one of the four main points of the compass. It is the direction in which you look to see the sun set. See **compass point**.

western ADJECTIVE

wet **wetter, wettest**

ADJECTIVE **1** If something is **wet**, it is covered in water or some other liquid.

ADJECTIVE **2** If the weather is **wet**, it is raining.

ADJECTIVE **3** If something such as ink or cement is **wet**, it has not yet dried.

whale **whales**

NOUN A **whale** is a huge mammal that lives in the sea. Whales breathe through an opening in the top of their head.

what

ADJECTIVE OR PRONOUN **1 What** is used in questions. *What time is it? What is your name?*

PRONOUN **2** You can use **what** to refer to information about something. *I don't know what you mean.*

what about PHRASE You say **what about** at the beginning of a question when you are making a suggestion or offer. *What about a sandwich?*

wheat

NOUN **Wheat** is a cereal plant grown for its grain, which is used to make flour.

wheel **wheels**

NOUN A **wheel** is a circular object which turns around on a rod fixed to its center. Wheels are fitted under things such as cars, bicycles, and carriages so that they can move along.

wheelbarrow **wheelbarrows**

NOUN A **wheelbarrow** is a small cart with a single wheel at the front.

wheelchair **wheelchairs**

NOUN A **wheelchair** is a chair with large wheels for use by people who find walking difficult or impossible.

when

ADVERB **1** You use **when** to ask what time something happened or will happen. *When are you leaving?*

CONJUNCTION **2** You use **when** to refer to a certain time. *I met him when we were at school together.*

where

ADVERB **1** You use **where** to ask questions about place. *Where is my book?*

CONJUNCTION **2** You use **where** to talk about the place in which something is situated or happening. *I don't know where we are.*

whether

CONJUNCTION You can use **whether** instead of **if**. *I don't know whether I can go.*

which

ADJECTIVE **1** You use **which** to ask for information about something when there are two or more possibilities. *Which room are you in?*

PRONOUN **2** You also use **which** when you are going to say more about something you have already mentioned. *Our car, which is falling to pieces, is fairly new.*

while

CONJUNCTION **1** If something happens **while** something else is happening, the two things happen at the same time.

NOUN **2** A **while** is a period of time. *She had to wait a little while.*

whimper whimpers, whimpering, whimpered

VERB When children or animals **whimper**, they make soft unhappy sounds, as if they are about to cry.

whine whines, whining, whined

VERB To **whine** is to make a long high-pitched noise because you are unhappy about something.

whip whips, whipping, whipped

VERB If you **whip** cream or eggs, you beat them until they are thick and frothy, or stiff.

whirl whirls, whirling, whirled

VERB When something **whirls**, it turns around very fast.

whirlpool whirlpools

NOUN A **whirlpool** is a small place in a river or the sea where the water is moving quickly in a circle, so that anything floating near it is pulled into its center.

whirlwind whirlwinds

NOUN A **whirlwind** is a tall column of air which spins around and around very quickly.

whirr whirrs, whirring, whirred

VERB When something like a machine **whirrs**, it makes a series of low sounds so fast that it seems like one sound.

whisk whisks, whisking, whisked

VERB If you **whisk** something like cream, you stir it very fast.

whisker whiskers

NOUN The **whiskers** of an animal, such as a cat or mouse, are the long stiff hairs near its mouth.

whisper whispers, whispering, whispered

VERB When you **whisper**, you talk very quietly, using your breath and not your voice.

whistle whistles, whistling, whistled

NOUN **1** A **whistle** is a small metal tube which makes a loud sound when you blow it.

VERB **2** When you **whistle**, you make a loud high noise by using a whistle or by forcing your breath out between your lips.

white **whiter, whitest; whites**

ADJECTIVE **1** Something that is **white** is the color of milk.
See Colors on page 271.

ADJECTIVE **2** If someone goes **white**, their face becomes very pale because they are afraid, shocked, or ill.

NOUN **3** The **white** of an egg is the transparent liquid surrounding the yolk.

who

PRONOUN **1** You use **who** when you are asking about someone. *Who told you?*

PRONOUN **2** You use **who** at the beginning of a clause when you want to say more about someone you have just mentioned. *I've got a brother who wants to be a vet.*

whole

NOUN **1** The **whole** of something is all of it. *It was the only pair in the whole store.*

ADJECTIVE **2** You use **whole** to describe all of something. *Take the whole cake.*

ADJECTIVE **3** **Whole** means in one piece.

whose

PRONOUN **1** You use **whose** to ask who something belongs to. *Whose book is this?*

PRONOUN **2** You use **whose** in front of information relating to a person or thing you have just mentioned. *That's the girl whose mother is a lawyer.*

why

ADVERB **1** You use **why** in questions when you ask about the reason for something. *Why did you do that?*

ADVERB **2** You also use **why** to talk about the reasons for something. *She wondered why he was there.*

wicked

ADJECTIVE Someone or something **wicked** is very bad.

wide **wider, widest**

ADJECTIVE **1** Something that is **wide** measures a lot from one side to the other.

ADVERB **2** If you open something **wide**, you open it a long way.

widow **widows**

NOUN A **widow** is a woman whose husband has died. See **widower**.

widower **widowers**

NOUN A **widower** is a man whose wife has died. See **widow**.

width **widths**

NOUN The **width** of something is the distance from one side to the other.

wife **wives**

NOUN A man's **wife** is the woman he is married to.

wig **wigs**

NOUN A **wig** is a false head of hair. People wear wigs because they are bald, or to cover their own hair.

wigwam **wigwams**

NOUN A **wigwam** is a kind of tent used by some North American Indians.

wild **wilder, wildest**

ADJECTIVE **1** **Wild** animals, birds, and plants live in natural surroundings and are not looked after by people.

ADJECTIVE **2** **Wild** behavior is excited and not controlled.

wildlife

NOUN **Wildlife** means wild animals and plants.

will

VERB **1** You use **will** to form the future tense. *Robin will be quite annoyed.*

VERB **2** You use **will** when asking or telling someone to do something. *Will you do me a favor?*

willing

ADJECTIVE **1** If you are **willing** to do something, you are ready and happy to do it if someone wants you to.

ADJECTIVE 2 A **willing** person is someone who does things cheerfully.

willow **willows**
NOUN A **willow** is a tree with long, thin branches and narrow leaves that likes to grow near water.

win **wins, winning, won**
VERB **1** If you **win** a race or game, you do better than the others taking part.
VERB **2** If you **win** a prize, you get it as a reward for doing something well.

wind **winds, winding, wound**
(*rhymes with* **sinned**) NOUN **1** A **wind** is a current of air that moves across the earth's surface.
(*rhymes with* **mind**) VERB **2** If a road or river **winds**, it has lots of bends in it.
(*rhymes with* **mind**) VERB **3** When you **wind** something around something else, you wrap it around several times.

windmill **windmills**
NOUN A **windmill** is a building with large sails which turn as the wind blows. This works a machine that pumps water or generates electricity.

window **windows**
NOUN A **window** is a space in a wall or vehicle. It has glass in it so that light can come in and you can see through.

windy **windier, windiest**
ADJECTIVE If it is **windy**, the wind is blowing hard.

wine **wines**
NOUN **Wine** is an alcoholic drink usually made from the juice of grapes.

wing **wings**
NOUN **1** The **wings** of a bird or insect are the two limbs on its body that it uses for flying.
NOUN **2** The **wings** of an airplane are the long, flat parts sticking out of its sides, which support it in the air.

wink **winks, winking, winked**
VERB When you **wink**, you close one eye for a moment. *She winked to show that she was joking.*

winner **winners**
NOUN If someone or something wins a prize, race, or competition, they are the **winner**.

winter **winters**
NOUN **Winter** is the season between autumn and spring.

wipe **wipes, wiping, wiped**
VERB If you **wipe** something, you rub its surface lightly to remove dirt or liquid.

wire **wires**
NOUN **Wire** is a long, thin, flexible piece of metal which can be used to make or fasten things or to carry an electric current.

wise **wiser, wisest**
ADJECTIVE Someone who is **wise** can use their experience and knowledge to make sensible decisions.
wisdom NOUN

wish **wishes, wishing, wished**
VERB **1** If you **wish** that something would happen, you would like it to happen.
NOUN **2** A **wish** is the act of wishing for something you would like to happen.

witch **witches**
NOUN In fairy stories, a witch is a woman who has magic powers. See **wizard**.

with

with

PREPOSITION **1** If you are **with** someone, you are in their company. *I was there with Mom and Dad.*

PREPOSITION **2 With** can mean using or having. *She worked with a big brush.*

wither withers, withering, withered

VERB If a plant **withers**, it shrivels up and dies.

within

PREPOSITION **1 Within** means not going outside certain limits. *Stay within the school grounds.*

PREPOSITION **2 Within** can also mean before a period of time has passed. *You must write back within ten days.*

without

PREPOSITION **1 Without** means not having or using. *You can't get in without a key.*

PREPOSITION **2 Without** can mean not in someone's company. *He went without me.*

PREPOSITION **3 Without** can also mean that something does not happen. *The phone rang three times without an answer.*

witness witnesses, witnessing, witnessed

NOUN **1** A **witness** is someone who has seen an event, such as an accident, and can describe what happened.

VERB **2** If you **witness** an event, you see it happen.

wizard wizards

NOUN In fairy stories, a **wizard** is a man who has magic powers. See **witch**.

wobble wobbles, wobbling, wobbled

VERB If something **wobbles**, it makes small movements from side to side.

wok woks

NOUN A **wok** is a pan shaped like a bowl that is used especially for stir-frying food.

woke

VERB **Woke** is the past tense of **wake**.

wolf wolves

NOUN A **wolf** is a wild animal that looks like a large dog. Wolves live in a group called a pack.

woman women

NOUN A **woman** is an adult female human being. See **man**.

won

VERB **Won** is the past tense of **win**.

wonder wonders, wondering, wondered

VERB **1** If you **wonder** about something, you wish you knew more about it.

VERB **2** If you **wonder** what to do about something, you are not sure what to do about it.

NOUN **3 Wonder** is a feeling of great and pleasant surprise.

wonderful

ADJECTIVE If something is **wonderful**, it makes you feel very happy.

won't

VERB **Won't** is a contraction of **will not**.

wood woods

NOUN **1 Wood** is the substance which forms the trunks and branches of trees.

NOUN **2 Woods** are large areas of trees growing near each other.

wooden

ADJECTIVE Something that is **wooden** is made of wood.

woodpecker woodpeckers

NOUN A **woodpecker** is a bird with a long, sharp beak. It drills holes in trees to find insects.

woodwork

NOUN 1 The **woodwork** in a house is all the parts that are made of wood, such as the doors and window frames.

NOUN 2 Woodworking is making things out of wood.

woof **woofs**

NOUN Woof is the noise that a dog makes when it barks.

wool

NOUN 1 Wool is the hair that grows on sheep and on some other animals.

NOUN 2 Wool is also the yarn spun from the wool of animals which is used to knit, weave, and make things like clothes, blankets, and carpets.

woolen

ADJECTIVE Something that is **woolen** is made from wool.

woolly **woollier, woolliest**

ADJECTIVE Something that is **woolly** is made of wool, or looks like wool.

word **words**

NOUN A **word** is a set of sounds or letters that has a meaning. A word can be written or spoken. When it is written, there are no spaces between the letters.

word processor **word processors**

NOUN A **word processor** is a computer which is used to store and print words that are typed into it.

wore

VERB Wore is the past tense of **wear**.

work **works, working, worked**

VERB 1 When you **work**, you spend time and energy doing something useful.

VERB 2 People who **work** have a job that they are paid to do.

VERB 3 If something **works**, it does what it is supposed to do.

work out **works out, working out, worked out**

VERB 1 If you **work out** the answer to a problem, you find the answer.

VERB 2 If you **work out**, you do exercises to make your body fit and strong.

world **worlds**

NOUN The **world** is the planet we live on.

worm **worms**

NOUN A **worm** is a small animal with a long, thin body. Worms have no bones and no legs. They live in the soil.

worn

VERB 1 Worn is the past participle of **wear**.

ADJECTIVE 2 Something that is **worn** is damaged or thin because it is old and has been used a lot.

worry **worries, worrying, worried**

VERB If you **worry**, you keep thinking about problems or about unpleasant things that might happen.

worse

ADJECTIVE 1 Worse is the comparative form of **bad**.

ADJECTIVE 2 If someone who is ill gets **worse**, they are more ill than before.

worship **worships, worshiping, worshiped**

VERB If you **worship** God, you show your respect by praying and singing hymns.

worst

ADJECTIVE Worst is the superlative form of **bad**.

worth

ADJECTIVE 1 If something is **worth** a particular amount of money, it could be sold for that amount.

ADJECTIVE 2 If something is **worth** doing, it is enjoyable or useful. *That movie is worth seeing.*

would

VERB 1 You use **would** to say what someone thought was going to happen. *We were sure it would rain.*

VERB 2 You also use **would** to say you want something to happen. *I would like to know how they do that.*

wound

wound **wounds**

(*rhymes with* **round**) VERB **1** Wound is the past tense of **wind**.
(*said* **woond**) NOUN **2** A **wound** is an injury to your body, especially a cut in your skin.

wove

VERB **Wove** is the past tense of **weave**.

woven

VERB **Woven** is the past participle of **weave**.

wrap **wraps, wrapping, wrapped**

VERB When you **wrap** something, you cover it tightly with something, like paper.

wrapping **wrappings**

NOUN **Wrapping** is the material used to cover and protect something.

wreath **wreaths**

NOUN A **wreath** is an arrangement of flowers and leaves, often in the shape of a circle.

wreck **wrecks, wrecking, wrecked**

VERB **1** If someone or something **wrecks** something, they destroy it completely.
VERB **2** If a ship is **wrecked**, it is so badly damaged that it can no longer sail.
NOUN **3** A **wreck** is a vehicle that has been badly damaged in an accident.

wren **wrens**

NOUN A **wren** is a tiny brown bird.

wrestle **wrestles, wrestling, wrestled**

VERB If you **wrestle** with someone, you fight them by holding or throwing them, but not hitting them.

wriggle **wriggles, wriggling, wriggled**

VERB When you **wriggle**, you twist and turn your body with quick movements.

wring **wrings, wringing, wrung**

VERB If you **wring** a wet piece of cloth, you squeeze the water out of it by twisting it.

wrinkle **wrinkles**

NOUN **1** A **wrinkle** is a line in someone's skin, especially on their face, that forms as they grow old.
NOUN **2** A **wrinkle** is also a raised fold in something like cloth or thin paper.

wrinkled

ADJECTIVE If something is **wrinkled**, it has folds or lines in it.

wrist **wrists**

NOUN Your **wrist** is the part of your body between your hand and your arm, which bends when you move your hand.

write **writes, writing, wrote, written**

VERB **1** When you **write**, you use a pen or pencil to make words, letters, or numbers.
VERB **2** If you **write** something such as a poem or a story, you create it.
VERB **3** When you **write** to someone, you tell them about something in a letter.

writing

NOUN **1** **Writing** is something that has been written or printed.
NOUN **2** Your **writing** is the way you write with a pen or pencil.

written

VERB **Written** is the past participle of **write**.

wrong

ADJECTIVE **1** Something that is **wrong** is not correct.
ADJECTIVE **2** If there is something **wrong** with a machine, vehicle, or piece of equipment, it is not working properly.
ADJECTIVE **3** If a person does something **wrong**, they do something bad.

wrote

VERB **Wrote** is the past tense of **write**.

wrung

VERB **Wrung** is the past tense of **wring**.

Xx

X-ray **X-rays**

NOUN An **X-ray** is a ray that can pass through some solid materials. X-rays are used by doctors to examine bones or organs inside people's bodies.

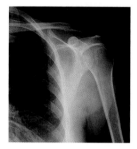

xylophone **xylophones**

NOUN A **xylophone** is a musical instrument made of wooden bars of different lengths which are arranged in a row. You play a xylophone by hitting the bars with special hammers.

Yy

yacht **yachts**

NOUN A **yacht** is a large boat with sails or a motor. Yachts are used for racing or for pleasure trips.

yam **yams**

NOUN A **yam** is a root vegetable which grows in tropical regions.

yard **yards**

NOUN **1** A **yard** is a unit of length equal to 3 feet or 36 inches.

NOUN **2** A **yard** is also an enclosed area that is usually next to a building.

yarn **yarns**

NOUN **Yarn** is thread made from something such as wool or cotton. It is used for knitting or making cloth.

yawn **yawns, yawning, yawned**

VERB When you **yawn**, you open your mouth wide and take in more air than usual. You often yawn when you are tired or bored.

a
b
c
d
e
f
g
h
i
j
k
l
m
n
o
p
q
r
s
t
u
v
w
Xx
Yy
z

year **years**

NOUN A **year** is a period of time. It is equal to 12 months, or 52 weeks, or 365 days (in leap year, 366 days).

yeast

NOUN **Yeast** is a kind of fungus that is used to make bread rise. It is also used in making drinks, such as beer.

yell **yells, yelling, yelled**

VERB If you **yell**, you shout loudly. People sometimes yell if they are excited, angry, or in pain.

yellow

ADJECTIVE Something that is **yellow** is the color of lemons or egg yolks.
See *Colors* on page 271.

yelp **yelps, yelping, yelped**

VERB If people or animals **yelp**, they give a sudden, short cry. This is often because they are frightened or in pain.

yes

You say **yes** to agree with someone, to say that something is true, or to accept something.

yesterday

ADVERB **Yesterday** is the day before today.

yet

ADVERB **1** You say **yet** when you mean up till now. *She hasn't come yet.*
ADVERB **2** If something should not be done **yet**, it should be done later. *Don't switch it off yet.*
CONJUNCTION **3** You can use **yet** to introduce something which is rather surprising. *He doesn't like math, yet he always does well.*

yew **yews**

NOUN A **yew** is an evergreen tree with thin, dark, green leaves. Some yew trees have red berries.

yogurt **yogurts**

NOUN **Yogurt** is a slightly sour, thick liquid food made from milk.

yolk **yolks**

NOUN A **yolk** is the yellow part in the middle of an egg.

young **younger, youngest**

ADJECTIVE **1** A **young** person, animal, or plant has not been alive for very long.
NOUN **2** The **young** of an animal are its babies.

your

ADJECTIVE **Your** means belonging or relating to the person or group of people that someone is speaking to. *Your teacher seems nice.*

yourself **yourselves**

PRONOUN If you do something **yourself**, no one else does it. *If you do that, you'll hurt yourself.*

by yourself PHRASE If you are **by yourself**, you are on your own. *What are you doing here all by yourself?*

youth **youths**

NOUN **1** A **youth** is a boy or young man.
NOUN **2** Your **youth** is the time in your life when you are young.

yo-yo **yo-yos**

NOUN A **yo-yo** is a round, wooden or plastic toy attached to a piece of string. You play by making the yo-yo rise and fall on the string.

Zz

zap **zaps, zapping, zapped**
VERB **1** If you **zap** something or somebody in a computer game, you get rid of them.

VERB **2** To **zap** is a slang expression meaning to heat in a microwave oven.

zebra **zebras**
NOUN A **zebra** is a type of African wild horse with black and white stripes all over its body.

zebra crossing **zebra crossings**
NOUN A **zebra crossing** is a place where you can cross the road safely. It's also called a crosswalk.

zero **zeros**
NOUN **1** Zero is the number 0.

NOUN **2** Zero also means nothing.

zigzag **zigzags**
NOUN A **zigzag** is a line which keeps changing direction sharply.

zinc
NOUN **Zinc** is a bluish-white metal which is used to make other metals, or to cover other metals, such as iron, to stop them from rusting.

zipper **zippers**
NOUN A **zipper** is a long narrow fastener with two rows of teeth that are closed or opened by a small clip pulled between them.

zone **zones**
NOUN A **zone** is an area of land or sea that is considered to be different from the areas around it. *My dad wants to turn the garden into a cat-free **zone**.*

zoo **zoos**
NOUN A **zoo** is a park where wild animals are kept so that people can look at them or study them.

zoom **zooms, zooming, zoomed**
VERB **1** To **zoom** somewhere means to go there very quickly.

VERB **2** If a camera **zooms** in on a person or thing being photographed, it gives a close-up picture of them.

a
b
c
d
e
f
g
h
i
j
k
l
m
n
o
p
q
r
s
t
u
v
w
x
y

Zz

Vegetables

celery

garlic

broccoli

eggplant

cabbage

radish

cauliflower

cucumber

lettuce

zucchini

asparagus

onion

beet

pea

potato

snow pea

pepper

turnip

bean

parsnip

brussels sprout

spinach

sweet potato

sweet corn

carrot

leek

apple

avocado

tomato

cherry

kiwi fruit

grape

grapefruit

lime

pear

plum

passion fruit

orange

lemon

mango

peach

strawberry

raspberry

melon

banana

pineapple

Your body

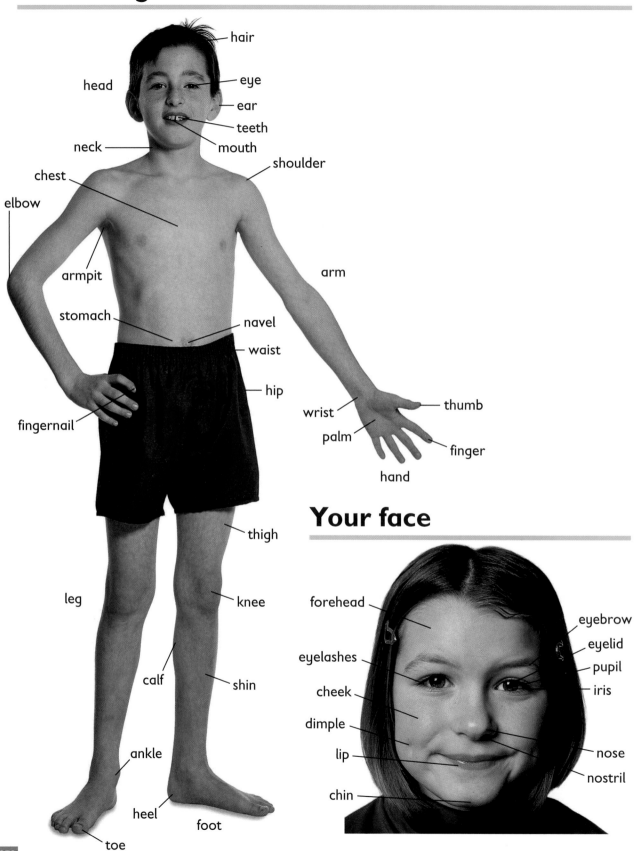

hair

head

eye

ear

teeth

mouth

neck

chest

shoulder

elbow

armpit

arm

stomach

navel

waist

hip

fingernail

wrist

thumb

palm

finger

hand

thigh

Your face

leg

knee

forehead

eyebrow

eyelid

pupil

iris

eyelashes

calf

shin

cheek

dimple

lip

nose

nostril

ankle

chin

heel

foot

toe

Insects

ant

bee

beetle

fly

butterfly

dragonfly

grasshopper

ladybug

mosquito

Amphibians

frog

newt

toad

Reptiles

alligator

crocodile

lizard

snake

tortoise

turtle

259

Young animals

bear and **cub**

cat and **kitten**

deer and **fawn**

goat and **kid**

goose and **gosling**

hare and **leveret**

horse and **foal**

kangaroo and **joey**

pig and **piglet**

rabbit and **kitten**

seal and **calf** or **pup**

sheep and **lamb**

tiger and **cub**

swan and **cygnet**

whale and **calf**

More young animals

bird and **chick**

chicken and **chick**

cow and **calf**

dog and **puppy**

duck and **duckling**

elephant and **calf**

fox and **cub**

lion and **cub**

wolf and **cub**

Words we use a lot

a	began	for	home	must	said	this	when
about	being	from	how	my	saw	three	where
after	but	get	I	name	say	to	which
again	by	go	if	next	seen	too	who
all	came	goes	in	no	she	took	why
along	can	going	is	not	should	two	will
am	can't	got	it	now	so	up	with
an	come	had	its	of	some	upon	woman
and	coming	hadn't	it's	off	suddenly	us	would
another	could	has	just	okay	take	very	wouldn't
are	couldn't	hasn't	last	on	than	want	yes
aren't	did	have	made	once	that	was	you
as	didn't	haven't	make	one	the	wasn't	your
at	do	he	man	or	their	way	
away	does	heard	many	our	them	we	
back	doesn't	her	may	out	then	went	
be	don't	here	me	over	there	were	
because	every	him	more	people	these	weren't	
been	first	his	much	put	they	what	

Silent letters

Each of these words has a silent letter. Can you think of any other words like these?

clim**b**	**k**nit
colum**n**	**k**nock
com**b**	**k**not
dou**b**t	**k**now
ghost	lam**b**
gnat	s**c**issors
gnaw	s**w**ord
gnome	**w**rap
hour	**w**riggle
knee	**w**rite
knife	

Confusable words

These words have different meanings but are easy to mix up.

its (belongs to it) *The dog wagged <u>its</u> tail.*
it's (it is) *<u>It's</u> not funny.*

loose *My tooth is <u>loose</u>.*
lose *Don't <u>lose</u> your pen.*

passed *I <u>passed</u> my test.*
past *It's ten <u>past</u> three.*

their (belongs to them) *The girls counted <u>their</u> money.*
they're (they are) *<u>They're</u> going to the shop.*
there *<u>There</u> are 26 chairs in this room.*
Put your bag down <u>there</u>.

than *I am shorter <u>than</u> you.*
then (at that time) *<u>Then</u> I heard footsteps.*

too *Can I come <u>too</u>? This is <u>too</u> hard.*
two *I'd like <u>two</u> cakes.*
to *I want <u>to</u> swim. Let's go <u>to</u> the beach.*

whose (belongs to whom) *<u>Whose</u> bag is this?*
who's (who is *<u>Who's</u> that?*
  or who has) *I know <u>who's</u> been sending you notes.*

Parts of speech

Noun

A **noun** is a person, place, thing, or idea. There are different types of nouns.

cat

cats

A noun can be **singular**, which means one ...

... or **plural**, which means more than one.

Common nouns name people, places, things, or ideas in general. For example, "boy," "dog," "school," "computer," and "happiness" are common nouns.

Proper nouns are the names of particular people, places, or things. They start with a capital letter. For example, "Ben," "France," and "White House" are proper nouns.

Collective nouns

A **collective noun** names a group of things.

a **bunch** of grapes

a **clutch** of eggs

a **flock** of sheep

a **pack** of wolves

a **litter** of puppies

a **herd** of cows

a **pride** of lions

a **school** of dolphins

a **shoal** or **school** of fish

a **swarm** of bees

Pronoun

A **pronoun** is used to replace a noun.

I	me	my	mine	myself
you	you	your	yours	yourself, yourselves
he, she, it	him, her, it	his, her, its	his, hers, its	himself, herself, itself
we	us	our	ours	ourselves
they	them	their	theirs	themselves

Personal pronouns are used for a person or thing that has already been named, for example "me," "her," "you," "it." *John jumped for the ball. <u>He</u> caught <u>it</u>!*

Possessive pronouns show that a noun belongs to a person or thing that has already been named, for example, "my," "their," "his," "our." *The bird flapped <u>its</u> wings.*

Adjective

An **adjective** describes a noun. For example, "tall," "happy," and "lucky" are all adjectives.

Some adjectives have a **comparative** and a **superlative** form. In most cases, these forms are made by adding "-er" or "-est" to the adjective.

adjective	comparative (more)	superlative (most)
tall	taller	tallest
hot	hotter	hottest
good	better	best
lucky	luckier	luckiest

Verb

A **verb** is an action word. It tells you what people and things do. For example, "sleep," "think," and "play" are all verbs.

Verbs have different forms called **tenses**. A tense shows whether you are talking about the past, present, or future.

past	present	future
I *played*	I *play*	I *will play*
	I *am playing*	

Adverb

An **adverb** tells you more about a verb. For example, "shyly," "brightly" and "happily" are all adverbs. Many adverbs end in the suffix "-ly."

How did Mary and Brian talk?
    *They talked **loudly**.*

Other adverbs tell you "where," "when," or "how often" something happens.

where: outside, inside, here, there
when: today, soon, immediately
how often: never, frequently, often, always

Punctuation

A B C	A **capital letter** is used at the beginning of a sentence and for proper nouns.	*My brother Jim lives in New Zealand.*
.	You put a **period** at the end of a sentence.	*This is a sentence.*
?	You put a **question mark** at the end of a question.	*Can you come to my party?*
,	You use a **comma** to separate parts of a sentence or items on a list.	*She brought sandwiches, chips, apples, and juice to the picnic.*
!	You use an **exclamation mark** at the end of a sentence to show a strong feeling.	*Wow!*
'	An **apostrophe** is used in contractions and to show belonging.	*I didn't mean to break my brother's toy.*
" " ' '	**Quotation marks** show where speech begins and ends.	*"I like your hair," she said.*
-	You use a **hyphen** to join together words or parts of words.	*I'm left-handed.*
( )	**Parentheses** are used to show that something is not part of the main text.	*My cousin (the one from Florida) is coming to stay.*
—	A **dash** can be used instead of parentheses, or to show a change of subject.	*My best friend – besides you – is George.*
:	You can use a **colon** for several things, for example in front of a list.	*You will need the following: strong walking boots, a map, and a compass.*
;	A **semicolon** is used to separate different parts of a sentence or list, or to show a pause.	*The pizza choices are: cheese; onions, peppers and mushrooms; ham and pineapple; pepperoni; or sausage.*

Prefixes

A **prefix** is a group of letters added to the beginning of a word to make a new word.

prefix	meaning	example	prefix	meaning	example
anti-	opposite of, against	antifraud	over-	too much	oversleep
			poly-	many	polygon
co-	together	copilot	pre-	before	prehistoric
de-	take away	decode	re-	again	rearrange
dis-	opposite of	disappear	semi-	half	semicircle
ex-	former	ex-husband	sub-	under, part of	subheading
micro-	very small	microscope	super-	larger, more than	supersonic
mid-	middle	midnight			
mini-	smaller	minibus	un-	not	unlucky
mis-	wrong	misspell	under-	under or not enough	underground
non-	not	nonfiction			

Suffixes

A **suffix** is a letter or group of letters added to the end of a word to make a new word.

Some suffixes can change nouns into other nouns:

-hood	child → child**hood**
-ist	art → art**ist** science → scient**ist**
-ship	friend → friend**ship**

Some suffixes can make nouns feminine:

-ess	lion → lion**ess** prince → princ**ess**

Some suffixes can form a diminutive (a small word):

-ette	disk → disk**ette**

Some suffixes can change nouns or verbs into adjectives:

-able	comfort → comfort**able** enjoy → enjoy**able**
-al	music → music**al**
-ary	imagine → imagin**ary**
-ful	help → help**ful**
-ible	sense → sens**ible**
-ic	angel → angel**ic** drama → dramat**ic**
-ish	child → child**ish**
-ive	act → act**ive** persuade → persuas**ive**
-less	care → care**less**
-like	life → life**like**
-ous	poison → poison**ous**
-worthy	trust → trust**worthy**
-y	thirst → thirst**y**

Some suffixes can change adjectives into adverbs:

-ally	automatic → automatic**ally**
-ly	slow → slow**ly** happy → happi**ly**

Some suffixes can change verbs or adjectives into nouns:

-ment	advertise → advertise**ment** enjoy → enjoy**ment**
-ness	ill → ill**ness** happy → happi**ness**
-sion	divide → divi**sion**
-tion	add → addi**tion** invite → invita**tion**

Some suffixes can change nouns into verbs:

-ate	illustration → illustr**ate**

Synonyms

Synonyms are words that have the same, or almost the same, meaning.
Here are some useful synonyms for everyday words.

angry
furious, mad, annoyed, outraged, indignant

bad
a bad person – wicked, nasty
a bad child – naughty, spiteful, defiant
bad food – rotten, decayed
a bad pain – severe
bad news – distressing, grave, terrible

big
huge, large, enormous, gigantic, vast, colossal

good
a good dog – well-behaved
a good painting – fine
a good film – enjoyable
a good worker – able, clever

happy
cheerful, contented, delighted, glad, pleased, thrilled

kind
kind of person or thing – type, class, group

level
grade, position, stage

lots or **a lot**
plenty, a great deal, heaps, loads, many, a large amount, masses, piles

lovely
a lovely day – pleasant, glorious, sunny, splendid
a lovely meal – tasty, scrumptious, delicious
a lovely person – warm, kind, helpful, friendly
a lovely time – enjoyable, great, fantastic, wonderful, fabulous

nasty
a nasty person – unkind, rude, unpleasant
a nasty taste – horrible, foul, disgusting, awful

nice
nice food – delicious
a nice person – kind, helpful, pleasant
a nice view – lovely

rough
a rough road – bumpy, stony
a rough sea – choppy, stormy

small
a small problem – unimportant, trivial
a small child – little, tiny, young
a small room – cramped, cozy, modest

What else can you say?

The word "said" is useful, but here are some more interesting words that you can use to describe speech.

answer
reply, respond, retort, admit, agree

ask
inquire, demand, beg, query, wonder

said
announced, whispered, shouted, stammered, mumbled, yelled, shrieked, screamed, cried, murmured, remarked, declared, groaned, snarled, whimpered, admitted

Antonyms

Antonyms are words that have the opposite meaning.

cold   hot

for   against

exact   approximate

on   off

left   right

old   young

old   new

wide   narrow

digital   analog

up   down

before   after

right   wrong

exciting   boring

to   from

above   below

formal   informal

gentle   rough

empty   full

under   over

deep   shallow

fiction   nonfiction

rough   smooth

with   without

in   out

sink   float

thin   thick

thin   fat

concave   convex

short   long

closed   open

short   tall

beginning   end

happy   sad

ascend   descend

hollow   solid

Time

9:50 a.m.

10 minutes to 10

7:25 p.m.

25 minutes past 7

Telling time

a.m.

p.m.

o'clock

half past

quarter past

quarter to

analog

digital

clock

watch

timer

More time words

yesterday
today
tomorrow

calendar
date
weekend
holiday
birthday

second
minute
hour
day
week
fortnight
month
year
leap year
decade
century
millennium

dawn
morning
midday
noon
afternoon
dusk
evening
night
midnight

bedtime
daytime
dinnertime
playtime

Months
January
February
March
April
May
June
July
August
September
October
November
December

How often?
never
once
twice
sometimes
often
usually
always

Days
Monday
Tuesday
Wednesday
Thursday
Friday
Saturday
Sunday

Seasons
spring
summer
autumn
winter

Weather words

bright   sunny   dry   breeze   clear   hot

freezing   cold   icy   snow   frost

dry   hot   drought   sun

cloudy   chilly   foggy   drizzle   misty

rain   windy   wet   sleet   cool

hail   lightning   gale   storm   thunder

showers rainbow sunshine warm breeze

Measures

Length
inch (in)
foot (ft)
yard (yd)
mile

Mass or weight
ounce (oz)
pound (lb)
ton

Capacity
ounce (oz)
cup (c)
quart (qt)
gallon (gal)

Abbreviations

a.m.	in the morning
°C	degrees Celsius
CD	compact disc (such as a music CD)
CD-ROM	a CD that is played on a computer (an abbreviation of "compact disc read-only memory")
cm	centimeter
cm²	square centimeter
COD	cash on delivery
Dr.	Doctor
DVD	digital video disc *or* digital versatile disc
ER	emergency room
ETA	estimated time of arrival
etc.	"et cetera," which means "and so on" in Latin
°F	degrees Fahrenheit
g	gram
hdbk	handbook
Jr.	junior
JV	junior varsity
kg	kilogram
km	kilometer
l	liter
m	meter

ml	milliliter
Mr.	a title used before a man's name
Mrs.	a title used before the name of a married woman
Ms.	a title used before a woman's name
p	page
PC	personal computer
p.m.	in the afternoon or evening
pp	pages
PS	PS is written at the end of a letter, before an extra message (an abbreviation of "postscript")
RIP	rest in peace
RSVP	please reply (an abbreviation of the French phrase "répondez s'il vous plaît")
SOS	a Morse code signal for help, especially used by ships or planes (sometimes said to be an abbreviation of "save our souls")
sp	spelling
TGIF	thank goodness it's Friday
TV	television
UFO	unidentified flying object
VIP	very important person
www	World Wide Web

Colors and flat shapes (2D)

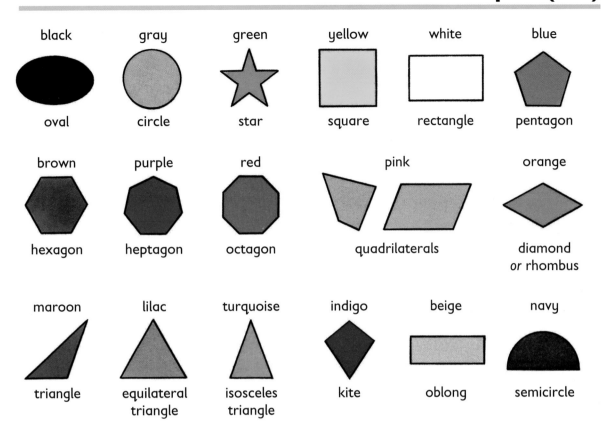

black — oval

gray — circle

green — star

yellow — square

white — rectangle

blue — pentagon

brown — hexagon

purple — heptagon

red — octagon

pink — quadrilaterals

orange — diamond *or* rhombus

maroon — triangle

lilac — equilateral triangle

turquoise — isosceles triangle

indigo — kite

beige — oblong

navy — semicircle

Solid shapes (3D)

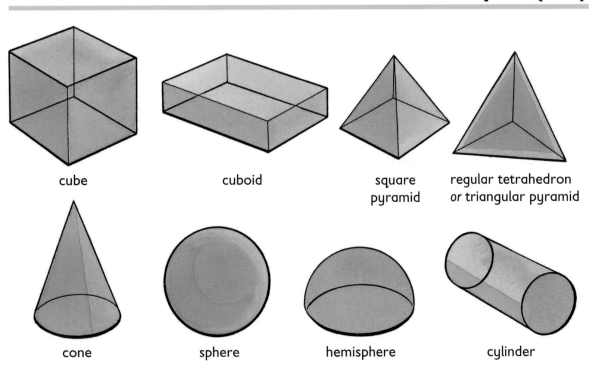

cube

cuboid

square pyramid

regular tetrahedron *or* triangular pyramid

cone

sphere

hemisphere

cylinder

Number bank

0	zero	30	thirty	1st	first
1	one	31	thirty-one	2nd	second
2	two	40	forty	3rd	third
3	three	41	forty-one	4th	fourth
4	four	50	fifty	5th	fifth
5	five	51	fifty-one	6th	sixth
6	six	60	sixty	7th	seventh
7	seven	61	sixty-one	8th	eighth
8	eight	70	seventy	9th	ninth
9	nine	71	seventy-one	10th	tenth
10	ten	80	eighty	11th	eleventh
11	eleven	81	eighty-one	12th	twelfth
12	twelve	90	ninety	13th	thirteenth
13	thirteen	91	ninety-one	14th	fourteenth
14	fourteen	100	one hundred	15th	fifteenth
15	fifteen	101	one hundred one	16th	sixteenth
16	sixteen	150	one hundred fifty	17th	seventeenth
17	seventeen	200	two hundred	18th	eighteenth
18	eighteen	1000	one thousand	19th	nineteenth
19	nineteen	10 000	ten thousand	20th	twentieth
20	twenty	100 000	one hundred thousand	21st	twenty-first
21	twenty-one	1 000 000	one million		

Fractions

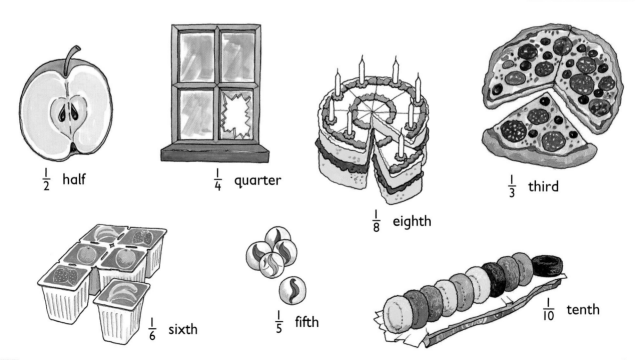

$\frac{1}{2}$ half

$\frac{1}{4}$ quarter

$\frac{1}{8}$ eighth

$\frac{1}{3}$ third

$\frac{1}{6}$ sixth

$\frac{1}{5}$ fifth

$\frac{1}{10}$ tenth